The Construction of Reformed Identity in Jean Crespin's *Livre des Martyrs*

Between 1554 and 1570, the Genevan printer Jean Crespin compiled seven French-language editions of his martyrology. In *The Construction of Reformed Identity in Jean Crespin's* Livre des Martyrs, Jameson Tucker explores how this martyrology helped to shape a distinct Reformed identity for its Protestant readership, with a particular interest in the stranger groups that Crespin included within his *Livre des Martyrs*.

By comparing each edition of the *Livre des Martyrs*, this book examines Crespin's editorial processes and considers the impact that he intended his work to have on his readers. Through this, it provides a window into the Reformed Church and its members during the outbreak of the French Wars of Religion. This is the first volume to comparatively study all seven French-language editions of Crespin's *Livre des Martyrs* and will be essential reading for all scholars of the Reformation and early modern France.

Jameson Tucker is Lecturer in Early Modern History at the University of Plymouth. His previous publications include 'From Fire to Iron: Martyrs and Massacre Victims in Genevan Martyrology' in *Dying, Death, Burial and Commemoration in Early Modern Europe*, edited by Liz Tingle and Jonathan Willis (2015).

Routledge Research in Early Modern History

In the same series:

Penury into Plenty
Dearth and the Making of
Knowledge in Early Modern England
Ayesha Mukherjee

**Violence and Emotions in Early
Modern Europe**
*Edited by Susan Broomhall and
Sarah Finn*

India in the Italian Renaissance
Visions of a Contemporary Pagan
World 1300–1600
Meera Juncu

**The English Revolution and the
Roots of Environmental Change**
The Changing Concept of the Land
in Early Modern England
George Yerby

Honourable Intentions?
Violence and Virtue in Australian
and Cape Colonies, *c.*1750 to 1850
*Edited by Penny Russell and
Nigel Worden*

**Social Thought in England,
1480–1730**
From Body Social to Worldly
Wealth
A. L. Beier

Dynastic Colonialism
Gender, Materiality and the early
modern House of Orange-Nassau
*Susan Broomhall and
Jacqueline van Gent*

**The Business of the Roman
Inquisition in the Early Modern
Era**
Germano Maifreda

Cities and Solidarities
Urban Communities in Pre-Modern
Europe
*Edited by Justin Colson and
Arie van Steensel*

**James VI and Noble Power in
Scotland 1578–1603**
*Edited by Miles Kerr-Peterson and
Steven J. Reid*

**Conversion and Islam in the Early
Modern Mediterranean**
The Lure of the Other
Edited by Claire Norton

Plural Pasts
Power, Identity and the Ottoman
Sieges of Nagykanizsa Castle
Claire Norton

The Construction of Reformed Identity in Jean Crespin's *Livre des Martyrs*

Jameson Tucker

LONDON AND NEW YORK

First published 2017
by Routledge
2 Park Square, Milton Park, Abingdon, Oxon OX14 4RN

and by Routledge
711 Third Avenue, New York, NY 10017

Routledge is an imprint of the Taylor & Francis Group, an informa business

© 2017 Jameson Tucker

The right of Jameson Tucker to be identified as author of this work
has been asserted by him in accordance with sections 77 and 78 of
the Copyright, Designs and Patents Act 1988.

All rights reserved. No part of this book may be reprinted or
reproduced or utilised in any form or by any electronic, mechanical,
or other means, now known or hereafter invented, including
photocopying and recording, or in any information storage or
retrieval system, without permission in writing from the publishers.

Trademark notice: Product or corporate names may be trademarks
or registered trademarks, and are used only for identification and
explanation without intent to infringe.

British Library Cataloguing in Publication Data
A catalogue record for this book is available from the British Library

Library of Congress Cataloging in Publication Data
Names: Tucker, Jameson, author.
Title: The construction of reformed identity in Jean Crespin's Livre
des martyrs / Dr. Jameson Tucker.
Description: New York : Routledge, 2017. | Series: Routledge
research in early modern history | Includes bibliographical references
and index.
Identifiers: LCCN 2016049695| ISBN 9781138125629 (hardback :
alk. paper) | ISBN 9781315203843 (ebook : alk. paper)
Subjects: LCSH: Crespin, Jean, –1572. Livre des martyrs. |
Martyrologies–History and criticism. | Christian hagiography–
History and criticism. | Martyrdom–Christianity–History–Sources. |
Church history–16th century.
Classification: LCC BR1608.5.C743 T83 2017 | DDC 272–dc23
LC record available at https://lccn.loc.gov/2016049695

ISBN: 978-1-138-12562-9 (hbk)
ISBN: 978-1-315-20384-3 (ebk)

Typeset in Sabon
by Wearset Ltd, Boldon, Tyne and Wear

For Laura

Contents

	Acknowledgements	viii
	Introduction	1
1	The Hussites and Protestant history	27
2	'What little true light they had': the Vaudois in history and martyrology	66
3	The alpine Vaudois in the 1550s and 1560s	98
4	'Luther n'est point mort pour moy': Crespin and Lutheran martyrs	120
5	The German Peasants' War	155
	Conclusion	177
	Bibliography	185
	Index	197

Acknowledgements

This book is based on my doctoral thesis, which was supervised by Penny Roberts at the University of Warwick. I'd like to thank her for all of her advice and direction, both then and since, in providing me with focus, advice, keen questions, and the necessary deadlines. I'd also like to thank my lecturers and tutors at the University of Birmingham, and Queen's University, including James Stayer, who first introduced me to the history of the Reformation, and Graeme Murdock, Alec Ryrie and Elaine Fulton, who have taught me much both about what I research and how to do it. Since completing my PhD I have benefitted a great deal from the advice and assistance of Liz Tingle and all of my colleagues at the University of Plymouth.

The research for this book was made possible by the help and expertise of, amongst others, Ian Holt of the Solothurn Zentralbibliothek, Margaret Thompson of Westminster College Cambridge, the Huguenot Library, London, UCL Special Collections, and the library of the Société de l'Histoire du Protestantisme Français in Paris. Professor Mark Greengrass has provided me with access to some key texts, as well as valuable advice and guidance during my research, while Dr Albert de Lange was able to assist me with a crucial text of Crespin's on the Waldensians.

I'd like to thank Laura Pilsworth for all of her help, and especially patience, in bringing this book to fruition, my copy-editor Penny Harper, who has done sterling work helping to prepare it, and my colleague James Daybell for the impetus he provided in getting this to publication.

I would not have been able to undertake this work without support from the Huguenot Society of London and the French Protestant Church, Soho Square, Mr Justice John Sutherland, and my family, to whom I owe a great deal of thanks.

Finally, above all, I would like to thank my wife, Laura, who has been a part of this project since the beginning, providing me with advice and support while working hard on her own several research projects.

Introduction

Writing about the 1523 execution of Henry Voez and Jean Esch in the second edition of his martyrology, Jean Crespin explained that they died 'for the Evangelical doctrine, and for the Apostolic writings, like good and true Christians'.[1] It was dying for the Gospel and for correct doctrine that made these two men true Christians in Crespin's eyes, and yet it is well known that he altered their confession of faith significantly, bringing their statements into line with those of his own Reformed Church.[2] His motivations for doing so stemmed from a contemporary controversy about sacramental issues, but also from Crespin's understanding of the essential nature of his Church.

In the first lines of the sixth edition of the martyrology, the *Actes des Martyrs*, Crespin expounded on the worthiness of the martyrs of his own age to be compared with those of the primitive Church:

> The ancient Martyrs, we say, were excellent in many ways. That is true, but if those who were spectators long ago, saw today the torment & afflictions of these last times, they would see new & marvellous things. The number of ancient [martyrs] was great: the number of ours, what is it? They have brought great profit & advancement to the Gospel: the constancy of ours is so well known today ... know that the fury of tyrants does not achieve what they desire: rather it has increased the number of those they would exterminate.[3]

This idea of a direct continuity with the ancient Church, as Frank Lestringant has noted, was a touch-stone for works like Crespin's martyrology.[4] The first edition of the martyrology, the *Livre des Martyrs*, or the *Recueil de plusieurs personnes qui ont constamment enduré la mort pour le nom de Nostre Seigneur*, began by placing martyrdom at the centre of the Christian experience, explaining that: 'among the marks of the true Church of God, this is one of the principal: to know that she at all times sustains the assaults of persecutions'.[5] This theme was continued through the editions of the martyrology, several of which began by stating that: 'there is today no region, nor country, not even the Turks & other barbarous people,

2   Introduction

where God has not raised some number of Martyrs, to render to all nations witness of his truth'.[6] In 1570, the introductory section was titled: 'Preface demonstrating the conformity of the persecutions and martyrs of these latter times to those of the primitive Church'.[7] This section depicted the deaths of some biblical martyrs, including John the Baptist, St Stephen, and Christ himself and, as the title suggested, compared them to the martyrs of Crespin's own time.[8]

If these men and women were the equals of the ancients, then they should be commemorated as the early martyrs had been, their deaths and more importantly the beliefs for which they died recorded for wide distribution. This was Crespin's mission in producing his martyrology, which he published under a variety of titles in seven French editions (and two Latin) in Geneva between 1554 and 1570.

Inclusion in the martyrology was therefore a sign of approval of the martyr and his message. As Crespin had noted in 1555, the Vaudois of Provence had written that their conception of the church was one of a: 'beautiful confraternity, in which are registered all the true Christians'.[9] Crespin took issue with many facets of the Vaudois congregation, but he shared their interest in collecting together all true Christians. If persecution was an inevitable companion to truth as Crespin suggested, then to understand the reach of the martyrs would be to understand the history and shape of the True Church itself. As a result, a number of martyrs are included in this very Calvinist book who come from a range of backgrounds – Lutherans, Vaudois, Lollards, and Hussites prominent amongst them. This book hopes to illustrate some of the ways in which this depiction of a relatively broad church shaped the message of the *Livre des Martyrs*, and the places in which this goal clashed with others, most notable the doctrinal purity, and usefulness, of the martyrology.

Jean Crespin

Jean Crespin's life, and career as a publisher in Geneva, have been extensively studied by Jean-François Gilmont. Crespin was born into a wealthy family at Arras around 1520, trained for the law at the University of Louvain, and became a legal assistant in Paris.[10] It seems to have been in this period that he converted to Protestantism. Forced to leave France in 1542 as a result of the Italian War between France and the Holy Roman Empire, he then left his homeland in stages, selling family property and finally establishing himself in Geneva in 1548.[11] Crespin was in close contact with the Genevan leadership as early as 1545, when he was writing to Calvin about his difficulties arranging to safely get his family and possessions out of Arras.[12] He continued to play a relatively prominent role within Geneva until his death, and served as a representative of the Genevan Church on a number of high-profile occasions, including at the Colloquy of Worms in 1557 and in the Low Countries during the critical period of 1566–67.[13]

Introduction 3

His career as a publisher began soon after his arrival in Geneva, in 1550, and seems to have been patronised from the beginning by Geneva's leading reformers. Of the eleven texts he published that first year, one was by Theodore Beza, and seven were by Jean Calvin. The next year's production was primarily Calvin's work and sections of Beza's French translation of the Bible.[14] Crespin produced his first martyrology in 1554, and continued to revise and publish versions of it until 1570, two years before his death.

Inclusion and the printing process

As with John Foxe, we have to regard Crespin as a presumptive, rather than actual author.[15] The question of his exact role in the production of the *Livre des Martyrs* is extended by his additional roles as printer and publisher, where he presumably took on some of the tasks which Foxe had been able to place in the hands of John Day. We cannot be certain exactly what role Crespin himself played in the process of composing or printing the *Livre des Martyrs*, although Jean-François Gilmont has given us a great deal of insight into the editing and production of Crespin's works in his bibliography and detailed study of the press. Crespin's workshop seems to have initially seen a period of co-production with another Genevan, Conrad Badius, before he was able to work on his own; this suggests that he was to some degree involved in the process of printing, rather than simply financing editions.[16] If the author's presence during the printing process was considered important enough that Foxe stayed with Day during the printing of the *Actes and Monuments* in 1562, then Crespin's dual role would have offered him some advantage, and a great deal of personal control over the final product.[17] Certainly there would have been many other people involved in the process, some of whom may have been crucial to the shaping of the martyrology as it emerged.

The *Livre des Martyrs* was primarily a collection, rather than a monograph (Crespin included the word 'recueil', meaning 'collection', in the title of four separate editions of the book), and so it is in his role as editor and compiler, rather than as an author, that he had the most impact on the work. This study will attempt to undertake an exploration of these editorial changes to shed light on the content of the book, specifically that relating to groups outside of Crespin's own Reformed denomination. It is these groups, holding as they did ideas that were divergent from (if not at odds with) those ascendant in Geneva, whose accounts would have required the most careful scrutiny from Crespin. The decisions made in composing the *Livre des Martyrs*, such as that to include the Hussites, Lollards, and Vaudois, but to entirely omit mention of the Cathars, reveal something of the conception of the Reformed Church held in one of its earliest and most influential historical works.

4   Introduction

The willingness to extend his editorial influence into the very content of the martyrs' beliefs suggests many things about Crespin's plan for the martyrology, and his means of achieving it. It appears that correct, Reformed, doctrine was paramount, and that doctrine was a point on which Crespin was unwilling to compromise. It suggests that this conformity could be gained through a tactful silence around the areas of disagreement, rather than insisting on a positive requirement for agreement on all subjects. It is also important that Crespin was willing to make these changes, and engage with these potentially difficult viewpoints, in order to broaden the breadth and depth of his martyrology. Lutheran and pre-Reformation subjects could have been avoided entirely, or placed within a second tier of reformers, flawed in their understanding of the Gospel. The changes he made in order to include Henry Voez and Jean Esch in the *Livre des Martyrs* are remarkable, but so too should be the fact that they were included at all.

Crespin's martyrology was, to a very great extent, made up of collected documents either by or about the martyrs. These were frequently primary sources, such as letters, trial documents, and eye-witness accounts, but Crespin also made extensive use of published material, drawing on pamphlets and books, including other martyrologies. Especially in the early editions, little of the text is presented in his own authorial voice. Outside of the introductions and prefaces (some of which were themselves derived from the writing of others), and later some marginalia, Crespin does not often assume the role of narrator or interpreter, instead simply introducing the documents to speak for themselves.[18] This was not simply a literary technique, although Crespin spent his career in Geneva working as an editor and publisher, rather than an author. Instead, this collecting, rather than authorship, of texts is central to the idea of a Protestant martyrology. Where the Catholics might covet the bones and possessions of the saints, the *Livre des Martyrs* aimed to collect: 'not their bones or their ashes, in the fashion of the baslisk, maker of idols and new monsters: but their constancy, their words and writings, their responses, the confession of their faith, their last words & adhortations'.[19] It is this idea of the martyrology as a cenotaph for, if not a reconstitution of, the martyrs which has been explored in the work of Catharine Randall Coats.[20] It is for these reasons that Crespin emphasised the importance of the original texts, and imbued them with a great deal of significance.

In many cases we are able to identify the likely source material for many of the accounts. The amount of overlap between the *Livre des Martyrs* and other Protestant martyrologies provides a useful frame of reference. In situations where we cannot identify the original source, or where a document is known but no longer exists outside of Crespin's pages, the editions of the *Livre des Martyrs* allow for detailed comparison between them. Some martyrs appear in four of the seven editions of the book; most appear in at least three. This sort of examination can often show revisions and editorial

Introduction 5

adjustments which shed light upon the aims of the author, and the concerns he may have had about the source material.

Modification, reduction, and replacement were all tools used regularly by Crespin as editor, and this must raise the question of the reliability of the martyrology. This is one of the most studied topics relating to Crespin, and has been subject to several works over the last century. Gilmont's assessment of Crespin's uncredited borrowing is that he reordered and recontextualised the material so that 'If he copies from other authors, he does not simply plagiarize. He exploits the model in order to explain a thought that is mostly new.'[21] Crespin's willingness to alter this uncredited material to express his own meaning must be considered when evaluating the content of the documents and accounts he reproduced. His approach to this, as in so many things, evolved over time. In the 1554 edition of the martyrology, Crespin apologised for his adherence to the sometimes-rough language of his sources, which allowed him to stress their authenticity:

> reader, do not be offended by the diversity of language, often very rough and rude. Because for greater confirmation of truth, we have left each one in its natural state – they speak some improper French – hoping that this will easily support itself: and yet it largely serves as much to verify the history as to declare the marvels of God...[22]

In 1570's introduction, by contrast, and using a passage heavily modified from Chandieu, Crespin expressed a degree of willingness to alter or improve the raw material with which he was working:

> I have sometimes found obscure things, like writings in dark dungeons, and often blood that the poor martyrs have drawn, for want of ink, others in rather bad language, as they are of diverse nations, or working men; that I have translated and recovered as faithfully as I could. Their interrogations and responses that have been sometimes taken from the clerks, all is customarily so confused, and framed to the appetite of the clerks, or the ignorant, or the malign, that it has been necessary to give a summary extract, keeping the same substance of questions and answers. Briefly, on this last point, my goal has been to write the life, the doctrine, and happy end of those who have sufficient testimony of having sealed with their death the truth of the Gospel.[23]

Even this admission of altering his quoted material suggests that he was careful to retain the content of the interrogations and confessions, though that this claim to editorial integrity was done through the modified words of another author should suggest to us that there is a great deal of complexity in Crespin's relationship to the texts with which he worked. There is no indication, however, that we should not follow Gilmont in seeing

6   *Introduction*

Crespin as an editor and shaper of texts, rearranging and cutting the original documents to his purposes, rather than adding new elements to them.

The editions

Jean Crespin's printing career saw him print a string of theological works by major reformers in both French and Latin, as well as more exotic languages such as Spanish and English. This works were largely intended for the stranger churches which had arrived in Geneva, and many of these were books of largely practical value to these communities.[24] They included, in 1556, *The Forme of Prayers Used in the English Congregation at Geneva*, combined with fifty-one psalms and an English translation of Calvin's *Catechism*.[25] A Spanish catechism was produced the same year, with the *Catechism* following in 1559, and Italian psalms, catechisms, and New Testaments were produced alongside Italian editions of Calvin's work.[26] These were all relatively practical works, designed for use in the Protestant communities within Geneva, but some were also clearly intended for covert export, being printed without a city of origin on the title page. These were also largely instructional works (although he also published Knox's *First Blast of the Trumpet*), aimed at educating new members of the Reformed faith, and Crespin's awareness of these needs helped to shape the *Livre des Martyrs*. In his later career, Crespin's workshop moved increasingly into more advanced educational works, publishing law textbooks, classical works like the Odyssey, and despite the competition from the formidable Estienne clan, dictionaries and lexicons of Italian, Latin, and Greek.[27]

Crespin was also involved in the publication of contemporary history, printing the works of Sleidan and Hainault.[28] These were authors with definite views of the practical utility of history, and skilled practitioners of the craft. Some of their techniques may shed light on the way in which Crespin may have worked. Like Crespin, Sleidan seems to have gathered official documents from prominent reformers, especially Calvin and Bucer, as well as receiving documents from the public, unsolicited.[29] Sleidan used these in a fashion that Alexandra Kas regarded as being influenced by Bucer's conciliatory approach at Strasbourg; he: 'tended to omit theological divisions'.[30] Sleidan seems to have seen an early draft or proof of the first edition of the *Livre des Martyrs*, as suggested by a letter he wrote to Calvin in 1554.[31]

The first edition of the *Livre des Martyrs* was published in 1554, the same year as Foxe's *Commentarii Rerum*, and two years after the first volume of Ludwig Rabus' martyrology. Later editions were seemingly compiled in full knowledge of the other martyrologies, and seem to have used material from them. The most dramatic example of this borrowing is the *Quatrieme Partie*, which was nearly entirely made up of translated passages from Foxe (having been first intended as a translation), but most of

Introduction 7

his editions borrowed from the words of others; it is also the case that Foxe and Rabus borrowed from Crespin.[32] Aside from using martyrological accounts already which others had already published, Crespin was influenced by the structure and philosophy of the other books, especially Foxe. Each of his editions after the Foxe-derived *Quatrieme Partie*, included an increasing amount of narrative history in which no martyr featured. This had the effect of binding the book more closely together, providing something closer to the grand narrative that has been identified with Foxe's martyrology.

As with the *Acts and Monuments* of John Foxe, the *Livre des Martyrs* cannot be treated as a single work; there is no single definitive edition. The title itself is an umbrella term (some studies have used *Histoire des Martyrs*); each edition of the martyrology was given a different title, and in one case, different states of the same edition received different titles. The history of the successive editions of the French-language *Livre des Martyrs* has been extensively outlined in Jean-François Gilmont's *Jean Crespin: Un editeur réformé du XVI siècle*, but the relationships between the seven primary editions require outlining if we are to be able to understand the changes between them.

There were at least two distinct phases to the production of the martyrology during Crespin's lifetime. In the first, lasting from 1554 to 1563, five successive editions were released, each providing the details of new events and martyrdoms. Crespin's 1554 *Livre des martyrs* was renamed the *Recueil de plusieurs personnes qui ont constamment enduré la mort pour le nom de N.S. Iesus Christ* in later states of its first edition, apparently due to objections to the word 'martyr' by the Genevan Council.[33] The fourth edition, of 1561, saw the return of the word 'martyr' in the title, though the now commonly used title *Livre des Martyrs* did not reappear until 1564's compendium edition.

The editions of the martyrology which came after 1554 were regarded as successive volumes of the same work, and later instalments were named accordingly: the *Troisieme*, *Quatrieme*, and *Cinquieme partie*. These were produced in octavo, often with a sextodecimo edition following in the next year, as happened with the first three volumes.[34] In addition to being portable, if thick, volumes (the first edition was more than 650 pages), these editions often showed signs of hurried production. Some quires were inserted between already-printed sections to allow for the inclusion of hastily added material, as was done in 1555 to add passages about the Hussite Wars and a number of Lollard martyrs.[35] This move was partially spurred by the publication of a pirate copy of his martyrology by the Rivery brothers in 1554, which incorporated elements from Foxe, including passages about Wyclif and the Lollards.[36]

In the 1563 *Cinquieme partie*, material was used which seems to have been printed for another purpose: there are two sets of quires with pages numbered 1–32, and the passage regarding the martyrs Varlut and Dayke

8 Introduction

has been separately paginated and signed; Gilmont has shown this was printed for an earlier work.[37] On a more minor level, it is quite common to see occasional compression of text, and increased use of abbreviations, in places where faulty casting-off has left the typesetter in a tight spot.

The two editions of the martyrology that Crespin published after 1564 were generally of a higher quality. The contents of the five volumes published between 1554 and 1563 were brought together, and added to, in a single folio volume. This 1564 edition (which also exists in a state from 1565), was generally speaking of a higher quality, with larger type and fewer abbreviations of the text.

David Watson has connected this change to the coming of the Wars of Religion, and the ability of Protestants in many areas to openly display their allegiances.[38] Gilmont also suggests that this change is likely to have changed how the book was used and read, with a greater ability to read the book communally and a more polemic tone than earlier editions.[39] This new format was divided internally into seven books, with the contents of the previous editions redistributed along chronological lines. Crespin published the second of these folio editions in 1570, this time running to eight books. This would be the final edition published in his lifetime.

The subsequent versions of the *Livre des Martyrs* published through to 1619 would be built on this model. The compendium editions of the martyrology were generally of a higher quality than the octavos which had preceded them. There was more space around the text, clearer demarcation between sections, more informative paratext and introductory material, and more thorough indexes. The 1564 and 1570 editions also included inside their title pages a full-page woodblock representation of Noah's Ark, the only illustration ever included in the martyrology.

As the *Livre des Martyrs* developed, so too did Crespin's approach to his subjects. In the early editions, the stress was strongly on the original words and documents of the martyrs themselves. Very little narrative material connected the martyrs' accounts, or provided context to their martyrdoms; instead the book emphasised its nature as a compilation of letters and documents contributed by its subjects and witnesses. At the same time that he was producing the *Livre des Martyrs* Crespin was publishing histories of the Church by authors such as Sleidan and de Hainault, and he seems to have drawn a distinction between these and the martyrology. When writing about the Vaudois of Provence, for example, he was careful to distinguish between the material included in the martyrology and the separate *Histoire memorable* that he produced on the same subject.

From 1563 onwards, however, this changed, as Crespin began to openly incorporate historical narratives into the martyrology. A series of historical accounts, each titled *Récit d'Histoire*, was inserted throughout the text, providing background and context for the individual accounts of the martyrs. This format allowed Crespin to include, amongst other things, the massacres which marked the French Wars of Religion, but also key events like the death of King Henri II of France, and the Reformation of Geneva, which would not have qualified under earlier versions of the book. These historical passages made up, by Crespin's last edition, approximately 18 per cent of the text.[40]

Two Latin editions were also produced, in 1556 and 1560, in octavo and quarto formats, respectively. The 1556 edition was a translation of the first two parts of the vernacular martyrology, done by Claude Baduel.[41] This was undertaken at about the same time that Crespin would have been engaged in the composition of the *Troisieme Partie*. The second was a larger volume, without an identified translator, and although it survives relatively widely, suggesting some success, it was the last to be published in Latin.[42] The 1560 edition was also Crespin's first attempt at a collected volume, subdivided into books.[43]

The martyrology was continued after Crespin's death, by his son-in-law and heir Eustache Vignon and Simon Goulart, who had succeeded Calvin and Beza as the head of the Genevan Company of Pastors. They produced Francophone folio editions in 1582, 1597, and 1619, making a series of new additions, including to the earliest phases of the book.

Identity and the *Livre des Martyrs*

Andrew Pettegree has made the important point that the Protestant martyrologies of this period can be read for their pedagogic value, and indeed may have been created for this purpose.[44] Already deeply involved in printing educational material, Crespin himself was clear on the use of the martyrology as an educational tool; his introductions stressed the 'utility of these collections', which derived from their presenting an ecclesiastical history, demonstrating how the Church was shaped and protected by God.[45] He wrote repeatedly in the introductions to volumes and to narratives that he hoped they could teach his readers; he hoped, for example, that the history of the Vaudois would: 'serve as instruction not only to all of the faithful, in particular, but in general to all peoples & republics'.[46]

The 1554 edition of the martyrology suggested that it was

> necessary that the faithful, to remedy their weaknesses ... place before their eyes the examples of those who have maintained the truth of the doctrine of the Son of God, and who have constantly endured death for the confession of it.[47]

The accounts of the martyrs were collected in the 'hope that it will serve you greatly as each one of you has need of consolation or of confirmation'.[48] Crespin argued that the martyrology was capable of providing advice and consolation to all categories of reader:

10   Introduction

are you old? You have here men of your age, who did not falter for the imbecility of their age. Are you young? There are in this collection examples of youths, who did not fear to lose the flower of their age ... [49]

Similar appeals to nobles, husbands, and women were made.

The martyrology could act as a conduct book for these people, giving examples of how to face up to persecution and defend one's faith, as David Watson has suggested, and it could also be useful as a guide to true belief. The stories of martyrs arguing with their captors contained long passages of theological argument, complete with biblical citation. A cover-to-cover reader of the *Livre des Martyrs* would be equipped with a series of tested arguments in favour of Reformed tenets, and against Catholic positions. Indeed, in a later edition of the martyrology, Crespin claimed that earlier editions had been put to exactly that use:

> We have well understood, that the faithful spread out here and there, have received great consolation, and have seized against the enemies of the truth, the responses and confessions contained in the First and Second parts ... this Third part, I hope that it will be of no less use than the other two preceding. [50]

The 1582 edition, published a decade after Crespin's death, was produced with this in mind. It contains an index organising the contents of the martyrology by theological topic, pointing the reader to key exchanges between martyrs and their interrogators on topics such as indulgences, the Virgin Mary, 'Limbo, invented by the Papists, refuted' and 'Intercession of the saints collected in heaven, neither commanded nor promised in Scripture'. [51] The most detailed entries are those discussing the Eucharist, the Papacy, and the confessions of the martyrs.

Crespin is likely to have been aware of the need amongst his audience for this sort of instruction. Amongst the martyrs whose accounts he edited are several men, like Benoit Romyen, Hugues Gravier, or Jean Rabec, who left their homes, travelling to Geneva to learn more about the faith, and live according to its dictates; several of their statements closely parallel John Knox's statement about the city being 'the most perfect school of Christ'. That many recent converts might still be in need of education in the faith would not have been an unusual or controversial idea to Crespin.

As a major publisher of Calvin's vernacular works, and a confirmed convert to the Reformed Church, Crespin was conversant with the reformer's views on a wide range of issues. If we cannot assume that Crespin's editorial standpoint on political and doctrinal issues can be identified with the official Genevan positions, then it at least seems that he was likely to be fully aware of them. Crespin's work on the Lutheran martyrs, coming at a time when he also published Calvin's polemic against certain Lutheran theologians, was likely to be affected by the public debate.

Introduction 11

In the other direction, the *Livre des Martyrs'* stance regarding some stranger groups became very influential amongst the Genevan establishment. Large early sections of the 1580 *Histoire Ecclesiastique* relating to the Vaudois and the early history of the Reformation have been excerpted directly from Crespin's own work. The *Livre des Martyrs*, therefore, may serve to illustrate Reformed attitudes toward Protestant history from the perspective of a man who was a member of Calvin's larger circle of influence.

Although he never took the concept as far as did Foxe, Crespin's martyrology acted as a history of the Reformed Church, defined in the broadest sense. The Hussites, Vaudois, and Lutherans (especially the early Lutheran martyrs in the *Livre des Martyrs*) all represented early opposition to the papacy and to Catholic doctrine, providing a genealogy for the Reformed Church. The appeal of these groups was, in part, that they provided an answer to Catholic charges of novelty. Luther had made a virtue of similarities between his programme and that of Jan Hus; Flacius Illyricus' *Catalogus Testum* worked to include more examples of historical dissent.[52]

This was a trend that would continue through the century; the French Reformed Church went so far as to formally acknowledge, at the 1572 Synod at Nîmes, that the Albigensians, members of the medieval dualist heresy, had been ancestors of the Reformed Church.[53] The Albigensians had been slightly rehabilitated by Jean de Hainault, whose 1557 history had depicted the Cathars as savages, indeed cannibals; his 1582 work described them as having seen the light, even if only to a small degree.[54] In the meantime, Foxe's second edition of the *Acts and Monuments* had included a lengthy defence of their inclusion in a protestant martyrology, though in doing so, he conflated them with the Vaudois.[55] Crespin himself never went so far as to praise or include the Cathars (whom Calvin had criticised) in his martyrology, but they appeared in editions published after his death.[56] The inclusion of older heretical groups to articulate Protestant history was by this stage an accepted tactic.

Crespin had clear criteria for including someone as a martyr. The primary test was twofold: the martyr had to have died, and done so for his faith. Both parts of that rubric were essential: a person had to have been executed as a result of refusing to recant his or her beliefs, and those beliefs had to have been correct. More so than other martyrologists, Crespin was reluctant to include in the *Livre des Martyrs* figures who had not been put to death, an attitude which only gradually shifted in 1563 and after, when he started to print separate historical sections. These were used to give context and continuity to the martyrological accounts, and had a distinctly secondary importance: several of these historical passages were not even listed in the index. Where Foxe had room for leading figures of the English Reformation, martyr or not, Crespin never included a biography of Calvin, for example, and his depiction of Luther came as part of a larger

12 Introduction

discussion of the decline of the Church. Rabus' use of prominent men as 'confessors of the faith', a category parallel to that of martyrdom, in his work does not appear to have been taken up by Crespin.[57]

David El Kenz, working from an unpublished work of Nadia Seré, has identified five marks of a true martyr in Crespin's work. These are, first, that he sheds blood for the truth of the Gospel; second, that (in a well-known passage from St Augustine) it is not the suffering, but the cause which makes the martyr (Crespin cited this dictum approvingly on at least one occasion); third, that it was important that a tribunal of some sort attest to the fact that it was for doctrine that the martyr was condemned; fourth, that the martyr must be condemned exclusively for reasons of religion – those suspected of sedition, for example, were excluded; and finally, that constancy, above all, was the essential principle.[58] In his introduction to the 1570 edition, Crespin stressed the importance of this sort of test:

> The infallible foundation of the truth, which alone shows the differences in suffering of true and false Christians. It is true that the heretics have, in appearance, attractive works, as wild trees also carry fruits which outwardly resemble good ones, and are adorned with very beautiful leaves: but so much as they are outside of Christ, and by consequence of the way, of the truth, and of the life, their faith is wicked, and their cross prevented from benediction. The doctrine therefore, and the confession of faith are amongst all others the most notable and certain fruits of a true foundation of faith: and which must be specially held in these Ecclesiastical collections which are compiled in eight books of this Ecclesiastical history, so as to judge the deeds of the Martyrs by the word of God.[59]

These marks of the martyr explain much that is distinctive about Crespin's work. Under this scheme, massacre victims would be counted as at best semi-martyrs, or 'persecuted faithful', in the absence of a court judgement explicitly condemning them for their beliefs.[60] This, according to El Kenz:

> Obedient, therefore, to the principal formulations of Calvin: the witnessing of Christ, the defence of doctrine, the condemnation for religion, excluding *ipso facto* the spirit of sedition and the patience before suffering. It follows the obligation of a legal process so that the respect of these critera is authenticated by a public demonstration.[61]

Amongst their other purposes, the short historical sections which appeared in the *Livre des Martyrs* from 1564 onward allowed Crespin to retain his criteria for martyrdom whilst providing space to the commemoration and discussion of those who had died in massacres or other persecution, a growing phenomenon in the Wars of Religion.

Introduction   13

A central reason why Crespin seems to have set such store by these marks of the true martyr was the martyrology's intended purpose as a pedagogical tool.[62] Aside from the question of eligibility to be a martyr, an account expressing doctrines contrary to Genevan orthodoxy would run the risk of misinforming its readers on issues of the highest importance. We can expect, therefore, that the *Livre des Martyrs* should broadly reflect Crespin's vision of his own Church, and its theological views. This emphasis on doctrinal matters shaped everything about the book, from the content of the martyrs' speeches to the format in which individual notices were presented. In the *Livre des Martyrs*, confessions of faith, interrogations, and trials were allotted far more space than were the sometimes-gory details of the executions themselves. This emphasis on the martyr's *acta*, rather than his *passio*, to use the language of the ancient martyrologies, betrays Crespin's interest in proving the Augustinian dictum that it was the cause, and not the punishment that mattered in defining a martyr.[63] In later editions, including those published after Crespin's death, the martyrology incorporated the victims of massacres and battles, initially as a lesser category of victim. As the wars progressed, and especially after the St Bartholomew's Day massacres, the two categories of martyr and massacre victim drew closer together, though they were never fully merged.[64]

Crespin's treatment of those of who died at the hands of the Catholic Church, therefore, reveals a great deal about his conception of his denomination and its history. His demonisation of the Anabaptists, for example, is consistent with the attitudes of others, but it confirms to us that there was more to his selection process than selecting the enemies of his enemies. The inclusion of Hussites and Lutherans, on the other hand, implies a broad Church, stretching across national boundaries, and embracing some contradictory stances on major issues. The acceptance of these groups was not, however, unconditional. Crespin edited and altered some of the doctrinal statements of these martyrs, seemingly to ensure that it was clear that they had died for the correct cause, and to advance an image of a united Protestant movement. Editing the *Livre des Martyrs* required Crespin to do more than select appropriate figures; it sometimes involved his intervention in the text itself.

Brad Gregory has written, in *Salvation at Stake*, about this willingness to alter core doctrinal statements; he noted the disparity between Calvin's public dispute with gnesio-Lutherans over the Eucharist at the same time that Crespin was compiling a martyrology which treated an earlier generation of Lutherans as integral members of his Church.[65] Indeed, Crespin was actually the publisher of a number of Calvin's anti-Lutheran tracts. In 1554, Crespin's martyrology omitted ten of their sixty-three articles, principally regarding the sacrament of the Eucharist, but also to do with purgatory.[66] John Foxe is known to have engaged in similar alterations to texts he reproduced, downplaying certain doctrines while still including as a martyr the man who held them.[67]

14   *Introduction*

Examining how Crespin handled a conventional Calvinist martyrdom may be useful for understanding the techniques he was using. The case of Pierre Brully, executed in Tournai in 1545, serves as a good example of how martyrs were presented. Brully had been sent from Strasbourg as a minister by Bucer and by Calvin, and visited several cities in the Low Countries on his tour. With Crespin's own strong links to the region, and to Calvin, he would have had good access to information about Brully. Brully represented a reliable, known quantity in a martyr. He had been chosen for the mission to the Low Countries by Calvin and Bucer themselves, and once captured had defended himself and his doctrine with skill and courage.

Crespin's first depiction of Brully was in the first edition of the *Livre des Martyrs*, in 1554. His account, which took thirty octavo pages, comprised two letters to his wife (addressed throughout as 'sister'), and two to his comrades. In this first version, the letter are presented with little introduction or context, simply a title block giving Brully's name, describing him as a 'Minister in the French Church of Strasbourg, who suffered death in the city of Tournai, 1545'.[68] It describes the letters that follow as his 'Confession of Faith'.[69] This is a fair description of the first letter, addressed to his wife, which states that as:

> you asked me that I tell you the interrogations that I have had, and the responses I gave also, to the Messiers as well as to the Doctors. Note that the thing would be too long if I mislead you writing of all the interrogations which I have done ...

he will provide instead 'the demands and responses touching the Christian faith and doctrine'.[70]

Brully then gives a lengthy reporting of his clashes with the Franciscan doctor Hazard, which allows him to state his religious views in great detail. A particular focus is given to the question of the Eucharist (a topic given a great deal of space in Crespin), but the letter also covers purgatory, several aspects of the cult of the saints, free will, justification, images, baptism, swearing, and confession. Each of these responses is relatively sophisticated, as befits a qualified minister, and usually takes the form of a long response to a short prompt:

> On the traditions of men, they asked if I held to such things, or if I rejected them. I said that I held as good those which have been made for a politic and civil purpose: but not the other, such as the prohibition of marriage to priests and monks, and the prohibition of eating meat on certain days, and the other jumbles and similar ceremonies to which they would oblige souls on pain of mortal sin.[71]

These responses, in the case of Brully like many others, are often full of biblical references and citations.

Introduction   15

This defence of Reformed ideas, and wholesale attack on Catholic ones, is augmented by the letters written to Brully's co-defendants, and to his wife, after being tried and sentenced. These are also full of biblical language, but rather than expounding on doctrine, they aim to console and encourage, urging a rejection of the world and a celebration of God's aid at this difficult time.[72] The only time that Brully appears to step out of his pastoral mode is the final letter to his wife, where he clearly acknowledges the realities of his coming execution, and declares himself happy to die 'for his Gospel and the edification of his people'.[73] He encourages her to remarry, and commends himself to her family, before signing off affectionately. In Crespin's 1554 edition, this series of letters comprises the entire entry on Pierre Brully. There is no narration of his execution, and little discussion of his preaching or his capture. His account in Crespin is presented almost entirely in his own words, with little obvious input from the editor.

Later editions of the *Livre des Martyrs* added narrative and context to the accounts of the martyrs, with the introduction of separate passages of history, and by developing more detailed introductions and conclusions to the core material. By 1570, Brully's account began with an introduction, two folio pages long, which gives a short history of the French Church in Strasbourg, and emphasising the links between Brully and Calvin.[74] Brully's travels in the Low Countries are described in some detail, as is his attempt to evade the authorities, and eventual capture, along with several others from the local congregation. The letters from Brully are then introduced, promising the reader:

> the Theologian monks interrogated him in the presence of the Magistrate, on many points of the religion, and above all on the Mass, on consecration, on adoration, on the host and on Purgatory, as the said Brully wrote to his wife.[75]

The rest of the account is the same as in the earlier editions, though marginal notes have been added throughout, glossing the biblical references and quotations used by Brully, increasing its value to the reader further. The 1570 edition also contains a short conclusion, describing attempts to intervene in his case by Protestant powers, and the actual execution of Brully. Such descriptions of the *passio* of a martyr were less frequent in Crespin than in Foxe, partly because of the difference in the sources available to the two martyrologists, but Crespin's later editions worked to include more of these narratives. Although only two sentences long, this description of Brully's death emphasises his personal bravery: 'the suffering was horrible, because he was burned at a small fire on a large platform', expressly ordered by the civic authorities.[76]

The account of Brully, though altered over its four appearances in Crespin's martyrology, were founded on the words of the martyr himself. Like most of the accounts in the *Livre des Martyrs*, its most important

16 *Introduction*

content was the doctrinal and devotional material in Brully's letters, which was emphasised above all else, even the martyr's own personal bravery and sad circumstances. The account of Brully's martyrdom, especially in the annotated later editions, provided a sort of catechism-by-demonstration, presented to the reader through the apparently unmediated words of a hero and martyr. The martyrology could also, increasingly, provide important context for the history of the Church and its development across Europe. Brully's close relationship with Bucer and Calvin helped to legitimate both him and them and gave the Church in the Low Countries a direct link to the wider Reformed movement.

One effect of the production of martyrologies was the polarised relationship with Catholic authorities which they encouraged. The *Livre des Martyrs* had fewer graphic descriptions of suffering than Foxe's martyrology, and no illustrations, which would have reduced the visceral impact of the executions, but the Catholic Church remained the central enemy, frequently identified with Satan himself. Indeed, as we shall see, a key organising principle, and a central point for qualification in the martyrology, was opposition to the Catholic Church. Catholic authorities are frequently depicted as both cruel and weak, inflicting physical suffering on Protestants after being outwitted by them during the trial. The martyrs, by contrast, are portrayed as confident, capable, and often kind, setting an example for readers not only in the abstract, but as a direct comparison to their Catholic opponents. The use of martyrologies as a conduct-book, as suggested by Pettegree, thus also worked through a process of separation, in encouraging distance from the ideas and behaviours shown by the Catholics.

The books appear to have been successful from a sales point of view. The early editions were pirated very soon after publication, and throughout the 1550s, Crespin compiled and published new editions in both octavo and sextodecimo. The decision to invest in producing a more prestigious folio edition in 1564 also suggests that the *Livre des Martyrs* was reasonably successful, and it appears that this larger edition was even more successful.[77]

The distribution of the books is harder to track. Relatively few copies survive, especially some of the later octavo editions: only two examples of the *Quatrieme partie* are known to exist, and only one of the *Cinquieme partie* of 1563. A great many must have been destroyed intentionally during the years when possession of such books was punishable by death under 1551's edict of Chateaubriant; only two copies of the fourth edition, and one copy of the fifth, are known to survive. Philip Benedict, however, looking at inventories in Metz in the middle of the seventeenth century, suggests that after bibles and psalters, the *Livre des Martyrs* was one of the most-owned books by Protestants in that city, owned at a rate similar to Calvin's *Institutes*.[78] David van der Linden has suggested that the martyrology continued to circulate fairly widely through the end of the

Introduction 17

seventeenth century, with new adaptations of it being published for the Walloon Church in The Hague in the 1680s.[79]

It appears that the martyrology had an important impact during the early years of Protestant growth. Given the material sent to Geneva and to Crespin, which included personal letters, official documents, and a small number of first-hand accounts, it is clear that some people shared Crespin's aims for the project. Susan Broomhall has written about the importance to survivors of such traumas finding that they, in effect, were not alone, and that the disasters visited on them were part of a good, and indeed divine, cause.[80] Both the deaths themselves, and the doctrines which were so carefully recorded, provided a set of shibboleths, which the *Livre des Martyrs* was careful to enshrine. Indeed, as Catherine Randall Coats says, this is nearly a literal enshrining, for Crespin pledged to collect from the martyrs 'not their bones or their ashes ... but their constancy, their words and writings'.[81]

The *Livre des Martyrs* also had an important impact on the development of Protestant historiography. It developed a conceptualisation of the True Church, previously seen in Bale and Foxe, which traced Protestantism's roots and legitimacy to the Apostles via medieval heretics and other groups persecuted by the Catholic Church. Crespin's depiction of the Vaudois, for example, which placed them in this succession, was taken up by both Beza and Foxe. It also appears to have been influential enough to have attracted serious Catholic opposition. Crespin's description of the True Church was attacked in detail more than a century later by Bishop Bossuet as part of his 1688 *History of the Variations of the Protestant Churches*.[82] In 1622, possibly spurred by the 1619 edition of the *Livre des Martyrs* published under Goulart's supervision, Jacques Severt published his *Anti-Martyrology*, which attempted to cast doubt on many of Crespin's claims. Severt was quick to pounce on any misprint or inaccuracy he could find in Crespin's text (and he claimed to find many), and in other places flatly contradicted the martyrology, claiming for example that rather than being the victim of a plot by his brothers, Juan Diaz was killed by robbers.[83]

This book aims to study how Crespin incorporated stranger groups into the *Livre des Martyrs*, with a particular interest in his editorial interventions, helping to construct an image of the church, its background, and its members. As suggested above, Crespin was well-connected, and theologically aware, and his presentation of these groups reflects important trends within Protestant, and especially Genevan, thought. Groups like the Vaudois and the Hussites presented the Reformed Church with a history that extended back centuries, while the close ties that Crespin advertised with the Lutherans and Anglicans helped to preserve an idea of Protestant unity.

This interest in forebears was not an innovation of Crespin's. Calvin had considered that the 'invisible church' of true believers had been

18   Introduction

continuous since the earliest days, a view he set out in his *Institutes*.[84] For Calvin, as for Luther, it had been the Catholic Church which had left the true path, with innovations ranging from the veneration of saints through to transubstantiation.

John Foxe's English martyrology conceived of the decline of the Church into corruption as having begun before the year 1000 (Calvin seems to have considered the process complete by 700 or so).[85] Although he placed special emphasis on the role played by John Wyclif, Foxe was careful to note that: 'there were divers and sondry before Wickliffe's time, whiche have wrasteled and laboured in the same cause & quarel', picking out for special mention John Scotus, Ockham, and John of Janduno, amongst others, for having resisted some of these changes.[86] Foxe's scheme here owed something to John Bale's conception of religious history, and to that outlined in the *Magdeburg Centuries* compiled under Matthias Flacius Illyricus.

A history of dissidents and objections against the Catholic Church, and its doctrines, should be able to trace itself back to the Apostolic Church. Later editions of Crespin stressed the conformity of Calvinist martyrs to those of the early Church, and insisted that even through the dark years of the middle ages there had been groups who had kept the true doctrine alive.[87] Like other Protestant authors, this was a response to what S.J. Barnett has called the question of: 'Where was your church before Luther?'.[88] Later Protestant historians became increasingly interested in tracing a direct line of genealogical descent (as opposed to simply doctrinal conformity) from the time when the Church had been pure.[89] Editions of the *Livre des Martyrs* produced by Simon Goulart, and following Crespin's lead, discussed persecutions under the Roman Empire, the Arians, and the Turks, helping to build a chain of martyrs reaching back to biblical times.

James Ussher, the Anglican bishop who famously calculated the date of the beginning of the world, in 1613 produced a work tracing Protestant doctrines back a millennium, and suggesting an apostolic succession for Martin Luther.[90] As Krumenacker and Racaut, amongst others, have noted, this search for links in the chain of successors led Protestant historians (including Ussher) to take an increasing interest in those groups who had been persecuted by the Catholic Church, notably the Vaudois, or Waldensians. These works often drew on Huguenot histories; Jean-Paul Perrin's history of the Vaudois found its way into English as 1624's *Luther's Fore-runners: Or a Cloud of Witnesses, Deposing for the Protestant Faith*.[91] The Genevan *Histoire Ecclesiastique* of 1580, which draws in places on the *Livre des Martyrs*, suggested that the Vaudois had their roots as early as the year 120, an idea that may have come from an early edition of Crespin's work. By the early seventeenth century, Protestant writers (including Simon Goulart) were often including the medieval heretic Cathars as forerunners of the Reformation as well.[92] This mode of thinking identifies almost all pre-Reformation opposition to the Catholic Church as

Introduction 19

belonging to a coherent movement, which would eventually make the Reformed Church its heir.

Within these theories, the Reformation was still an important and discrete event. Crespin was careful to note the ways in which earlier groups like the Vaudois had been deficient in their beliefs. As will be described below, Luther's appearance on the scene was held to represent the positive return of true doctrine to the Church in ways that other persecuted groups had not done. Groups like the Vaudois were described by Crespin as erring, as having 'little of the true light', and they were shown as eager for the advice and leadership of the Reformed Church.[93] Later discussions of the Vaudois, particularly in Savoy, showed them as integrated members of the Church, with Genevan-trained ministers, and diplomatic support from a number of Swiss cities.

It is clear that for Crespin, the unity he described had to be not simply organisational, but doctrinal. Not only was correct belief the main qualification for martyrdom, above even one's suffering, but given the martyrology's uses as an instructional tool, the theological statements in it had to be both correct and useful. Readers were encouraged to identify with and learn from the martyrs, and incorrect statements could not be included in this context, even to be critiqued. It was exactly this idea of unity that Bossuet attacked a century later, demonstrating some of the liberties Crespin had taken with his sources.[94]

Historiography

Much of the academic study on Crespin's martyrology has tended to focus on the reliability of the *Livre des Martyrs* as a historical source, a debate which has been under way for most of the last century. Piaget and Berthoud, writing in 1930, were critical of Crespin's accuracy, noting a series of deviations from the source materials. Moreau, writing in 1957, argued that Piaget and Berthoud had overstated their case, estimating that in the cases of executions near Arras, Crespin had correctly represented eight of ten verifiable facts.[95] Using court records, William Monter has found another method of assessing Crespin's accuracy, by calculating what percentage of known heresy trials found their way into the *Livre des Martyrs*. He concludes that Crespin's information for periods before the reign of Henri II was 'grossly inadequate', but it became much more reliable, particularly after 1555.[96] Pierre Cameron's PhD thesis similarly suggests a certain degree of reliability in the martyrology over the period in which it was active; his study includes the later editions which continued to 1619.[97]

Monter calculates that for the period 1540–47, Crespin included 13 per cent of the executions recorded in parlementary documents, a figure which rose to 77 per cent for the period 1555–59.[98] David Watson's thesis, which argues for a great deal of caution when using Crespin as a historical

20 *Introduction*

source, uses Gilmont's bibliographical analysis to take into account the divergences between the successive editions of the *Livre des Martyrs*.[99]

Much of the most recent work on Crespin has come in the context of research on broader subjects, or in combination with other publications. Brad Gregory's *Salvation at Stake* places Crespin in context with martyrologies from other confessions, and especially with those of Foxe, Panteleone, de Haemestede, and Rabus, with which the *Livre des Martyrs* shares many aims and much material. This approach engages more fully with the purposes and content of the martyrology than some earlier studies, which often treated Crespin primarily as a source, more concerned with its reliability and its production. The clarification of the extent of exchange of ideas and content amongst the sixteenth-century compilers has also resulted in an increased understanding of Crespin's sources, not least through the work of the John Foxe Project.

This more recent, often comparative, work has also directed more attention to questions of the content of the martyrology: what its aims were, for whom it was written, and what techniques were used to achieve its ends. Andrew Pettegree's suggestion, made about the Dutch martyrologist Adriaan van Haemstede, that martyrologies may have functioned primarily as a pedagogic tool is one which can be applied to Crespin, as Donald Kelley suggested in 1983.[100] This would require us to approach the contents of the *Livre des Martyrs* with a view not simply to their value as historical record, or work of Protestant propaganda, but also as a sort of catechism, a history, and a conduct-book of sorts.

The particular themes and interests to be found in the *Livre des Martyrs* have begun to be addressed, as well. Charles Parker's work has shown that the *Livre des Martyrs* showed an especial tendency to use Old Testament language, compared to other Protestant martyrologies.[101] In addition, literary analysis has been brought to bear on Crespin in Frank Lestringant's *Lumière des Martyrs* and the work of Amy Graves-Monroe; Lestringant, too, notes the identification amongst the Reformed congregations with the wandering tribes of Israel.[102] The work of Catharine Randall Coats has studied the use of themes and ideas which recur throughout the *Livre des Martyrs*, though this approach demands an assumption of a great deal of authorial intent and editorial unity which runs counter to the somewhat magpie approach depicted by Gilmont and others.[103] Nikki Shepardson's *Burning Zeal* also professes the importance of post-modernist techniques of close reading, while wanting to retain the centrality of belief in the actions of the martyrs themselves.[104]

Chapters

As the *Livre des Martyrs* was primarily composed of reprinted tracts and collected letters, with relatively little text penned by Crespin himself, it is in his editorial decisions that we may most easily see his own hand.

Introduction 21

Crespin's interest in doctrinal matters, and his willingness to intervene in the text of his martyrs, can be examined by studying the portrayal of outside groups within *Livre des Martyrs*. Although small in proportion against the mainstream Reformed martyrs, these groups were central to his conception of the Church, and of the historical import of the Reformation. Almost every introduction to the martyrology stated: 'There is today no region, nor country, not even the Turks & other barbarous people, where God has not raised some number of Martyrs, to render to all nations witness of his truth.'[105] The *Livre des Martyrs* was founded on the idea that the Church was universal; there was no assumption that Reform was present in Geneva, or in France, alone.

Important though these stranger groups might be, they often held views critical of the Reformed consensus, or in conflict with it; including them without change could damage the martyrology's utility as a guide to doctrine, or reveal the kinds of tensions within the Protestant movement which were so attractive to Catholic controversialists. Including martyrs from outside of the Genevan or Reformed circles had its attractions, however. They provided a genealogy to reform, giving the movement a pedigree of resistance to papal power and Catholic doctrine, and they asserted a commonality of purpose and history with other Protestant denominations. The way in which Crespin balanced the competing imperatives of doctrinal orthodoxy and historical scope can tell us much about his conception of his Church. In many ways, this represents an early attempt to impose structure upon what Lucien Febvre called the 'magnificent anarchy' of early sixteenth-century heterodoxy.[106] This study will investigate the relationship of the *Livre des Martyrs* with three of these groups: the Hussites, the Vaudois, and the Lutherans.

Of these groups, the Hussites represent nearly the earliest limit of the *Livre des Martyrs*. However, their presence in Crespin was largely limited to their two primary martyrs, Jan Hus and Jerome of Prague, and a short passage detailing the Hussite Wars. The descriptions of the Hussites were full of doctrinal discussion and criticism, and presented challenges to Crespin primarily in their insufficient criticism of the Church as it stood in the early fifteenth century. In the rubric of the *Livre des Martyrs*, they and the Lollards still belonged to a period that imperfectly saw the light, which Crespin eventually identified with the coming of Luther. By comparing the original sources with the martyrology's version of the trials of Hus and Jerome, and the Hussite wars that followed, we can see the ways in which Crespin addressed these issues, including omitting many of the points of difference.

Compared to the Hussites, the Lutherans were regarded by Crespin as full members of the True Church, despite doctrinal clashes with the Reformed Church. The Lutherans presented in the *Livre des Martyrs* are primarily from 1520s Germany, and they represent a period where Crespin considered that the Gospel had begun to return, but for which there were

22 Introduction

no Reformed martyrs. The Genevan relationship with the Lutherans at the time of publication was ongoing and complex, with Crespin involved in both the publication of Lutheran works and polemical tracts attacking Lutheran positions. The treatment of the Lutherans, above all, was informed by the need for a balance between correct doctrine and a show of outward unity with a group over whom they could exercise no control, and who were themselves producing works of history and martyrology.

The immense upheaval of the Peasants' War presented Crespin, and many other Protestant writers, with a radical cause against which they contrasted their own movements. Crespin included a small number of martyrdoms from this period, representing the martyrs (who were primarily Lutheran pastors) as suffering not only for their opposition to the rebels, but in the repression that followed the victory of the authorities. The martyrology's later editions also associated the peasant risings of the 1520s with the Anabaptists and the events at Münster in 1534–35. These martyrological and historical accounts were not strongly focussed on doctrinal matters, being more concerned with questions of resistance to established authority and the legitimate use of force.

The Vaudois had a long history of opposition to the Catholic Church, although by Crespin's time they had formally come under the leadership of the Reformed Church. During the 1540s, 1550s, and 1560s, the Vaudois of Provence, Savoy, and Italy faced periods of persecution and outright military attack, requiring Crespin to frequently update his passages on the Vaudois from edition to edition. As a heretical group who had willingly joined the Reformed Church, the Vaudois testified to Genevan religious leadership, and their clashes with French and Savoyard authorities gave Crespin space in which to discuss their resistance to authority.

When they first appeared in the *Livre des Martyrs*, they represented an early example of a congregation subjected to persecution and massacre; in later editions, the alpine communities of the Vaudois were exemplars of successful resistance to Catholic force. The final editions of the *Livre des Martyrs* featured Vaudois martyrs who were full members of the Reformed Church, and indeed were indistinguishable from Genevan Calvinists.

Looking at the depiction of these groups in the *Livre des Martyrs* allows us to see something of how influential early Calvinists saw their church, and its place in history. Groups like the Vaudois and the Lutherans forced Crespin to draw lines on what doctrines were acceptable material for his audience, and were sometimes the target of criticism that explicitly measured them against the Reformed Church. If we accept that the *Livre des Martyrs* was, like other martyrologies, intended to provide examples of behaviour and of doctrinal instruction, then these groups suggest that there was value to be had in marginal cases. The doctrinal weaknesses of allies like the Vaudois were rarely spelled out, particularly not in official documents like confessions of faith or interrogations; they were instead alluded to indirectly, and in contrast to the positions of the Reformed Church.

Introduction   23

Doctrine was not the only reason that Crespin discussed these groups and included them amongst his martyrs. They provided the Reformed Church with a history and even, perhaps, a sort of alternative apostolic succession. They also provided the Reformed Church with a greater geographical spread. The *Livre des Martyrs* was always an explicitly international publication; 1556's *Troisieme Partie* arranged its index by country of origin, rather than alphabetically, and English martyrs drawn from Foxe made up a very high proportion of later editions of the martyrology.[107] Examining groups like the Vaudois, the Hussites, and the Lutherans, as presented by Crespin, allows us to understand where this influential series of books placed the Reformed Church in time, and in space.

Notes

1 Jean Crespin, *Recueil de plusieurs personnes qui ont constamment enduré la mort pour le nom de Nostre Seigneur* ([Geneva]: Jean Crespin, 1555), pp. 146–47.

2 Brad Gregory, *Salvation at Stake: Christian Martyrdom in Early Modern Europe* (Cambridge: Harvard University Press, 2001), p. 185.

3 Jean Crespin, *Actes des Martyrs* ([Geneva]: Jean Crespin, 1565), sig. *a* iii verso.

4 Frank Lestringant, *Lumière des Martyrs* (Paris, Honoré Champion, 2004), p. 194.

5 Jean Crespin, *Recueil de plusieurs personnes qui ont constamment endure la mort pour la nome de N. S. Jesus Christ* ([Geneva: Jean Crespin], 1554), sig. ii recto.

6 Crespin, *Recueil de plusieurs personnes* (1554), sig. iiii verso.

7 Jean Crespin, *Histoire des vrays tesmoins de la verité de l'Evangile* ([Geneva: Jean Crespin], 1570), sig. *a* iiii recto.

8 Crespin, *Histoire des vrays tesmoins* (1570), sig. *a* iiii verso to [vi] recto.

9 Jean Crespin, *Histoire memorable de la persecution de Merindol et Cabrieres* ([Geneva: Jean Crespin], 1555), p. 47.

10 Jean-François Gilmont, *Jean Crespin: Un éditeur réformé du XVIe siècle* (Geneva: Droz, 1981), p. 32.

11 Gilmont, *Jean Crespin*, pp. 32, 45.

12 Gilmont, 'La Correspondence de Jean Crespin', *Lias*, VI, p. 9.

13 Gilmont, *Jean Crespin*, pp. 222–28.

14 Gilmont, *Jean Crespin*, p. 246.

15 See Devorah Greenberg, ' "Foxe" as a Methodological Response to Epistemic Challenges', in David Loades (ed.), *John Foxe at Home and Abroad* (Aldershot: Ashgate, 2004), p. 242.

16 Gilmont, *Jean Crespin*, p. 66.

17 Elizabeth Evenden, *Patents, Pictures and Patronage: John Day and the Tudor Book Trade* (Aldershot: Ashgate, 2008), p. 64.

18 Gilmont, *Jean Crespin*, pp. 179–87.

19 Crespin, *Recueil de plusieurs personnes* (1554), sig. [vi], recto–verso.

20 Catharine Randall Coats, *(Em)bodying the Word: Textual Resurrections in the Martyrological Narratives of Foxe, Crespin, de Bèze and d'Aubigné* (New York: Peter Lang, 1992).

21 Coats, p. 187.

22 Crespin, *Recueil de plusieurs personnes* (1554), sig. [viii] verso.

24 Introduction

23 Crespin, *Histoire des vrays tesmoins* (1570), Preface, sig. [*a* vii recto].
24 Gilmont, *Jean Crespin*, p. 129.
25 Gilmont, *Bibliographie des éditions de Jean Crespin* (Verviers: Gason, 1981), Vol. I, p. 68.
26 Gilmont, *Jean Crespin*, pp. 130–35.
27 Gilmont, *Jean Crespin*, pp. 255–60.
28 David Watson discussed these two in the context of Crespin's writing in 'Jean Crespin and the Writing of History in the French Reformation', in Bruce Gordon (ed.), *Protestant History and Identity in Sixteenth-Century Europe*, Vol. 2 (Aldershot: Scolar Press, 1996), pp. 40–41.
29 Alexandra Kess, *Johann Sleidan and the Protestant Vision of History* (Aldershot: Ashgate, 2008), pp. 93–94.
30 Kess, p. 106.
31 Kess, p. 95.
32 Gilmont, *Jean Crespin*, p. 177.
33 Gilmont, *Jean Crespin*, p. 166.
34 Gilmont, *Bibliographie*, Vol. I, pp. 248–55. This excludes the pirated sextodecimos made of the first edition, printed by the Rivery brothers.
35 Crespin, *Recueil de plusieurs personnes* (1555), p. CXXXIIII.
36 Gilmont, *Jean Crespin*, p. 170. Elizabeth Evenden and Thomas Freeman, *Religion and the Book in Early Modern England: The Making of John Foxe's 'Book of Martyrs'* (Cambridge: Cambridge University Press, 2014), pp. 59–60.
37 Gilmont, *Bibliographie*, p. 163.
38 Watson, 'Jean Crespin and the Writing of History in the French Reformation', p. 57.
39 Gilmont, *Jean Crespin*, p. 180.
40 Gilmont, *Jean Crespin*, p. 181.
41 Gilmont, *Jean Crespin*, p. 250.
42 Gilmont, *Bibliographie*, p. 131.
43 Gilmont, *Jean Crespin*, p. 175.
44 Andrew Pettegree, 'Adriaan van Haemstede: The Heretic as Historian', in Bruce Gordon (ed.), *Protestant History and Identity in Sixteenth Century Europe* (Aldershot: Scolar Press, 1996), p. 69.
45 Crespin, *Actes des Martyrs* (1565), sig. *a* ii verso.
46 Crespin, *Actes des Martyrs* (1565), p. 189.
47 Crespin, *Recueil de plusieurs personnes* (1554), sig. *ii recto.
48 Crespin, *Recueil de plusieurs personnes* (1554), f. [*vi verso].
49 Crespin, *Recueil de plusieurs personnes* (1554), f. [*vii recto].
50 Crespin, *Troisieme Partie du recueil des martyrs* ([Geneva]: Jean Crespin, 1556), p. 4.
51 Jean Crespin and Eustache Vignon, *Histoire des Martyrs persécutez et mis à mort pour la vérité de l'Evangile* (Geneva, 1582), ff. *i–*ii verso.
52 Yves Krumenacker, 'Les genealogie imaginaire de la Reforme Protestante', *Revue Historique*, 638 (2006), p. 262.
53 Krumenacker, p. 271.
54 Krumenacker, p. 271.
55 Luc Racaut, *Hatred in Print, Catholic Propaganda and Protestant Identity During the French Wars of Religion* (Aldershot: Ashgate, 2002), p. 119.
56 Jean Calvin, *Institutes of the Christian Religion*, trans. Beveridge (London: James Clarke & Co, 1953), p. 292.
57 Robert Kolb, *For All the Saints: Changing Perceptions of Martyrdom and Sainthood in the Lutheran Reformation* (Macon, GA: Mercer, 1987), p. 63.

Introduction 25

58 David El Kenz, *Les bûchers du roi: la culture protestante des martyrs (1523–1572)* (Paris: Seyssel, 1997), p. 128. Brad Gregory discusses the appearance of this theme in martyrology in *Salvation at Stake*, pp. 329–32.

59 Crespin, *Histoire des vrays tesmoins* (1570), sig. *a* iiii, verso.

60 El Kenz, *Les bûchers du roi*, p. 128.

61 El Kenz, *Les bûchers du roi*, p. 128.

62 David Watson, *The Martyrology of Jean Crespin and the Early French Evangelical Movement, 1523–1555* (PhD Thesis, St Andrew's, 1997), p. 2. Watson, 'Jean Crespin and the Writing of History in the French Reformation', pp. 39–58.

63 Maureen Tilley, *Donatist Martyr Stories: The Church in Conflict in Roman North Africa* (Liverpool: Liverpool University Press, 1996), pp. XIX–XXI.

64 Jameson Tucker, 'Fire and Iron', in Elizabeth Tingle and Jonathan Willis (eds), *Dying, Death, Burial and Commemoration in Reformation Europe* (Aldershot: Ashgate, 2015).

65 Gregory, p. 183.

66 Gregory, p. 185.

67 Gregory, p. 185, gives the examples of [Jorgen] Wagner.

68 Crespin, *Recueil de plusieurs personnes* (1554), p. 186.

69 Crespin, *Recueil de plusieurs personnes* (1554), p. 186.

70 Crespin, *Recueil de plusieurs personnes* (1554), p. 187.

71 Crespin, *Recueil de plusieurs personnes* (1554), p. 194.

72 Crespin, *Recueil de plusieurs personnes* (1554), p. 205.

73 Crespin, *Recueil de plusieurs personnes* (1554), p. 214.

74 Crespin, *Histoire des vrays tesmoins* (1570), p. 135 verso.

75 Crespin, *Histoire des vrays tesmoins* (1570), p. 136 recto.

76 Crespin, *Histoire des vrays tesmoins* (1570), p. 240 recto.

77 Gilmont, *Jean Crespin*, p. 179.

78 Philip Benedict, 'Bibliothèques protestantes et catholiques à Metz au XVIIe siècle', *Annales. Économies, Sociétés, Civilisations*, 40:2 (1985), p. 354.

79 David van der Linden, *Experiencing Exile: Huguenot Refugees in the Dutch Republic, 1680–1700* (Aldershot: Ashgate Publishing, 2015), p. 183.

80 Susan Broomhall, 'Disturbing Memories: Narrating Experiences and Emotions of Distressing Events in the French Wars of Religion', in Erika Kuijpers, Judith Pollmann, Johannes Mueller, and Jasper van der Steen (eds), *Memory before Modernity: Practices of Memory in Early Modern Europe* (Leiden: Brill, 2013).

81 Crespin, *Recueil de plusieurs personnes* (1554), sig. [vi], recto–verso.

82 Jacques-Bénigne Bossuet, *Histoire des Variations des Eglises Protestantes* (Paris: Veuve Mabre Cramoisy, 1688).

83 Jacques Severt, *L'anti-martyrologe ou Verité manifestée contre les histories des supposées martyrs de la Religion pretendue reformee ...*, (Lyon: Rigaud, 1622), p. 490.

84 Calvin, *Institutes*, Book IV, Chapter 1, 2, p. 282. Krumenacker, p. 263.

85 *The Acts and Monuments Online*, 1563 edition, p. 17. Calvin, *Institutes*, Book IV, Chapter VII, pp. 365–88.

86 *The Acts and Monuments Online*, 1563 edition, p. 137.

87 Crespin, *Actes des Martyrs* (1565), [sig. A vi].

88 S.J. Barnett, 'Where Was Your Church Before Luther? Claims for the Antiquity of Protestantism Examined', *Church History* 68 (1999), p. 15.

89 Krumenacker, p. 261.

90 Krumenacker, p. 266.

91 Jean-Paul Perrin, *Luthers Fore-runners: Or a Cloud of Witnesses, Deposing for the Protestant Faith* (London, for Nathanael Newbery, 1624). Barnett, p. 25.

26 Introduction

92 Théodore de Bèze, *Histoire Ecclésiastique des Églises Réformées au Royaume de France*, Vol. 1, G. Baum and E. Cunitz (eds) (Nieuwkoop: De Graaf, 1974), p. 57. Racaut, *Hatred in Print*, p. 126.

93 Crespin, *Recueil de plusieurs personnes* (1554), p. 657.

94 Bossuet, *Histoire des Variations*, pp. 508–13, e.g.

95 Georges Moreau, 'Contribution à l'Histoire de Livre des Martyrs', *Bulletin de la Société de l'Histoire de Protestantisme Français*, 103 (1957), p. 179. As it was Crespin's hometown, Arras might have been expected to be a particular area of strength.

96 William Monter, *Judging the French Reformation: Heresy Trials by Sixteenth-Century Parlements* (London: Harvard University Press, 1999), p. 183.

97 Pierre Cameron, *Le martyrologe de Jean Crespin, etude de ses editions au XVIe siecle* (PhD Thesis, Université de Montreal, 1996).

98 Monter, *Judging the French Reformation*, p. 183.

99 David Watson, *The Martyrology of Jean Crespin*.

100 Andrew Pettegree, 'Adriaan van Haemstede: The Heretic as Historian', in Gordon, *Protestant History and Identity*, p. 69. Donald Kelley, *The Beginning of Ideology: Consciousness and Society in the French Reformation* (Cambridge: Cambridge University Press, 1983), p. 248.

101 Charles Parker, 'French Calvinists as the Children of Israel: An Old Testament Self-Consciousness in Jean Crespin's *Histoire des Martyrs* before the Wars of Religion', *Sixteenth Century Journal*, 24 (1993).

102 Lestringant, *Lumière des Martyrs*.

103 Coats.

104 Nikki Shepardson, *Burning Zeal: The Rhetoric of Martyrdom and the Protestant Community in Reformation France, 1520–1570* (Cranbury, NJ: Associated University Presses, 2007).

105 Crespin, *Recueil de plusieurs personnes* (1554), sig. iiii verso.

106 Lucien Febvre, *Au Coeur religieux du XVIe siècle* (Paris: Sevpen, 1968).

107 Crespin, *Troisieme Partie du recueil des martyrs* (1556), p. 531.

1 The Hussites and Protestant history

The first edition of Crespin's martyrology, 1554's *Livre des Martyrs*, begins with a section depicting the: 'History of the Holy Martyr Jan Hus', the Bohemian theologian who had been burned at the Council of Constance in 1415. This idea, that Hus had a central role to play in the history of the Reformation, was not new to Crespin. Hussite documents, works, and histories had been published in Germany almost since the beginning of the Reformation there. Translations of Peter of Mladonovice's eyewitness account of Hus' trial and execution were published in Nuremburg in 1528 and 1529, Poggio Bracciolini's *Historia Johannis Huss* ... was published in 1528, and Aeneas Sylvius's *Historia Bohemica* was published in Basel in 1551. German authors also produced their own confessionally inflected histories of Hus, with the Catholic controversialist Johannes Cochlaeus producing a *Historia Hussitorium* in 1549, and the Lutheran Matthias Flacius Illyricus publishing his 1558 *Johannis Hus et Hieronymi Pragensis* ... *Historia et Monumenta*, which brought together many of the key Hussite letters and documents into a large-scale history.[1] Johannes Agricola even wrote a drama based on the *Relatio* of Philip of Mladonovice, Crespin's principal source.[2]

This wide, and almost immediate, interest in Hus was driven by an awareness of parallels between his situation and that of Luther. The emperor's promise of safe-conduct to and from the Diet of Worms for Luther was contrasted with the similar promise offered to Hus in 1414, which had not been upheld.[3] Luther himself seems to have been behind some of this renewed interest in Hus. In 1521 he was said to have declared that:

> if [Jerome] Emser produces Aristotle and crowns me with the name of Huss and Jerome, I would rather share Huss's disgrace than Aristotle's honor ... Huss, who, by the grace of God, is again coming to life and tormenting his murderers, the pope and the popish set, more strongly now than when he was alive.[4]

Luther's 1520 *Address to the Christian Nobility* contains the suggestion that the claims of the Bohemians be seriously considered, and goes on to

28 *The Hussites and Protestant history*

state that he has found no error in what he has read of Hus, though he had specifically stated: 'I do not wish to make John Huss a saint or martyr, as some of the Bohemians do.'[5] In a letter of the same year to George Spalatin, Luther identified himself strongly with Hus:

> I have taught and held all the teachings of John Huss, but thus far did not know it. John Staupitz has taught it in the same unintentional way. In short we are all Hussites, and did not know it. Even Paul and Augustine are in reality Hussites ... I am so shocked that I do not know what to think when I see such terrible judgements of God over mankind, namely, that the most evident evangelical truth was burned in public and was already considered condemned more than one hundred years ago. Yet one is not allowed to avow this. Woe to this earth.[6]

The publication of Mladonovice's *Relatio* in Latin, in 1528 and German in 1529 by Johannes Agricola seems to have been done at Luther's instigation, and in 1538 Luther published a series of Hus' sermons alongside one of his own.[7] By this point, he was seemingly less reserved in his praise of Hus; in his 1537 sermon on John 16, Luther even went so far as to call him 'St. John Hus – we can surely do him the honor of calling him a saint, since he had far less guilt than we have ...'.[8] By the 1550s a tradition had developed of linking contemporary Lutherans back to Wyclif, via the intermediary of Jan Hus.[9] Indeed, some Lutherans were eager enough to claim a direct connection that some Hussite tracts were falsified, in order to better agree with Protestant doctrine.[10] Thus by the time that Crespin produced the *Livre des Martyrs*, starting the martyrology with Hus and the Hussites would have seemed a relatively uncontroversial choice. From the beginning, the *Livre des Martyrs* presented Hus as a forerunner of Luther's in a genealogical, and not simply doctrinal, sense, as the Lutheran books of the 1530s and 1540s had already argued.[11]

The position of Hus at the very beginning of the *Livre des Martyrs* did not last long, however. From 1555's edition onwards, Hus and the Hussites lost their position as the first martyrs of the book to the English theologian John Wyclif, who would retain this position in all of his following editions. This was achieved by adding new pages to the first volume, creating two new quires, with pages numbered i–xxxii, before the Hussite section, allowing the passages on Hus that had been printed in 1554 to be reused. Indeed, Gilmont demonstrates that these sections of the 1554 and 1555 editions of the martyrology were interchangeable.[12] This suggests a certain degree of opportunism in the addition of the English martyrs, as it appears that no major reworking of the structure of the book was being considered. Even with addition of a great deal of material from Foxe on the subject of Wyclif and the Lollards, Hus and his followers provided the bulk of the theological discussion, and narrative thrust, of the early sections of the martyrology.

John Wyclif

In 1555, in the second edition of the martyrology, Crespin provided a lengthy description and defence of his decision to include Wyclif in the martyrology, placing him in a context of Satan's campaign against the True Church, which has taken place at all times, and in all corners of the world.[13] He described how even in darkest times, God has 'in a marvellous fashion always guarded some sparks to relight the great illumination of his truth' in 'times he knew were opportune, by His divine prudence'.[14] Wyclif and other early figures are explicitly said to provide a link back to the Apostles themselves, as: 'since the beginning of the preaching of the Gospel, there has been a continual order of good Doctors and Ministers, which will be easy to show ...', but trusts that his readers will 'be content this time, if we begin with the times of M John Wyclif, Englishman, to show how this sentence is true, that "The gates of Hell can do nothing against this invincible truth of God"'.[15] Wyclif, then, represented for Crespin only one of a number of potential beginnings for the martyrology, as Hus had in the previous edition, and a particular emphasis is laid on the idea that the Reformed Church can trace its own form of Apostolic succession.

This introduction to the subject of Wyclif provides the reader with a description of the state of the Church during the middle ages, outlining a time when:

> the Christian kings and princes, for all the affection and all the zeal that they had to emphasise the religion, employed all of their forces to recover the wood of the cross of Christ, which was in the city of Jerusalem. As if all the religion consisted of that, and as if there were no other cross, than that which was in the city of Jerusalem.[16]

It was into this corrupted and misguided climate that Wyclif emerged. Using language also used about Luther and of Vualdo, Crespin suggests that Wyclif's prominence had a divine origin, that: 'our Lord and good God raised this good person'; God, 'by his great mercy, awakened the world, buried under the dreams of human traditions, and this by means of the said Wyclif'.[17] Wyclif, from his position at Oxford, had seen that the 'true Theology had been villainously corrupted', and began to dispute small issues, planning to move to greater ones.[18] These took place in debates against the monk John Kenningham, which helped to attract the attention of the Pope.

This interest in Wyclif, and in the history of the Church, derived fairly directly from John Foxe's *Commentarii Rerum* of 1554, from which Crespin drew of his information on Wyclif and the Lollards, and a great deal of the introductory material with which he introduced them, including his conception of the state of the medieval Church.[19] Crespin also used the

30 *The Hussites and Protestant history*

Commentarii Rerum to expand his existing section on Jerome of Prague, to which he added an extra quire of sixteen pages; like the section on Wyclif, this was added to the existing pagination, and had to be paginated in roman numerals.[20] This edition of the *Livre des Martyrs* did not draw on Foxe for the narrative of Hus, however, but continued to use the version published the year before.

Crespin drew heavily on Foxe's Latin edition for his information on Wyclif, and did not materially change it in the later editions. He included not only a history of Wyclif's life, but also two of the propositions (to list them all 'would be too lengthy'), purportedly from an assembly of bishops at Lambeth, in 1377.[21] The extent to which we can take these as genuinely representing his theology is open to question: Wyclif would later complain about being misrepresented when a series of articles from a later meeting was condemned by the Pope.[22] The articles selected attack the Church's temporal power, questioning the Church's right to hold property, as it had been given under 'a tacit condition: that God be honoured, and that the faithful be edified'; and arguing that the Pope could be legitimately reprimanded, for he 'can sin like the others, and if he sins, he must be fraternally corrected'.[23] There is no other serious theological discussion in this passage, which goes on to describe Wyclif's condemnation, and eventual death. The passage also describes the burning of Wyclif's bones in 1428 with reference to martyrdom: 'these cruel tyrants exercise their barbarity not only on the living, but also against the dead'.[24]

Crespin moved his narrative on from Wyclif, suggesting that 'it would not be possible to amass all the histories of so many martyrs, who by all regions of the whole world spent their blood to maintain the truth'.[25] Some were caught by fraud, others imprisoned, and some publically tortured, while many died in secret, or of hunger, in prisons.[26] This text connects the discussion of Wyclif to a series of other martyrs of the middle ages, some of whom died before Wyclif. These are all taken from Foxe's *Commentarii*: forty men burned in Narbonne, and twenty-four in Paris, in 1210, were claimed for the cause (at least some of these would appear to be the followers of Amalric de Bène), while the 'Prince Armeric' who was hanged in 1211, corresponds to Aimery de Montréal, killed during the Albigensian Crusade, an early example of Protestant adoption of that sect, whom Crespin held were 'burned by the enemies of truth'.[27] The Lollards, the Hussites, and by extension, the Reformed Church were all connected to this history of dissent against the Catholic Church, connections which Crespin made more explicit at the end of this section of the martyrology.

Crespin's history of the Lollards grew substantially in 1564, when he included a number of Lollard martyrs drawn from Foxe's English-language martyrology. Primarily, they were long accounts relating prosecutions from the fifteenth century, and served to flesh out the history of opposition to the Catholic Church after Wyclif and Hus, and before Luther. Crespin begins the *Livre des Martyrs* of 1564 with Wyclif on the first page, and shows his doctrine travelling to Bohemia on the ninth.[28] This is followed by seven martyr's accounts, most of them relatively short, before the case of Jan Hus is reached. Crespin was working to maintain chronological order in this edition of the martyrology, where some earlier editions had divided the martyrs by geographical location. Hus and Jerome of Prague were followed by a number of passages not derived from Foxe, including Catherine Saube, burned at Montpellier in 1417 for denying the power of corrupt priests, by Henry Grunfelder and others executed in Germany in 1420, and by a long passage drawn from the work of Nicholas Clemangis on the corruption of the Church in this period.[29] A number of Lollard accounts, including a lengthy passage on John Oldcastle, and another on William Taylor, were interspersed with the accounts of the Hussite wars from the 1420s, and indeed Savonarola, until the first Lutheran martyrs appear on the scene in the form of the Brussels martyrs Voez and Esch.[30]

Even after these additions of Wyclif and the Lollard martyrs had been made, however, Hus and his followers remained the largest and most detailed accounts that Crespin presented of the Church in the fifteenth century. Unlike with Wyclif and his followers, whose doctrinal positions had been mediated by Foxe, when constructing his accounts of Hus and the Hussites Crespin was for the most part drawing upon contemporary accounts, often reprinted due to the Lutheran interest in them. The editorial changes and doctrinal positions taken, therefore, reflect Crespin's work on an early stage of Reformation history.

Sources

Crespin's lengthy narration of the trial and execution of Hus was largely based on Peter of Mladonovice's eyewitness account of the trial and execution at the Council of Constance, the *Relatio de Magistri Joannis Hus causa*. This work was reasonably well-known in Protestant circles, having already been adapted by Agricola and Flacius Illyricus, and reprinted in 1528 and 1529. Mladonovice had been a student of Hus', and in 1414 was secretary to Hus' protector Lord Chlum, a companion on the voyage from Bohemia to Constance.[31] This work was almost immediately treated as the definitive account of Hus' death by his followers, and passages of it were read in church on the anniversary of his death, after the Gospel lesson.[32] Vaclav considered the chapters describing the hearings at the Council to have been written contemporaneously, while the description of Hus' death were perhaps written shortly after the fact.[33] This *Relatio de magistri Joannis Hus causa*, was published, as we have seen, in 1528 and 1529, in Latin and German respectively. However, no examples of the Latin printed edition are known to have survived, and so Novotny and Spinka have based their editions on the fifteenth-century manuscript examples; it is possible that some of the changes seen in the text were made by the German editors of 1528, and not by Crespin himself.[34]

32 The Hussites and Protestant history

The sections on the Hussites were not restricted to Mladonovice's narration of Hus' death. The trial and execution of Jerome of Prague, one of Hus' followers and a Hussite leader in his own right, had been recorded by Poggio Bracciolini, a Florentine humanist present at Constance in his capacity as a functionary of the papal *curia*. The letter he wrote, which was later published, describing Jerome's defence of himself, and casting his suffering in a Stoic mould, became famous in humanist circles during the fifteenth century. Well before the development of Protestant martyrology, Poggio's description of Jerome was a well-known piece of writing.[35]

The Hussite Wars were described in Crespin through the history produced by Aeneas Sylvius Piccolomini, later Pope Pius II, whose 1458 *Historia Bohemica* was rooted in his mission to Bohemia, which had secured the Compacts of Basel, allowing the Hussites to remain in communion with Rome which practising Utraquism.[36] Aeneas Sylvius's work betrays a particular interest in the radical Taborite faction of the Hussites, which he had visited, and was a major source for Crespin's narrative of the Hussite wars. This material was replaced in the next edition, with more of a focus on Zizka, citing different sections of the *Historica Bohemica*.[37] In addition to the *Historica Bohemica*, Crespin could draw on other publications by Aeneas Sylvius, including the *Commentariorum Aeneae Sylvii Piccolominei Senensis, de Concilio Basileae* ... published in 1523 in Basel. The Bohemian civil wars, and the nature of the Taborites, were less discussed at the beginning of the sixteenth century than the trials of Hus and Jerome had been.

The narrative

Crespin's accounts of Hus' death, and the events afterwards, are marked by their reliance on one or two sources for any given topic. Despite the existence of other sources, like Poggio's *Historia*, or the work of John Bale, in Crespin the discussion of Hus' trial and execution at the Council of Constance derives almost entirely from the *Relatio* of Peter of Mladonovice. This recognition of the value of the eyewitness account followed the example of Flacius Illyricus and Agricola in their use of Mladonovice. This narrative, however, was presented and mediated by Crespin in a manner that stressed the links with Calvinist doctrine.

In the first edition, Crespin began relating the story of Hus with no fanfare and little introduction. The first page of the *Livre des Martyrs* is simply titled: 'The history of the Holy Martyr Jan Hus'. In 1555, in accordance with the Council of Geneva, the word 'martyr' was removed, and the first page of this edition was headed with: 'The history and acts of Jan Hus, true witness of the doctrine of the Son of God.'[38] This page was otherwise unaltered; there is still no introduction, or context given to Hus specifically. This page (its entire quire, in fact) was reprinted as a direct copy of the 1554 edition; new pages were appended before and after it to

The Hussites and Protestant history 33

include the discussion of Wyclif and the Lollards that appeared in this edition.[39] In both cases, there was relatively little space given to explaining Hus' background or significance to the reader.

Crespin made the connection between Wyclif and Hus clear in two pages at the end of this section, describing 'How the doctrine of Wyclif came to Bohemia'.[40] Like Foxe, he appears to have drawn this material from the *Historia Bohemica* of Aeneas Sylvius. This section brings the inserted quires up to the required thirty-two pages, describing a Bohemian scholar named Nicholas (and unkindly referred to as 'the rotting fish') returning to his native land with a copy of Wyclif's *Des Universales*, and the difficulties that these works caused between the Czech and German factions at the university.[41] Crespin relates the victory over the German masters, and their departure to found a new university at Leipzig in 1409.[42] Hus' personal qualities are praised, and Crespin describes the foundation of the Bethlehem chapel and its population with Czech-language preachers as if it happened as a result of, and not before, the rise of Hus to prominence.[43] The section concludes, and links to the account of Hus, with a description of Hus' work in the Bethlehem chapel. Hus began to teach from Wyclif's books,

> affirming that all truth was contained in them, and often saying that after his passing he hoped that his soul went to where Wyclif's was, so assured was he that he had been a man of substance, holy and worthy of going to Heaven.[44]

Hus was introduced again in the 1564 edition, as Crespin collected together all of the information from the previous volumes. This edition, which placed Hus on page 27 of the first book of the martyrology, represented Crespin's first real opportunity to alter the text of his section on Hus. As in 1555, however, the only real changes were to the presentation and paratext around the narrative. In a short introduction, he describes the basic arc of Hus' story, emphasising his personal goodness, his being lured to Constance, and his death, which 'has further advanced the growth of this truth', and claims that his work is drawn directly from the records of the Council.[45] While the Mladonovice work from which Crespin drew his account does include some official documents, it must have been clear to Crespin that his source was not an official document in any form; Mladonovice makes clear in places his status as an eyewitness, and appeals for correction if he has erred. Crespin also added marginalia to this edition, giving reference points and biblical glosses.

Mladonovice's *Relatio* was divided into five chapters, translated by Spinka as 'Events prior to the Journey to Constance', 'The Trial to the Beginning of the Imprisonment, and in what Matter it Originated', 'Here Follow the So-called Hearings, but in Truth not Hearings but Jeerings and Vilifications', 'About the Hearing on the Eighth Day of June', and 'The

34 *The Hussites and Protestant history*

End of the Saintly and Reverend Master John Hus'. They cover a period of about ten months, from the summons by the council in October 1414 to Hus' death in July 1415. Crespin's version follows it closely, though there are some areas where cuts to the text have been made, which reduce the document's length by nearly a third in total.

The narrative begins with the calling of the Council, and Hus' summons to it by Sigismund, who provided Hus with a safe conduct, reproduced by Crespin in full.[46] This places one of the most controversial parts of Hus' martyrdom – his betrayal by the Imperial powers – in the first section of the account. The trust Hus put into the safe-conduct of the king is emphasised: 'seeing such pretty promises, and the assurances that the Emperor gave, he responded that he was going to the Council', as is the care that he took to ensure that no authority in Prague claimed that he held heretical beliefs by offering a debate on his doctrines, a stratagem to reduce accusations of disobedience to Bohemian authorities.[47]

Perhaps displaying a lack of confidence in these promises, Hus left letters to his friends and the people of Prague, which Mladonovice and Crespin reproduced.[48] These are joined by a series of letters which serve to narrate Hus' voyage through Germany, and arrival at Constance. Crespin was familiar with this approach to including letters within a martyrological framework, and largely maintained it in the *Livre des Martyrs*.

The next chapter in the *Relatio* (the chapter divisions are not clearly made in Crespin) begins with Hus' arrest at the hands of two bishops and a number of armed men.[49] This section is presented in described speech, presumably witnessed first-hand by Mladonovice, who was in Hus' party. Early in his captivity, Hus was engaged by a theologian posing as a simple Minorite friar, but avoided the Council's trap with the aid of his companion and patron Lord Chlum.[50] The Cardinals and other members of the Church hierarchy are shown in an unflattering light, from their attempt to entrap Hus above, to their glee at his arrest, and the ease with which they are defeated in debate by members of Hus' party.[51]

Hus is also shown answering the first of many sets of articles created to try and define his positions. This list of forty-four articles was compiled by his old friend and colleague, Stephen Palecs, from some of Hus' existing writings. Mladonovice and Crespin stress their convictions that Palec's list was fraudulent, and designed to condemn Hus, although neither quotes the list itself.[52] The last section of this chapter – amounting to nearly half of its length, and a quarter of the entire *Relatio* – was cut, presumably by Crespin, although it is not possible to fully rule out that it was missing from his source version.

The third chapter of Mladonovice's account gave his readers eye-witness information from the hearing before the Council. Hus was charged primarily with teaching and defending the errors of Wyclif, as well as holding the doctrine of remanence, a denial of transubstantiation which had long been implied by Wyclifite teaching.[53] The questioning of Hus by the

The Hussites and Protestant history 35

Council is given supposedly verbatim (Mladonovice was present at these events), over the course of the first day's hearing. The sometimes tumultuous nature of the hearings is emphasised throughout, and the dialogue centres on the theological issues for which Hus was on trial, as well as the political ramifications of the safe-conduct given by Sigismund. The next chapter takes in another day's hearings, and consists largely of articles excerpted from Hus' writings by Palecs, and Hus' article-by-article responses to them, followed by the Council's condemnation. The debate, including interventions from Sigismund himself, continues from the previous chapter.

The final chapter details the degradation and execution of Hus. The defrocking process was described in detail, particularly the reading of the articles which had been decided against him, including some points that had not been aired before. The chapter also sees repeated discussions of Hus' stance towards recanting: Hus repeatedly offered, in Mladonovice's account, to recant should he be shown, through scripture, to be wrong.[54] After his degradation, a paper crown painted with devils was placed on Hus' head (Hus immediately compared it to the crown of thorns), he was tied to the stake, and burned.[55] He met his death singing religious songs, and his body was broken up and thrown into the river to ensure that there was no chance of his followers taking relics.[56]

Doctrine

Within this narrative, Hus' doctrine is discussed in detail at several points, all within the context of his hearings before the Council of Constance, the details of which are taken from Mladonovice, and usually in his own reported words. First, there is a letter from the Bishop of Litomysl, explaining to the Council the way in which Hussite agitation was proceeding across Bohemia, showing the impact Hus' movement was having in Prague, and the accusations being levelled against his followers. Second, the charges against Hus are reproduced, and his initial defence of himself. The most in-depth discussion, however, comes with the presentation of thirty-nine articles against Hus, and his subsequent defence. These were mainly assembled by Palecs, taken from Hus' works *De Ecclesiastica* and *Contra Palecs*; the reader is told that they were presented falsely, in order to condemn Hus.[57] The central issues on which Hus was being challenged were those which questioned the power of the Church hierarchy, rather than his views on the Eucharist, for which his followers would become notorious. At many points, Hus defended himself by denying these charges, and insisted that he held to more conventional Catholic positions. Crespin, like other Protestant authors, felt that the positions that Hus was accused of holding represented premonitions of his own doctrine, and in several places altered Hus' responses, weakening them in a way that gave the impression of a more radical Hus.

36 *The Hussites and Protestant history*

The letter from the Bishop of Litomysl was tabled at the conference in response to a letter by the lords of Bohemia. It made frequent references to the rising tensions within Bohemia, suggesting that there was a growing public support for Hus, and refers to accusations that the people of Bohemia were carrying the blood of Christ about in bottles, accusations the nobles wanted to deny.[58] Crespin did not reproduce this letter in full; he paraphrased, instead, the first part of this letter touching on the safe-conduct, and the request that the Emperor honour it.[59] Crespin removed several of the later passages, however, most importantly one which complains of the stories being told that 'the sacrament of the most precious blood of the Lord is being carried about Bohemia in bottles and that cobblers are now hearing confessions and administering the most holy body of the Lord to others'.[60] In order to protect the reputation of their nation, the lords had implored the council not to believe such rumours.

It was in response to this letter by the lords that the Bishop of Litomysl intervened. Having been told that his accusations of profaning the Eucharist have defamed the Bohemians, the bishop repeats the accusation at length – a central argument was that Hus' teachings were reshaping Bohemians' relationship with the sacrament. He stresses that laymen are taking both the bread and the wine, and that consecrated wine is being carried about in bottles and flasks.[61] He also introduces, second-hand, an incident wherein a woman had grabbed the Eucharist from the hands of a priest and administered it to herself.[62]

Crespin cut three sections of this short document. The first section he removed continued the bishop's accusation that the bread and wine were being given to laymen by saying that 'they stubbornly assert that the clergy who administer it in the contrary manner err and consent to a repugnant sacrilege'.[63] The second passage removed followed the bishop's complaints about consecrated wine being carried in bottles, and claimed:

> on the basis of the erroneous assertion of the afore-mentioned Wyclifites that it is necessary for salvation that people commune in both bread and wine, it follows necessarily that just as the body of Christ is [carried] in a pyx, so also the blood of Christ should be carried from place to place in bottles and other utensils, particularly for the use of the sick.[64]

The third omission, and the largest, followed shortly after. The bishop's letter touches on the incident of the woman taking the Eucharist for herself. In Crespin's reproduction it ends there, but in Mladonovice's, the bishop relates some of the woman's beliefs; she 'maintained the opinions that a good layman or laywoman consecrated better than a bad priest ...' and dismissed the rumours that working men had been hearing confession in public.[65] Aside from this last retraction of an accusation against the Hussites, the omitted articles each attributed to the people of Bohemia

The Hussites and Protestant history 37

radical views on the nature of the Church. Their omission did not change the essential points of conflict between the followers of Hus and the Catholic hierarchy, but it did remove the most dramatic examples of that conflict, examples which raised the spectre of rebellious activity by the Hussites.

Contemporary Reformed doctrine on the Eucharist, which Crespin knew well, agreed with the taking of both bread and wine by the entire congregation. The carrying about of the consecrated wine, and the serving of the communion to one's self, however, were not behaviour recommended by Reformed ministers. Amongst the elements Crespin left out of the *Livre des Martyrs*, however, were those which suggested radical beliefs, or doctrines that the Reformed Church did not hold. The first among these, the woman's assertion that clergy who administered the sacrament in only one kind did so erroneously and, indeed, sacrilegiously, was perhaps one with which the Reformed could agree. The second, in which the bishop claims that the Hussites believe that the bread and wine are necessary for salvation, is more directly opposed to Protestant doctrine on the nature of the Eucharist. This emphasis on the salvatory nature of the Eucharist was of course inimical to Protestant thought; the Hussites, according to this accusation, were placing undue faith in the powers of the Eucharist. To carry the consecrated wine about was offensive to Catholic minds, but to Hussites, it mirrored the way in which the host was sometimes used, as the letter makes clear. As written in Mladonovice, the Hussite practice of carrying the Eucharist was clearly an extension of Catholic belief about its efficacy which underlay much of the rebellion; as written in Crespin, the practice is not explained, being mainly an example of the tensions between the Bohemians and the institutional church. The third omission, whereby the woman who served herself the Eucharist explained her convictions, stresses the belief of some of Hus' followers, that a good layperson had a stronger right to administer the sacraments than a sinful priest.[66]

This assertion essentially amounted to an accusation of the old heresy of Donatism, a charge which Hus had faced before. In an exchange of treatises with Palecs in Prague, before the trial, Hus had defended himself by arguing that corrupt, sinful, or evil priests still had the power to administer the sacraments, but that such a thing was unworthy.[67] Palecs' position, repeated during the trial in Constance, was that the authority of the hierarchy came parcelled with the office, and not due to any personal merit.[68] It was, as Spinka notes, Hus' acknowledgement of the validity of the sacramental acts of unworthy priests that saved him from 'the thin ice of Donatism'.[69] The statement by the Bohemian woman, that a layperson could better consecrate than a priest, was on the contrary unambiguously Donatist. This complaint by the Bishop of Litomsyl, though by an enemy, was potentially damaging to Hus' cause, tarring it with accusations of long-gone heresy. It was inevitable that Hus would be tainted by the

38   *The Hussites and Protestant history*

supposed actions of his followers, even if he had not taught the specific doctrines that they were defending. In some cases the differences between his doctrine and that of the radical Bohemians were subtle, while the links were very apparent.

Donatism was attacked by the Reformed as well as the Catholic Church; Calvin had no sympathy for other groups such as the Cathars who put a great deal of emphasis on the purity of their clergy.[70] Crespin, whilst editing this section, retained these accusations, which could have been damaging to Hus' reputation. On the other hand, he removed from his version some of the details most embarrassing to Hus, and least compatible with contemporary Reformed thought. It is worth noting, however, that Crespin did not excise any of the three accusations completely, either. Instead, he altered each separate accusation, removing the second half. Perhaps more importantly, this technique allowed the central ideas of the document to be presented while saving space, and Crespin made use of it fairly regularly, though rarely did he alter the meaning of the passage so completely. Later letters by the Czech and Polish lords were also edited, primarily removing their discussions of Hus' safe-conduct, but also their concern with defending the honour of Bohemia against the accusations of heresy. As such, it strongly insisted on the Catholic status of the Bohemian nobility, and it is not surprising that they were removed.

The narrative then moved to Hus' hearings at the Council, omitting a large portion of Mladonovice's Chapter II, more than a quarter of the entire *Relatio*, made up largely of letters written by Hus' supporters, insisting on his loyalty to the Catholic Church.[71] Crespin's narrative stresses the ways in which Hus' doctrines were: 'falsely collected from his books', especially with regard to the sacraments.[72] Hus was accused of remanence, holding that some of the sacramental bread remained bread after consecration.[73] This idea had grown out of Wyclif's ultra-Realist views, which rejected the idea that the category of 'bread' could be entirely annihilated and replaced with that of 'Christ'.[74] Hus, though a close follower of Wyclif in many respects, rejected the teaching and argued in favour of the doctrine of transubstantiation.[75] Mladonovice related that Hus denied having ever argued such a thing, and indeed had never expressed an opinion on the material bread.[76] Crespin, however, removed this denial and its implicit support for Catholic doctrine on this aspect of the Eucharist.[77] The impression given to a reader of this passage, as with several others, would be that Hus acquiesced in this description of his doctrine, a technique used at several points in the passages about Hus.

In the same debate, according to Mladonovice, Hus again affirmed his belief in transubstantiation; he: 'responded that truly, really, and totally that same body of Christ that had been born of the Virgin Mary ... and that was seated at the right hand of the Father, was in the sacrament of the altar'.[78] He denied, again, that he held Wyclif's doctrine of remanence to be true.[79] Crespin cut these passages, as well, retaining only a few lines

The Hussites and Protestant history   39

where Hus insisted on the sincerity of his testimony, even in the face of contradicting evidence.[80] Hus was then accused of teaching and holding the doctrines of Wyclif; he replied, as he had done elsewhere, that he did not hold Wyclif's errors, and that if Wyclif: 'had spread some heresies or errors in England, it is for the English to make provision' for them.[81]

In response, the Council began to question Hus about his defence of the '45 Articles' of Wyclif (which appear to have been assembled with hostile intent). Hus responded by saying that there were some articles there which he would not condemn, giving the example: 'that the Emperor Constantine had done badly to have conferred such donations upon the Church', an attack on the very roots of the Church's temporal power.[82] It also established a divide between the primitive Church and the current, established one, suggesting that the previous 1,000 years of Catholic history were to some degree tainted. This identification of the Donation of Constantine with the beginning of the decline of the Church was used by other heterodox groups, as well: some Vaudois traditions drew on the same trope in establishing their foundation to that event, and this critique appeared in some editions of Crespin's work.[83] Further comments that related to the question of Donatism, and which traced back to Wyclif's writings, were largely dropped from Crespin's version of these passages.

The narrative then moves onto the thirty-nine articles supposedly derived from his writings. Hus acknowledged that many of the articles were indeed his, but claimed that others had been forged to his disadvantage.[84] Distancing Hus from some of these accusations, Crespin specifically added that these misleading excerpts had been made by Hus' former friend Palecs, the: 'principal author of this argument: & they were not found in the books of which they claimed were drawn and collected: or if they were, they were corrupted by slander, as we can easily see'.[85]

Mladonovice's original work contrasted the articles put to Hus by the Council with Hus' own writings from which they were drawn, along with any commentary by Hus himself. This makes clear to the reader the alterations made by the prosecution, and disputed by Hus. Crespin retained this format, printing a numbered list of the articles, and stating each before including Hus' response. Most of the responses are slightly shortened, leaving out some of Hus' explanation, and often omitting the original phrasing of the article in question. Crespin therefore removed many of the minor objections Hus had to their wording, and has the effect of placing Hus in agreement with more of the articles he was accused of supporting than might otherwise appear to be the case. The articles are based on Hus' writings, which means that they deal primarily with the more technical and less dramatic aspects of Hus' thought: there is no discussion of the more dramatic developments in Hussite thought, such as the Utraquism which was beginning to become so important back in Prague.

Of the thirty-nine articles, the first twenty-two are drawn from Hus' *De Ecclesia*. Eleven of these deal with the question of membership of the

40   The Hussites and Protestant history

Church, an issue prominent in Wyclif's own thinking. Hus argued that the Universal Church (as opposed to the Church Militant, or Terrestrial) was composed only of the predestined, and was therefore an example of an 'invisible Church'.[86] As in Calvin's work, predestination and the nature of the Church were inherently linked. These articles were reduced in length, with Crespin making small but significant changes around the question of predestination. For example, the first article as recorded by Mladonovice argues: 'The holy catholic Church, that is the universal [Church], is then the totality of all the predestined, present, past, and future' before going on to give proofs from Augustine.[87] Crespin's rendering shortens Hus' defence, only referring to St Augustine rather than quoting him. In the rendering in the *Livre des Martyrs*, Hus confesses that: 'There is but one holy catholic or universal Church, which is the universal community of all the faithful and elect.'[88]

Several subsequent articles parse the question of membership in the Church (meaning the invisible, eternal Church), such as whether St Paul had ever been 'member of the devil' or if he had been a servant of God even when persecuting the earliest Christians, whether members of the Church could fall away from her.[89] Through these questions Hus was probing ideas around predestination and election – as those foreknown to be doomed were never part of the invisible, universal Church, they cannot fall away from her. Similarly though Paul acted against the Church at first, his was not the sort of permanent separation from the Church suffered by the foreknown.[90]

The ninth article, in both Hus and Crespin, argues that only Christ could be described as the head of the Church, striking at papal claims.[91] The tenth, like the others up to this point, addresses questions of membership in the Church and possible Donatism, by asserting that:

> If he who is called the vicar of Jesus Christ, follows Jesus Christ in life, then he is his vicar; but if he walks in contrary paths, then he is the messenger of the Antichrist, opposed to St. Peter & to Jesus Christ, & the vicar of Judas Iscariot.[92]

The eleventh article attacks priests living badly, saying that they therefore also think faithlessly with regard to their use of the seven sacraments.[93] This passage, by acknowledging the continued effectiveness of sacraments given by such men, insulates Hus from an outright Donatist position. Furthermore, Crespin, while repeating the list of 'Offices, keys, censures, customs & ceremonies, divine service of the Church, veneration of relics, orders founded in the Church' and 'indulgences', is careful to avoid repeating Hus' claim that there are seven sacraments.[94]

The twenty-first article touches the question of whether a person excommunicated by the Pope can appeal to Christ, which is what Hus had done in the years before his arrival before the Council of Constance. The article as

The Hussites and Protestant history 41

put to Hus had not appeared in his works, and Mladonovice instead included an explanation by Hus of his struggles over his excommunication.[95] He had appealed to the Pope and had no satisfaction; he had appealed to a Council, which had taken too long, and so he had appealed to Christ.[96]

These first articles being concluded, Crespin gives the reader a page of Hus' pleading, under a sub-headline reading: 'As mention is made to the appeal of the said Hus, it seems appropriate to insert the form thereof.'[97] After this interruption, Mladonovice and Crespin return to Hus' defence of articles taken from *De Ecclesia*. The twenty-second article voices his concerns on man's wickedness: 'The vicious man lives viciously, and the virtuous man lives virtuously'.[98] Hus' lengthy explanation of his point, drawing from Augustine, Luke, and Corinthians as found in Mladonovice is replaced with a short summary: 'There is no middle between the two, or human works are virtuous or vicious.'[99] This somewhat Manichean polarity, with everything being either good or evil, is not something that Mladonovice recorded, although it is implicit in some of Hus' examples.[100] The twenty-third article demands preaching from priests as essential to their role, even should the Pope order them to stop.[101] This, again, is a subject ostensibly drawn from Hus' teaching, but in fact it relates to his recent experience: Hus was being forced to defend his recent actions as much as his writings. Hus' argument, that priests were commanded by God to preach, in Crespin's translation avoids the word 'priest', in favour of 'man of the Church', or 'minister of the Word'.[102]

Hus was then interrogated on articles drawn from his work against Palecs, who had had a hand in composing the charges against him. There were seven, most of them on questions about the papacy, and the questions of a Pope foreknown to be damned. The first article, that: 'If the pope, or some bishop or prelate is in mortal sin, then he is no longer the pope, bishop or prelate', echoes much of what had already been debated.[103] The third and fourth articles also deal with the question of a Pope who is wicked, or foreknown, the fifth claims that the Pope should not be called 'most Holy', while the sixth questions the very legitimacy of a Pope who lives contrary to Christ, for he has only obtained the post through human action, and not divine.[104] Each of these articles was reduced in length for the martyrology, although Crespin retained at length an exchange between Hus and King Sigismund. In this, Hus seemed to have won a point, for when the King questioned him on his first article, Hus was able to ask of Palecs: 'if Pope John is the true Pope, why have you deprived him of his office?'[105] This particular charge was later dropped.[106] As the questioning continued, Hus' relationship to Wyclif's writing remained difficult, given its recent condemnation by the council. He refused to condemn all of Wyclif's articles, while at the same time saying that: 'I do not maintain the errors of Wyclif, nor those of anyone.'[107]

The final six articles were taken from a 'small book composed against Stanislaus of Znoyme'. They, again, deal with the election and the power

42 *The Hussites and Protestant history*

of the papacy, using the legendary example of Agnes, elected Pope John (or 'Pope Joan') to argue his point about the status of the Pope. His more subtle point is largely ignored by Crespin, who in many ways repeats the Council's accusations against Hus, though this time with approbation.[108] The nuance of the argument, that 'It also happens that they elect a wicked person whose passive election God approves ... whether the electors have chosen well or ill, we should believe the works of the elected', is missed in favour of more eye-catching statements such as: 'And that [the Church] elected a thief, a robber, and a devil, and in consequence we could elect an Antichrist.'[109] The argument moved on to whether the Church militant even requires a head on earth, as Christ could: 'at the glorious right hand of his Father, govern the Church here below on Earth by the grace and virtue of his Spirit'.[110] As there was at the time of the hearings no Pope, Hus argued that the Church could evidently survive without one (a point cut from Crespin's translation of this passage).[111] The Church's current state, without a Pope, and the legend of Agnes, Pope John, are used as evidence toward this point.[112]

Hus' beliefs were raised again, when he was condemned by the Council, which passed judgement on his doctrines. Even at this stage, Hus was demanding that the members of the Council explain to him which of his articles was heretical, and in what fashion, for he as elsewhere, promised to recant any which could be shown to be false.[113] In Spinka's translation of Mladonovice, the first article read against Hus regarded his claims that 'the holy universal Church is one, which is the totality of the predestinate, etc.' – concerns voiced throughout his trial.[114] Crespin's interpretation of this is that the prosecution had 'inserted amongst the others, to wit, that Jan Hus had dogmatised that the two natures, to wit, the divinity & humanity, are one Christ', an idea which is expressed nowhere in this section of the Mladonovice.[115] Hus is accused of wishing himself to be the fourth person of the divinity – an absurd accusation, which Novotny has explained by suggesting that it represented a *reductio ad absurdum* from Hus' tenets of philosophical realism.[116]

These points, excerpted from the full summing-up against him, are the final articles of doctrinal argument in Crespin's account of Hus. The bulk of the discussion of Hus' trial, and almost all of his formal questioning on doctrinal points had been included in the *Livre des Martyrs*. Crespin also included some of the discussion in the Council from these hearings, which will be discussed briefly below. Crespin dedicated the bulk of his space to the reported doctrines of Hus, and to the Catholic criticisms of his positions. The execution of Hus, and the controversies over the imperial safe-conduct granted him – potentially important features for a Protestant martyrologist – are dwarfed by a full-length airing of Hus' recorded beliefs. Much of this is due to Crespin's reliance on his source, for the same emphases are present in Mladonovice's text. The majority of Hus' doctrines are represented as they are found in Mladonovice, but there was a series of changes made. The accusations made by the Bishop of Litomysl were edited, seemingly bearing in mind the potentially dangerous subjects of the Eucharist and of Donatism.

Crespin's editing of Hus' articles maintained this pattern. Hus' adherence to the doctrine of transubstantiation was omitted entirely, with the effect that the Council's charges against him were in some areas no longer denied. The discussion of the first two articles put to Hus by the Council evinces several cuts of Eucharistic material in the space of a single page.[117] Arguments which suggest Donatism, often centring on the question of a sinning or unworthy priest, were consistently either shortened or cut entirely. The articles themselves, which engage these problems in more detail, were less affected by Crespin's editorship, but the pattern remains. The articles also bring into question Hussite doctrines around predestination, another area where Crespin made some minor changes. Hus' language is also policed for Catholic terminology, with substitutions being made for the seven sacraments and for 'priests'. Hus is again made to agree with accusers more often than was the case in the source material, such as in the attacks on the Papacy, where Hus' claims to have been misrepresented are replaced by his agreement; his nuanced responses and clarifications to the Council become, in the *Livre des Martyrs*, explanations of the doctrine he was originally trying to defend himself against.

The execution of Hus

After the lengthy sentence of condemnation, the text depicts the degradation and defrocking of Hus, and his execution. Mladonovice, who was an eye-witness to this event, gives it in great detail; it was this section of his account which was read in Bohemian churches on the anniversary of Hus' execution.[118] Crespin clearly saw the value of this passage, and included it in nearly its entirety. However, even in the midst of Hus' heroism, there were details which were altered. As Hus was being led to the stake, a priest 'in a green suit with a red silk lining' said that Hus should not be heard, nor given a confessor.[119] What Mladonovice relates approvingly, and Crespin omits, is that 'Master John, while he was still in prison, had confessed to a certain doctor, a monk, and had been kindly heard and absolved by him, as he himself stated in one of his letters to his [friends] from prison.'[120] Among his final words were a plea: 'Jesus, son of God, help me, that by your holy aid I might constantly and patiently endure this cruel and shameful death, to which I have been condemned, for having preached the word of your holy Gospel.'[121]

He also told the crowd not to believe the accusations against him, for he had never held or taught such things; this plea is related by Crespin as: 'he showed to the people the cause of his death, as he had done previously'; another example of Crespin weakening Hus' defence, and implying a greater break with Catholic orthodoxy.[122] On the pyre, Hus refused to

44 *The Hussites and Protestant history*

recant, again denying he had done the things of which he had been convicted.[123] After his death, his body was burned further and mutilated on the orders of the marshal, according to Mladonovice: 'so that the Czechs would not regard it as relics', and thrown into the river.[124] Crespin, who was unlikely to view the collection of relics favourably, declared that Hus' body had been destroyed: 'that there was nothing remaining of the man's body, as small as it was', which, although true, omits the question of relics.[125] This question of veneration amongst Hussites is not something on which Crespin had a consistent line: Palecs had earlier accused members of Hus' faction of venerating a piece of Wyclif's tombstone 'like a reliquary', an accusation which Crespin kept in his text, as he would later accusations that Hussites took and revered parts of Wyclif's tomb.[126] Crespin concludes the passage with a subtitle that stresses: 'he who recorded this history in writing was present at all that he has related here: so that no-one thinks this is an account by hearsay'.[127]

Letters

Crespin followed Mladonovice's narrative of Hus' trial and execution with a collection of Hus' letters, introducing them by stressing the editorial role he had played in selecting them: 'among the letters that master Jan Hus wrote since his decision to depart Bohemia to go to the Council of Constance, up to his death, those that seem most worthy to be collected in writing'.[128] Fourteen letters were reproduced in the first and second editions of the *Livre des Martyrs*, with fifteen included in 1564 and 1570, although the addition was simply an edited and reduced version of the fourth letter. This oversight is repeated and so does not seem to have been spotted.[129] The letters are largely concerned with Hus' facing up to his imprisonment and trial; only two of them were written before his arrest. The letters reproduced by Crespin are largely ones written with a public audience in mind. Of the fourteen, three are either to his patron Lord Chlum or to Chlum and Lord Duba, five are to 'Friends' or 'Faithful Friends' in Bohemia, one to 'Friends in Constance', with another to 'Faithful Czechs' and one each to his parishioners and to Praguers in general, employing the consolatory mode often seen in letters from martyrs at this stage of their proceedings. The letters reproduced spend little time on the specifics either of Hus' doctrine, or of the progress of his trial. They focus instead on a defence of his principles, and on admonitions to his readers to live good Christian lives and not to be dissuaded by the actions of the Council.[130] The fourth letter, the one printed twice by Crespin, deviates from this pattern, directly attacking the Council's organisation and conduct.[131]

The letters are increasingly informed by Hus' knowledge that he is to be executed, and provide an example of preparation to make a good death. In the sixth, he dwells on the varied ways in which the martyrs of the primitive Church met their end (presumably a topic newly important to him), and makes arrangements to ensure that his helpers are safe, his debts paid, and due acknowledgement given to his supporters and patrons. He also relates the actions of members of the Church hierarchy to persuade him to abjure his positions or admit to his heresy. He relates to his friends in Constance, in the ninth letter that 'There have already been a great many exhorters, persuading me by many words that I ought and lawfully can recant, subjecting my will to the holy Church which the sacred Council represents.'[132] Hus, however, refused to consider such a course on the basis that he had never held any such heresy, and would not confess to something he had not held.[133] Hus' interlocutors tried to convince him there was merit in confessing to things he had not held or done, drawing examples from the *Lives of the Fathers*, and saying that 'if the council told me that I had only one eye, & notwithstanding that I have two, nevertheless I must confess with the council that it is thus'.[134]

The central theme of the letters, however, is of Hus' preparation for his death. He tried to aid the progress of the Bohemian reform movement, telling them not to fear that his books were being burned, for the Israelites had once burned the writings of the prophet Jeremiah.[135] The Antichrist was manifesting himself in the Pope, and in parts of the Council now, and Hus wanted his followers to be able to defeat him:

> What pleasure it would give me, if I had some freedom to uncover, now that I know, such horrible wickedness, so that the faithful servants of the Son of God were able to take guard! But I have a good partner in my God, that he will send after me (as there are already) the bravest of preachers, who will discover much more openly the malice of the antichrist & his fine tricks, & will expose themselves to death for the truth of the Son of God.[136]

Jerome of Prague

Amongst the earliest of these followers of Hus was his compatriot and ally Jerome of Prague. Jerome was a significant figure in the Bohemian reform movement in his own right, and was included in the *Livre des Martyrs* in his own section alongside Hus, though not at nearly the same length. Jerome's status within the Hussite movement has long been contested. As we have seen, within months of his execution he was being treated by some Bohemians as the equal of Hus in holiness and in martyrdom, indeed, as a saint.[137] In 1554, Crespin wrote about Hus and Jerome as a linked pair, narrating that as news of their executions reached Bohemia: 'their disciples & followers assembled, & in the first place commemorated the memory of them, & ordained that they would be celebrated each year'.[138]

Later historiography has not always been so positive. Lutzow, writing in the early twentieth century, took pains to suggest that Jerome's role as

46 *The Hussites and Protestant history*

'church-reformer has been greatly exaggerated'; his frequent absences from Bohemia gave him less influence than Hus, based at the Bethlehem chapel in Prague, had held, while comparison 'between the saintly and truly evangelical simplicity of the character of Hus, and the sophistical insincerity of Jerome, who represents an early type of the humanist' also relegated Jerome to a supporting role.[139] R.R. Betts, writing in 1948, acknowledged the subordinate role in which Jerome had been cast since the seventeenth century, and theorised that this was due to a 'greater interest in ideas than actions' amongst modern scholars.[140] However, Jerome's actions have also proved difficult to quantify: unlike Hus, he held no post with the importance of the Rectorship of the University, or the stature of the Bethlehem chapel, and his contributions to the Bohemian movement have sometimes escaped precise definition.

Jerome of Prague had studied at the Charles University alongside Hus, but left sometime before 1400 for Oxford, taking advantage of the recent links between the two institutions forged by the royal marriage.[141] On his return he brought with him several of Wyclif's works which had not previously been available in Bohemia, most importantly the *Dialogus* and *Trialogus*, which amongst other things argued for the secularisation of Church property.[142] When the forty-five articles of Wyclif were condemned by the University, Jerome was absent, perhaps in Jerusalem; he returned in time to take place in the debates on indulgences.[143] At Hus' summoning before the Council of Constance, Jerome felt himself bound to attend. Arriving in Constance after Hus' arrest, and shortly before his trial, Jerome managed to only temporarily escape arrest himself. After Hus' execution, Jerome recanted his position, and even his loyalty to Hus, declaring that the Council had been right to burn Hus.[144] He eventually returned to his original position, and declared before the Council that he regretted his abandonment of Hus and Wyclif, an action that allowed them, as he would have known, to declare him a relapsed heretic and have him burned.[145]

Jerome was executed on 30 May 1416, nearly a year after Hus. The situation in Bohemia had changed dramatically in that period; the Hussite League had formed, and issued a protest to the Council of Constance which declared that 'John Hus confessed to no crime, nor was he legitimately and properly convicted of any, nor were any errors or heresies cited and demonstrated against him.'[146] The eight copies delivered to the Council bore the names of 452 members of the Bohemian nobility, an indication of the potential power of an embryonic Hussite movement.[147] The surge of support which had grown up around Hus did not seem to dissuade the Council from trying and executing him; indeed, this addition of secular disobedience made the embryonic Hussite movement more threatening to the Church hierarchy, and more in need of repression. Spinka has suggested that it was this volatile situation which gave the Council increased motivation to secure Jerome's recantation.[148] Thus, Jerome was a problematic character, as his recantation called into question his status as a witness

The Hussites and Protestant history 47

for the divine truth, and his career before Constance had not contained much to allow him to be depicted as a dedicated reformer.

Jerome's trial and death were not only well-documented, but relatively famous: the important Florentine humanist Poggio Bracciolini, present in his capacity as a functionary of the papal *curia*, wrote about Jerome's trial in a letter which was later published. This only detailed the last few days of Jerome's trial, and his death, and did not portray his abjuration. Instead, Poggio focussed on the rhetorical skill and learning with which Jerome defended himself, presenting him as a humanist, and drawing comparisons to the ancients. Renee Neu Watkins, indeed, has suggested that the differences between Poggio's letter and other accounts of Jerome's death can be explained by the Florentine's interest in portraying a type of contemporary Stoic: 'Jerome seeks to remind us, and did remind his sympathisers, of the Passion. Only to and through Poggio could his death call up the memory of the tranquil Socrates, the imperturbable Cato.'[149]

Jerome was included in Crespin from the first edition, which devoted slightly more than ten pages to him. The passage begins with a large headline, and a couple of lines of introduction, claiming the following to be drawn from Poggio's writing: 'Poggio the Florentine, adversary though he was, has been obliged to render testimony in his letter of the constancy & happy death of the Holy Martyr, as having been a spectator of it.'[150] Poggio's letter (to Bruni, aka Leonardo Aretino, though Crespin does not mention the recipient) is reproduced nearly in full, only omitting primarily introductory material, is the only material to be found on Jerome in this edition. Crespin's gloss gives Jerome status as a martyr, and emphasises his bravery in the face of death, Poggio's account having already worked to cast him as a stoic figure. Crespin was clearly not entirely comfortable with the use of a hostile source to illustrate Jerome's execution, and concluded his account by discussing Poggio's suitability as a messenger:

> the constancy of one such servant of the Son of God [Jerome] merits a man of better faith than the author of this narrative, who is Poggio the Florentine ... nevertheless one may see that this description is out of all suspicion: see that this profane man Poggio the Florentine, that gave well to knowledge by his writings, is obliged to praise this Martyr of Jesus Christ, against all his will and intention.[151]

Poggio's letter described only Jerome's final appearance before the Council; it is an account of one impressive speech, and Jerome's execution. It therefore does not include, or mention, Jerome's arrest, his initial admission of heresy, recantation, or denunciation of Hus and Wyclif. The Jerome portrayed by Poggio, and included in the first edition of the *Livre des Martyrs* is defiant, eloquent, and doomed.

Poggio's letter does not touch on Jerome's theology in any detail at all. It mentions that Jerome 'responded publicly to all the articles which were

48   *The Hussites and Protestant history*

proposed against him, but mentions only one specific point of disagreement: the Eucharist.[152] Asked: 'if you maintain this position that the bread remains the same after consecration', he replied that 'the bread is at the baker's'.[153] The discussion then moves away to more *ad hominem* arguments, and does not return to the subject. Jerome delivered a long oration on men who had been condemned by unjust trials, including Socrates, Plato, Anaxagoras, Boethius, amongst the Jews, Isaiah, Jeremy, and Daniel and to John the Baptist, Stephen, and the Apostles before turning his attention on the witnesses whom he thought had ensured his conviction.[154] He lamented the period where men could disagree on doctrinal matters 'without any suspicion of error or heresy', as had Saints Augustine and Jerome.[155] It was, in short, a noteworthy demonstration of the orator's art, furnished with classical allusions and forms, and it is largely this aspect that Poggio, the arch-humanist recorded and which caused him to remark that: 'this man is worthy of perpetual memory amongst men'.[156] Poggio also gave an eye-witness account of Jerome's death at the stake, which was borne with great courage, as he sang a hymn and reminded the executioner to light all parts of the fire.[157]

As Crespin had noted, Poggio was a member of the *curia*, and potentially suspect to Protestants, so that his version of events could only confirm Jerome's bearing, confidence, and the elements of his defence. The articles which Jerome had to defend, the central issue of the hearings, are never elucidated, and the only time Poggio makes reference to doctrinal difference is to show Jerome's wit, not his learning, which Watkins argues is central to Poggio's conception of Jerome.[158]

In 1555's edition, Crespin expanded his account of Jerome of Prague; an extra quire (which had to be paginated in Roman numerals) provided sixteen more pages of space for this. Part of this seems to have been done using information, including a list of articles, taken from Foxe's *Commentarii Rerum*, (itself derived from Bale) which had been published the previous year, as part of the same series of changes (first attached to Crespin's editions in the pirate Rivery editions) that saw the addition of Wyclif and a number of Lollards, although Crespin did not use information from Foxe to alter his section on Hus.[159]

Instead of Poggio's letter, the 1555 edition's version begins with a two-page section of narrative, describing events up until Jerome's final confrontation with the Council. When Hus was taken before the Council, Jerome travelled to Constance to aid him, and was arrested. Crespin acknowledges and addresses the question of Jerome's abjuration by saying that Jerome, like St Peter, may offer an example of human fragility, for after he was imprisoned:

> long endured great afflictions and cruel oppressions. On this he was threatened with terrible menaces: and he had also some hope of escaping amongst the mix, that he agreed to say the word, that Jan Hus had been justly condemned.[160]

The Hussites and Protestant history 49

Crespin immediately noted that: 'although this confession was extracted in fear, he was made of greater constancy thereafter, as will be shown in the trial'.[161]

Jerome was soon overtaken by guilt for having betrayed his friend, and was in part driven by his love for the true religion. He resolved to appear before the Council to complete Hus' work, and to redeem himself.[162] His captors amassed a series of accusations against him, and Crespin presents here a list of twenty-one articles, for which Jerome was eventually condemned. These articles had appeared in 1554 in Foxe's *Commentarii Rerum*, after that work's own reprinting of Poggio and would later appear (in slightly truncated form) in de Haemstede's 1559 Dutch martyrology.[163] However, both Foxe and Crespin omitted this list in their respective later editions. Although Foxe's *Rerum in Ecclesia gestarum* repeated the same twenty-one articles in 1559, his 1563 martyrology and Crespin's 1564 edition both omitted such detailed examination of Jerome's beliefs.[164] It is possible that just as Crespin decided to follow Foxe in including the twenty-one articles in 1555, he took his cue from the English martyrologist when excluding them in 1564. There was, therefore, only a single edition of the martyrology containing this particular set of twenty-one articles.

These articles were presented, unnumbered, as a list across two pages. They were framed as Jerome's own propositions rather than accusations for him to answer, as had been done for Hus. The articles naturally share much with Hus' philosophy, and several are repeated from Hus' trials. Compared with Hus, Jerome's articles are less concerned with the scholastic philosophical underpinnings of doctrine, but instead with the correction of Christian belief and practice. Overall, they argue for a reduction in the power and influence of the Church hierarchy, and challenge its ability to intercede with God for its members. Jerome betrays his interest in the concept of the invisible Church of believers that he had shared with Hus; his fifth article argues that St Paul was never of the devil, and is the same as the second of Hus' twenty-one articles from the previous year.[165] Like Hus, he believed that authority was at least partially contingent on personal sanctity, rather than title.

Jerome devoted more attention to specific criticisms of Church practice, some fundamentally – indeed, the first article denies that the Pope has power over other bishops, and the third denies the existence of purgatory. The ninth article states that auricular confession is a lie, and the tenth that it is sufficient that all confess their sins before God. Jerome denies the existence of purgatory in his third article, from which it follows (in the seventeenth article) that one wastes time appealing to the holy dead, or (in the eighteenth) by singing the canonical hours.[166] These theses attack the clergy's special standing, powers, and, in the fifteenth article, vestments by denying their power in saving the souls of laymen.

Other articles pushed against ideas of sacrality, denying in successive points (the twelfth and thirteenth) the sanctity of cemeteries, and arguing

50 The Hussites and Protestant history

that 'It is all the same where bodies are buried.'[167] Central to this mode of thinking was the fourteenth article, which claimed that the church of God is the world, thus temples and chapels only serve to restrict sanctity. Similarly, as feast days should be abolished, the twentieth article argues that one could work any day but Sundays. Most importantly, in the sixteenth article Jerome asserts that the Eucharist can be given to all who repent, at any time, and at any place. Taken together, these articles argue for a view of the world with few intermediaries between God and man. Holy places, holy days, and holy men were all to be discarded, reducing the Church's agency in tending to its flock.

The *Livre des Martyrs* tells us that the Council condemned the articles, and then Jerome: 'for greater attestation of all of this story, we have here inserted the sentence pronounced against the said Jerome, which we have translated almost word for word ...'[168] Crespin included the sentence pronounced against Jerome, a document which takes nearly three pages of the octavo edition.[169] The sentence of condemnation's primary charge against Jerome is his rejection of his recantation, on the grounds that 'he had falsely lied'.[170]

The first edition, which had been based entirely on Poggio's letter, had attested only to Jerome's eloquence and constancy in the face of death. The second edition added information about Jerome's own views in the form of the twenty-one articles and acknowledged his earlier recantation through both the narrative section and his condemnation by the Council. As the addition of the extra quire suggests, these were changes which may well have been inconvenient to Crespin, as a printer, to make, and they contained material which was not to Jerome's credit, but they were made anyway.

Like Hus, Jerome of Prague next appeared in the *Livre des Martyrs* in the 1564 edition. He again directly followed Hus. Unlike Hus' account which had not changed materially since the first edition, Jerome's only found any sort of stability with this edition, which differed from the 1555 edition in a number of ways, amongst which was the exclusion of the list of Jerome's articles. Crespin presented a new narrative, based on new sources, reducing the relative importance of Poggio's letter to the account.

This is consistent with the increased focus on narrative history which emerged in the compendium editions. This edition begins by stressing the ties between Jerome and Hus in their ideas and their biographies.[171] This expansion of his existing text is typical of Crespin's wider approach; the greatest growth can be found in the section leading up to Jerome's imprisonment and abjuration. This is partly because Crespin, in keeping with the chronology, moved to this section the episode of Jerome's attempts before his arrest to obtain a safe-passage back to Constance, but it is also due to the insertion of a tranche of new material. This depicts Jerome's posting of provocative letters on the doors of cardinals and churches around Constance which declared his willingness to answer to charges on the basis of

The Hussites and Protestant history   51

doctrine, and a series of exchanges, after his arrest, with Jean Gerson, the Chancellor of the University of Paris, which help to show him as more of an activist than previous editions had suggested.[172] In total, the section preceding Jerome's recantation was expanded from perhaps half of one octavo page in 1555 to nearly two pages in folio, as many as 1,800 words.[173] This would be the place for Crespin to reproduce the twenty-one articles found in 1555, but he refrained from doing so; none of the articles alleged against Jerome at this hearing are detailed. Instead, he included a strongly worded retraction by Jerome of his abjuration. Further attacks by Jerome on the established order, and against Jerome by members of hierarchy, appear in Crespin for the first time; much of their content consists of mutual denunciation.

In 1564, Crespin also introduced new material, drawn perhaps from Flacius Illyricus, or from Flacius Illyricus via Foxe, which overlaps with Poggio's description of Jerome's last appearances before the Council. In these appearances, he gave a strong defence of himself and his doctrines, firmly aligning himself with Hus and Wyclif. Echoing Poggio, Crespin draws attention to how he 'spoke well of the diverse disciplines of philosophers, and of holy Scriptures' and used examples of men wrongly condemned drawn from amongst the philosophers, prophets, and Apostles.[174] This edition also shows Jerome approving 'the sermons of Jan Hus, and also of John Wyclif, by which these two have repeated sharply the intolerance, the malice, the beggary, and the avarice of Priests', a line of argument which Crespin highlighted in a marginal note.[175]

This new account gives us more detail on the execution of Jerome. Like Hus, Jerome was adorned with a paper crown painted with devils. It also tells us some of what he said at the stake: besides his claim that: 'my faith is not other than that I have just sung', he commended his spirit to God and, in Czech, asked for forgiveness for his sins.[176] His bed and other possessions were then taken from the prison and burned on the same fire and the remains thrown in the Rhine; as with Hus, it seems as if the authorities were planning to eliminate any relics of Jerome from emerging.[177]

Jerome's place in history has long been controversial, and his portrayal in the *Livre des Martyrs* contains most of the reasons why that has been so. Throughout, he is presented as a companion, or a subordinate to Hus, and the smaller space he has been given reflects that, as does the narrative, included from 1555, of him rushing to Hus' aid, and then betraying him. Jerome, too, was portrayed more in terms of his actions and trial than his ideas and his doctrines. In 1555, twenty-one articles against him were detailed, but they were omitted from the compendium editions. In 1564, the reader is told about more than 100 articles levelled against Jerome, but these are not given in detail as they were against Hus. Some of this emphasis is surely due to the sources available to Crespin: in 1554, he appears to have only had available Poggio's letter to Aretin which, as we have seen,

52   *The Hussites and Protestant history*

was concerned with Jerome as an exemplar of Stoic behaviour rather than as a challenger to the doctrines of the Church. The later additions, if they do not greatly expand our knowledge of Jerome's beliefs, at least attempt to portray him in a better light. They never attempt to deny his recantation, but they do stress his loyalty to Hus from the earlier days, and so implicate him more fully in the reform movement, as do the passages where Jerome swears his loyalty to Hus' doctrines. Crespin was also forthcoming about Jerome's recantation, including it consistently from 1555, and comparing it to St Peter's denial of Christ. Jerome's inclusion was predicated primarily on his relationship with Hus, and his behaviour. The recantation attacked both of those factors, but was retained throughout Crespin's editions.

The Hussite Wars

Like many of its sources, the *Livre des Martyrs* placed its primary focus on Hus, and to some degree Jerome of Prague. These accounts were focussed on theological matters, and featured a very clear trial format which pitted the papacy against the protagonists. In contrast, the descriptions of events in Bohemia were a more conventional history of battles and politics, and did not directly feature the trial and defence of martyrs which formed the core of the book. The history of the Hussite Wars also discussed resistance to an unjust and unfaithful ruler, which took the form of sacking monasteries, killing Catholic clergy, and outright civil war. These were dangerous topics for a Genevan text to discuss in the 1550s, and by the 1560s some of this material could be considered inflammatory in the context of the French Wars of Religion. Crespin's inclusion of it also prefigured the changes that were developing in Genevan history-writing as a whole, which were becoming more focused on secular, narrative, history.

In 1554, the passage entitled 'What happened after the death of Jan Hus, and of Jerome of Prague, martyrs', ran for nearly five pages. This version focussed on tensions in Prague in the years immediately after news of the executions in Constance arrived. As Crespin suggests, Hus and Jerome were treated as martyrs nearly immediately:

> the ashes of these two Martyrs were thrown into lake Constance, out of fear that the Bohemians would take them. Nonetheless, their disciples carried away the earth of the place where they had been burned, and took it to their country like a sacred and holy thing. And these two good men were honoured in Bohemia like excellent Martyrs of Jesus Christ. For after news had come to Bohemia about what had happened in Constance to M Jan Hus and Jerome, their disciples and adherents assembled, and in first place commemorated the memory of them, and ordained that it be celebrated every year.[178]

The Hussites and Protestant history   53

This is consistent with reports from other sources that as early as 1416:

> [o]thers hold services in churches, before many people, for John Hus and Jerome of Prague, condemned public heretics, as though for deceased faithful Christians. Others celebrate festivities for them, and sing the Gaudeamus and other songs as though for martyrs, comparing them in merits and sufferings to St Laurence the martyr, and preferring them to St Peter and other saints.[179]

At this stage, the Hussites were able to obtain some churches (described consistently here as 'temples') in which they could preach, and render sacraments to the people.[180] Seemingly by way of contrast, the richness of the Catholic temples of Bohemia is discussed at some length, in a passage mirroring that of Aeneas Sylvius' description of the monastic church of Glatouiam.[181] These churches were attacked by the more radical Hussites, and Crespin relates this destruction in some detail.

Attacks on ecclesiastical properties continued, and the narrative openly describes how the people of the city of 'Slavonie' (Slavonice, in Moravia) demolished a church belonging to the Jacopins (Dominicans), and that this was not the last of the churches demolished by the followers of Hus: 'For they razed many others, down to the foundations, fired many others which had been sumptuously built.'[182] Shortly after the death of Wenceslas IV, they moved on the monastery where he had been buried (today known as Zbraslav), and 'destroyed everything there'.[183] Crespin's text does not condemn these attacks, although the narrative does not include some of the more lurid anecdotes told about the sacking of Zbraslav, which described the recently deceased king's body being hauled from its tomb, mocked, and plied with wine although this may be due to his reliance on the *Historia Bohemica*, which made similar omissions.[184]

A shorter passage then follows which describes a mass assembly of 30,000 on the hill which they named Tabor, near Bechingue (Bechyne), where 300 tables in the open air were set up and: 'administered the Eucharist to people in both kinds, in bread as well as in wine', partly through being driven out from their own towns and church.[185] This passage closely follows Aeneas Sylvius' account of the first popular masses.[186]

This Taborite movement was the radical, 'left' wing of Hussitism, informed by a chiliasm and communalism which Crespin did not spend much time on; the site of 'Tabor' itself would eventually be crystallised into a new, fortified, town. The rural movement concerned King Wenceslas (the chronology here is confused – this event occurred in 1419), with its overtones of sedition and even rebellion. This account places the priest Coranda at the centre of the unrest, urging followers to pray for the king, drunkard and coward though he might be, for he would not dare to clamp down on their reforms.[187] Curiously, this is said to have endeared him to Wenceslas. At the same time another priest, Jean (Jan Zelivsky), was

54 The Hussites and Protestant history

encouraging more action within Prague. On his urging, the Hussites seized for their use the Carmelite church, Mother of God of the Snows, and then: 'carrying nearly every day their host by their temples', they petitioned the king through a gentleman named Nicholas for more churches.[188] These details, too appear to have been derived from the *Historia Bohemica*.[189] The king's reaction is to retire across the river to his castle of 'Vissegrade' (Vyšehrad), and thereafter even farther from his rebellious capital.[190] The account ends there, in mid-1419, with Tabor rising and the king under pressure, before the Defenestration of Prague and the death of Wenceslas, although a glimpse is given of that violence, in the form of the attacks on churches which followed that event.[191]

The 1554 edition of the *Livre des Martyrs* thus focussed on the very earliest years of the Hussite movement, openly depicting iconoclastic attacks on Church property, and even the royal mausoleum. The narrative ended, however, before the outbreak of open conflict, and avoided showing the Hussites in direct opposition to royal authority. This passage was entirely reworked in the next edition. Whereas the first edition largely gave an account of events in Prague before the Defenestration of 1419, the new account in the 1555 edition starts after it, and makes no mention of the action and the deaths of the city councillors.[192] In this edition, the section begins by explaining the rage which the execution of Hus and Jerome caused in Bohemia, and the immediate reaction by their followers: 'who by their means had taken some taste of the word of God ... had some temples, at which they could sincerely preach the word & administer the Sacraments'.[193]

To protest the actions of the Council, and preserve the memory of Hus his followers had minted 'Hussite money', which bore the inscription 'After one hundred years you will have to answer to God, and to me', which were supposedly the words of Hus himself to those condemning him.[194] Luther had developed a version of this prophecy in his 1531 *Gloss on the Alleged Imperial Edict*, helping to develop the idea of Hus as a genuine prophet; more than simply a forerunner of Luther.[195] Crespin repeats Luther's reading, suggesting that what Hus had actually meant by this was that he could be confident that a century hence, all of those would have died and gone before God's judgement, and made to account for their conduct at the Council.[196] The martyrology reproduces the prophecy as follows:

> Saint Jan Hus (he said), to be the precursor or forerunner of the contempt of the Papacy, as he to them prophesised in spirit, saying: After one hundred years you will answer to God and to me. And again: Now certainly they have cooked the Goose (for in the Czech language Hus means that), but they will not cook the Swan, who comes after me.[197]

Crespin then points out the coincidence of dates, with Hus' execution at Constance occurring in 1416, and Luther's arguments with the Papacy

The Hussites and Protestant history   55

from 1517 (though as is established elsewhere in Crespin's own narrative, Hus died in 1415).

Having established this link between Hus and the sixteenth-century reformers, the *Livre des Martyrs* then returns its focus to the events in Bohemia itself. This narration of the Hussite wars is viewed almost entirely through the biography of Jan Zizka, the nemesis of Zelivsky (the protagonist of the 1554 account), one of the primarily military leaders of the Hussite movement, and certainly the most iconic. Although the material derived from Aeneas Sylvius that was used in 1554 had been entirely removed, Crespin returned to the work for his material on Zizka. The *Historia Bohemica* is cited in Crespin's text twice in one paragraph, with the immediate qualification that it came from: 'Aeneas, their mortal enemy, who later became Pope of Rome, called Pius the Second'.[198] His life and connections with the royal court are rehearsed, as are his military background and eye lost in battle.[199] The reader is told that Zizka regarded the execution of Hus and Jerome as an insult to the Bohemian Kingdom (as other documents show, he would not have been alone in this view) and gathered together:

> many knights, proposing to avenge the outrage of the Council of Constance. Because he could not get to the authors of the deed, he decided to throw himself on their accomplices & those of their league, namely, on the Priests, Monks, & similar other vermin. Following thus his point, he began to demolish & waste Churches, to break images to pieces, to destroy monasteries & drive out the Monks, because that he said that it was for those, that he entered in these cloisters. Finally, he amassed more than forty thousand men, all well determined to maintain by the sword the doctrine of Jan Hus.[200]

Even amongst the Taborites Zizka seems to have been notable for his hostility to monks, and he showed them no mercy when captured.[201] Sigismund, who had inherited the Bohemian throne from his brother, and thus was the rightful king, was kept out of the kingdom by Zizka as an enemy of their faith, mistrusted for his abandonment of Hus earlier.[202]

As a result, Zizka – who is again made to stand for the Hussite movement as a whole – was assaulted by papal forces (indeed, Sigismund arranged for a crusade to be declared against his rebellious and heretical subjects) and showed his military genius by repelling them. Zizka's exploits were apparently too good to resist printing, and Crespin outlines how he defeated one mounted force by the fact that he: 'commanded their women … to strew their long veils on the ground, in which they hoped the Knights would be entangled'.[203] This seems to have been drawn from Aeneas' account of the battle of Sudomer, in 1420; most other relations of this battle have the royalist knights bogged down in the marshy ground rather than women's attire.[204] The participation of women in Zizka's armies was

56 *The Hussites and Protestant history*

a commonly used trope.[205] In another encounter he seized horses and taught his men to ride, establishing a fully capable army.[206] Amongst Zizka's varied victories are omitted those over the more conservative Praguer faction in 1423 and 1424, in a series of conflicts between Hussite groups.

The text also credits Zizka, and not the Hussite masses, with the foundation of the town of Tabor, which in this telling was a settlement for the Hussite armies. No mention is made of the mass-meetings outlined in 1554's edition. In the version of events in the *Livre des Martyrs*, Zizka founded it when he realised that his troops had nowhere to which to retreat, and selected a place himself. His soldiers were thus ever afterwards known as 'Taborites'.[207] They were viewed with some concern by the moderates in Prague.[208] Zizka's role was to give some order to the fledgling community, and he was elected as one of its four captains some months after its foundation in 1420.[209] At no point are the beliefs or actions of the Taborites explained to the readers of the martyrology.

The remainder of the account celebrates Zizka's defence of Bohemia against ever-increasing imperial armies, the loss of his remaining eye, and his death of plague (in 1424) en route to negotiate with Sigismund about a settlement that would supposedly have granted 'all charge and authority under him'.[210] It ends by reinforcing Zizka's legend: he supposedly requested that his skin be made into a drum to lead armies against his enemies, and his tomb to read: 'terror of the Pope, ruin of the Priests, the death and destruction of Monks etc.'.[211] This macabre story is also drawn from Aeneas Sylvius, building again the legend of Zizka. The warlord's primacy came again at the expense of the other actors; the account of Bohemia post-Hus ends with Zizka's death, and the reader is never told what happened to the remaining Hussites, or the outcome of the war.

This focus on Zizka removes the responsibility for the sackings of monasteries from the unruly mob and gives it to one man with a coherent plan of action. Aeneas Sylvius's depiction of Zizka, as a powerful and dynamic force – almost superhuman, if malign – may have been influenced by his role in winning the Utraquists back to the Catholic fold, 'in part from a desire to make the most out of this anticipated crusade against the Turks'.[212] It was certainly an image well-suited to Crespin's purposes.

Crespin did not engage with the doctrinal elements of the wars. His account has the Hussites fighting for the doctrines of Hus, but in reality the situation had long moved past Hus' own positions. Utraquism, communion in both kinds, had become the central issue, agreed by both Prague moderates and Taborite radicals, and had only been approved by Hus in a letter, rather than formulated by him. The question appears nowhere in the lengthy discussion of Hus' beliefs before the Council of Constance; it was cut from the accusations made against the Hussites by the Bishop of Litomysl. The 1555 version of events was to remain Crespin's main depiction of years after Hus' death, though in 1564, he added some phrases to

The Hussites and Protestant history   57

Zizka's epitaph, describing him as 'Protector of his country, Terror of the Pope, Flail of the Priesthood', and two more lines comparing Zizka to heroes of the Roman Republic, and his assurance of lasting fame 'if the envy of his adversaries does not prevent it'.[213] Emphasis is taken off Zizka's nationalist motivations for revolt, leaving religion as the dominant factor.

In 1570, Crespin added new material to the Hussite Wars section. A letter was added from a group of Moravian nobility, a document rooted in injured national pride at the accusation of having harboured heretics. Indeed, the letter condemns the execution of Hus on the basis of the: 'false accusations & evil calumnies of his mortal enemies, traitors to our Kingdom, that of the marquisate of Moravia'.[214] The letter defends Hus against all accusations of heresy, attacking those who:

> said that there are heresies seeded in Bohemia or Moravia, that we have infected and other faithful of the Kingdom. This person, we say, falsely lied by his venomous tongue and stinking throat, as a wicked traitor of the said Kingdom & Marquisate: and as a perverse & unhappy heretic himself.[215]

The letter appears to have been reproduced verbatim aside from one paragraph, in which the lords declared their kingdom and marquisate's longstanding loyalty to the Catholic Church, throughout the periods of schism and antipopes, which was cut entirely.[216]

The lords proclaim their intention to one day plead their case before the Apostolic throne (against which Crespin added a marginal note reading: 'the simple faith which they still had in the seat of Rome, was abused').[217] This letter became a basis for the Hussite League, founded three days later by fifty-five of the fifty-eight original signatories.[218]

The Hussite wars were hugely important to the survival of the Utraquist movement in Bohemia, and they could have been used by Crespin as a demonstration of resistance to Catholic forces (by a motivated nobility, no less). However, they received relatively little space within the *Livre des Martyrs*, and much of that focussed on a few specific events. Much of this must be due to Crespin's own conception of the martyrology, which was always more concerned with individuals than with historical moments. From this point of view, it is somewhat remarkable that any such history was included as early as 1554's edition, although even by 1570, when historical sections were more common, it was still almost a footnote to the deaths of Hus and Jerome. More material could have been included, from a number of the sources Crespin had already used – Foxe's 1563 edition, for example, presented a much longer version of the Hussite wars which included elements found in each of Crespin's accounts, and in more detail. That this was not done should not suggest that he was entirely content with the section; it was modified in each subsequent edition, and had another edition been produced, it may have changed again.

58   *The Hussites and Protestant history*

There were two main versions of the events after the executions at Constance: that in the 1554 edition, which focussed on the events in Prague in 1419, and that in the later editions, which covered some of Zizka's battles up to his death in 1424. Though there is little overlap in the material which the two narratives cover, there are some similarities of theme and of approach. Both main versions mention the iconoclasm, and anticlericalism, of the Hussite movement, with the 1554 account spending a significant amount of time describing the riches of the Bohemian Church. Both versions also mention the foundation of the town of Tabor, though 1554's describes it as the outgrowth of mass meetings held to receive the sacrament, a view closer to the modern consensus. In 1555, 1564, and 1570, Tabor's foundation is the work of Zizka, done primarily to house his army. These later accounts give more prominence to the noble Hussite League, and the Taborite general than to the mass demonstrations in Prague and in the countryside. This more closely accords with Aeneas Sylvius' account, and indeed with Crespin's technique of portraying events primarily through their leading members, but it also reduces the role of the masses, and thus the more radical elements in Hussite history.

Conclusion

Between Hus, Jerome, and the Hussite wars, Crespin devoted a substantial amount of space to the Bohemians – 143 pages of octavo in 1554, and fifty-four of folio in his 1570 edition. The majority of that space was devoted to the account of Hus, which was itself primarily an account of his trial; the ratio of *acta* to *passio* is in Hus' case near to 100:1. As such, the Hussite pages contain a high proportion of religious discussion, of which a great deal is very sophisticated. Hus' doctrines, so far as they were presented at the trial, and related by Mladonovice, were included by Crespin in the Livre des Martyrs, though not without a series of small cuts and modifications. Most significantly, Crespin removed the portions of Hus' defence in which he claimed that his doctrines were compatible with the Catholic doctrine of transubstantiation.

As we shall see in relation to the Lutherans, Eucharistic theology was of the highest importance to Crespin, and indeed to the Reformed movement in this period. Hus' statements on the sacraments were thus brought into line (by omitting the offending passages, not altering them), which ensured that he could be presented as being in opposition to the Catholic Church on the single most important area of disagreement. This Eucharistic interest, however, seems not to have extended to the most striking of the Hussite stances: the Utraquist insistence on the sacrament being given in both kinds. The topic would have been difficult to raise in Hus' or Jerome's accounts, for they left Bohemia before the practice was widely spread, and only a single letter connects Hus to the practice. The writings on which Hus was being examined contained no mention of Utraquism.

The Hussites and Protestant history   59

However, whatever evidence is given, the accusations levelled by the Bishop of Litomysl were purged of their mention of the Utraquist practice, which had appeared in Mladonovice. Utraquism, which had been practised by the Hussites and was acceptable to the Reformed, was removed from the list of accusations along with other, more damaging, ones. Jerome's trial similarly did not touch on the question. He, too, had left Bohemia before the practice became common, and there was nothing in his trial to indicate that he was accused of participating in it. Even the list of twenty-one articles that appeared in the 1555 edition makes no reference to his sacramental theology beyond the sixteenth, which states 'The Eucharist can be given at all times and places to all who repent', an inclusive attitude which was shared by the Utraquists without approaching their position. With the question of Utraquism avoided in both Hus and Jerome's accounts, it could have been addressed in the short history of the Hussite wars. This it was, passingly, in the 1554 account, where Tabor was described as a place where thousands would gather to be given 'the Eucharist ... under both kinds, of bread and wine'. This recognition of the Taborite movement's early days was not expanded on, and was excluded from all subsequent editions of the Livre des Martyrs. Rather than being the central motivating force of the Hussites, Utraquism was briefly presented as part of the rural mass movement, and quickly removed.

Crespin was, naturally, reliant on his sources, and on this front, too, there is real difference between the different Hussite accounts. Hus' remained static, indeed nearly identical from the first edition to the last, while those of Jerome and the Hussite Wars changed several times. In Jerome's case, this was probably because the first edition's source was both incomplete, and furnished by an author presumed to be hostile. When Crespin had the ability, the following year, to add information from elsewhere, such as Foxe, he did so. What is unusual, however, is that if he did add to Jerome's account from Foxe, he did not take anything from Foxe's version of Hus. He did not use information from official trial documents not included in Mladonovice, which would have contained more information on the beliefs of his antagonists, perhaps due to difficulty in obtaining them through a source he trusted. Crespin did not make as much use as he could have from Aeneas Sylvius, either, although including more from the *Historia Bohemica* would have given him more narrative history, rather than martyrological material. His depiction of the Hussites was therefore largely based around the narrative of Mladonovice, who was, like so many of Crespin's sources, an eye-witness and friend of the victim.

Hus and his followers were the first entries in Crespin's first edition, and though they were soon superseded by Wyclif, they never lost their prominence in the martyrology's scheme of late medieval reform. Along with the Lollards, who joined them in 1555, they represented almost the entirety of pre-Reformation resistance to the Catholic Church. Their role was such that they could not simply be excused faults on the basis that they did not

60 The Hussites and Protestant history

know any better, and were at least opposed to the fallen Catholic Church: dispensations that Crespin would extend to the Vaudois for their errors. Instead, the Hussites were portrayed as explicit forebears to the coming of the Reformation a century later. In 1554, the Hussites concluded on page 143. On page 144, the first Lutheran martyr was introduced. From 1555 onwards, the two movements were instead brought together by the legend of Hus' prophecy, which was linked to Luther by the reformer's own writing. Thus, Crespin knit the Hussites into the *Livre des Martyrs* as fully fledged members of the True Church.

Notes

1 Philip Haberkern, *Patron Saint and Prophet: Jan Hus in the Bohemian and German Reformations* (Oxford University Press, 2016), p. 250.
2 Haberkern, p. 239.
3 Heiko Oberman, *Luther Between God and the Devil* (New Haven, CT: Yale University Press, 2006), p. 197.
4 Martin Luther, 'Concerning the Answer of the Goat in Leipzig', *Works*, Vol. 39 (Philadelphia: Fortress Press, 1970), p. 134.
5 Luther, 'Address to the Christian Nobility', *Works*, Vol. 44 (Philadelphia: Fortress Press, 1966), p. 196.
6 Luther, 'To George Spelatin', February 1520, *Works*, Vol. 47 (Philadelphia: Fortress Press, 1971), p. 152.
7 Matthew Spinka, *Hus at the Council* (London: Columbia University Press, 1965), p. 81. Yves Krumenacker, 'La généalogie de la Réforme protestante', *Revue Historique* 638 (2006), p. 261.
8 Martin Luther, 'Sermon on John, Chapter 16', *Works*, Vol. 24 (St Louis: Concordia, 1961), p. 413.
9 Thomas Fudge, *The Magnificent Ride: First Reformation in Hussite Bohemia* (Aldershot: Ashgate, 1998) gives several examples of this, e.g. pp. 1, 133.
10 David El Kenz, *Les bûchers du roi: la culture protestante des martyrs (1523–1572)* (Paris: Seyssel, 1997), p. 70.
11 Krumenacker, pp. 261, 263.
12 Jean-François Gilmont, *Bibliographie des éditions de Jean Crespin* (Verviers: Gason, 1981), p. 58.
13 Jean Crespin, *Recueil de plusieurs personnes qui ont constamment enduré la mort pour le nom de Nostre Seigneur* ([Geneva]: Jean Crespin, 1555), Vol. I, pp. I–II.
14 Crespin, *Recueil de plusieurs personnes* (1555), Vol. I, p. I.
15 Crespin, *Recueil de plusieurs personnes* (1555), Vol. I, pp. I–II.
16 Crespin, *Recueil de plusieurs personnes* (1555), Vol. I, p. III.
17 Crespin, *Recueil de plusieurs personnes* (1555), Vol. I, pp. II–III.
18 Crespin, *Recueil de plusieurs personnes* (1555), Vol. I, pp. II–III.
19 John Foxe, *Commentarii rerum in ecclesia gestarum* (Strasbourg: Rihel, 1554). Gilmont also discusses this.
20 Crespin, *Recueil de plusieurs personnes* (1555), Vol. I, pp. 129–CXXXIII. See also David Watson, *The Martyrology of Jean Crespin and the Early French Evangelical Movement, 1523–1555* (PhD Thesis, St Andrew's, 1997), p. 150.
21 Crespin, *Recueil de plusieurs personnes* (1555), Vol. I, p. X.
22 Anne Hudson, 'Notes of an Early Fifteenth-Century Research Assistant, and

The Hussites and Protestant history   61

the Emergence of the 267 Articles against Wyclif', *The English Historical Review*, 118 (2003), p. 693.

23 Crespin, *Recueil de plusieurs personnes* (1555), Vol. I, p. X.

24 Crespin, *Recueil de plusieurs personnes* (1555), Vol. I, p. XVI.

25 Crespin, *Recueil de plusieurs personnes* (1555), Vol. I, p. XXVI.

26 Crespin, *Recueil de plusieurs personnes* (1555), Vol. I, p. XXVII.

27 Elizabeth Evenden and Thomas Freeman, *Religion and the Book in Early Modern England: The Making of John Foxe's 'Book of Martyrs'* (Cambridge: Cambridge University Press, 2014), p. 57.

28 Jean Crespin, *Actes des Martyrs* ([Geneva]: Jean Crespin, 1565), pp. 1, 9.

29 Crespin, *Actes des Martyrs* (1565), pp. 58–60.

30 Crespin, *Actes des Martyrs* (1565), p. 87.

31 Spinka, *Hus at the Council*, p. 81.

32 Spinka, *Hus at the Council*, p. 80.

33 Spinka, *Hus at the Council*, p. 80.

34 Spinka, *Hus at the Council*, p. 80.

35 Renee Neu Watkins, 'The Death of Jerome of Prague: Divergent Views', *Speculum*, 42: 1 (1967), p. 120.

36 Howard Kaminsky, 'Pius Aeneas Among the Taborites', *American Society of Church History*, 28: 3 (1959), p. 281.

37 Jean Crespin, *Histoire des vrays tesmoins de la verité de l'Evangile* ([Geneva: Jean Crespin], 1570), p. 42 verso.

38 Crespin, *Recueil de plusieurs personnes* (1555), Vol. I, p. 1.

39 Gilmont, *Bibliographie*, p. 58.

40 Crespin, *Recueil de plusieurs personnes* (1555), Vol. I, p. XXXI.

41 Crespin, *Recueil de plusieurs personnes* (1555), Vol. I, p. XXXI. A discussion of this nickname can be found in Michael Van Dussen's *From England to Bohemia: Heresy and Communication in the Later Middle Ages* (Cambridge: Cambridge University Press, 2012), p. 70.

42 Crespin, *Recueil de plusieurs personnes* (1555), Vol. I, p. XXXII.

43 Crespin, *Recueil de plusieurs personnes* (1555), Vol. I, p. XXXII.

44 Crespin, *Recueil de plusieurs personnes* (1555), Vol. I, p. XXXII.

45 Crespin, *Actes des Martyrs* (1565), p. 27.

46 Jean Crespin, *Recueil de plusieurs personnes qui ont constamment endure la mort pour la nome de N. S. Jesus Christ.* ([Geneva: Jean Crespin], 1554), p. 1. 1570, p. 15 verso.

47 Crespin, *Recueil de plusieurs personnes* (1554), pp. 2–3.

48 Spinka, *Hus at the Council*, pp. 95–98.

49 Spinka, *Hus at the Council*, pp. 110–11.

50 Spinka, *Hus at the Council*, p. 113.

51 Spinka, *Hus at the Council*, p. 115.

52 Spinka, *Hus at the Council*, p. 121.

53 Spinka, *Hus at the Council*, p. 167.

54 Spinka, *Hus at the Council*, p. 228.

55 Spinka, *Hus at the Council*, p. 232.

56 Spinka, *Hus at the Council*, p. 233.

57 Crespin, *Histoire des vrays tesmoins* (1570), p. 21.5.

58 Crespin, *Histoire des vrays tesmoins* (1570), p. 125.

59 Crespin, *Histoire des vrays tesmoins* (1570), p. 18 recto.

60 Crespin, *Histoire des vrays tesmoins* (1570), p. 125.

61 Crespin, *Histoire des vrays tesmoins* (1570), p. 18 verso.

62 Spinka, *Hus at the Council*, p. 128. Crespin, *Histoire des vrays tesmoins* (1570), p. 18 verso.

63 Spinka, *Hus at the Council*, p. 128.

62 The Hussites and Protestant history

64 Spinka, *Hus at the Council*, p. 128.
65 Spinka, *Hus at the Council*, pp. 128–29.
66 Spinka, *Hus at the Council*, p. 128.
67 Spinka, *John Hus' Conception of the Church* (Princeton, NJ: Princeton University Press, 1966), p. 232.
68 Spinka, *John Hus' Conception of the Church*, p. 232.
69 Spinka, *John Hus' Conception of the Church*, p. 232.
70 See, for example, Calvin's 1559 *Institutes*, 4.1.12–16, 20.
71 Spinka, *Hus at the Council*, p. 138.
72 Crespin, *Histoire des vrays tesmoins* (1570), p. 19 recto.
73 Crespin, *Histoire des vrays tesmoins* (1570), p. 19 verso. Spinka, *Hus at the Council*, p. 167.
74 Spinka, *John Hus: A Biography* (Princeton, NJ: Princeton University Press, 1968), p. 64.
75 Spinka, *Hus at the Council*, pp. 167–68 n.
76 Spinka, *Hus at the Council*, pp. 167–68.
77 Crespin, *Histoire des vrays tesmoins* (1570), p. 19 verso.
78 Spinka, *Hus at the Council*, p. 169.
79 Spinka, *Hus at the Council*, p. 169.
80 Crespin, *Histoire des vrays tesmoins* (1570), p. 19 verso.
81 Crespin, *Histoire des vrays tesmoins* (1570), p. 20 recto.
82 Crespin, *Histoire des vrays tesmoins* (1570), p. 20 verso.
83 Gabriel Audisio, *Les Vaudois: Histoire d'une dissidence XIIe–XVIe siècle* (Paris: Fayard, 1998), pp. 16, 68, 216.
84 Spinka, *Hus at the Council*, p. 182. Crespin, *Histoire des vrays tesmoins* (1570), p. 21 verso.
85 Crespin, *Histoire des vrays tesmoins* (1570), p. 20 recto.
86 Spinka, *Hus at the Council*, p. 183. Crespin, *Histoire des vrays tesmoins* (1570), p. 22 recto.
87 Crespin, *Histoire des vrays tesmoins* (1570), pp. 183–84.
88 Crespin, *Histoire des vrays tesmoins* (1570), p. 22 recto.
89 Crespin, *Histoire des vrays tesmoins* (1570), p. 22 recto.
90 Spinka, *Hus at the Council*, pp. 184–85.
91 Crespin, *Histoire des vrays tesmoins* (1570), p. 22 verso.
92 Crespin, *Histoire des vrays tesmoins* (1570), p. 22 verso.
93 Spinka, *Hus at the Council*, p. 189.
94 Spinka, *Hus at the Council*, p. 189. Crespin, *Histoire des vrays tesmoins* (1570), p. 22 verso.
95 Spinka, *Hus at the Council*, p. 189.
96 Crespin, *Histoire des vrays tesmoins* (1570), p. 23 verso.
97 Crespin, *Histoire des vrays tesmoins* (1570), p. 23 verso.
98 Crespin, *Histoire des vrays tesmoins* (1570), p. 24 recto.
99 Crespin, *Histoire des vrays tesmoins* (1570), p. 24 verso.
100 Spinka, *Hus at the Council*, p. 197.
101 Crespin, *Histoire des vrays tesmóins* (1570), p. 24 verso.
102 Crespin, *Histoire des vrays tesmoins* (1570), p. 24 verso. Spinka, *Hus at the Council*, p. 24 verso.
103 Crespin, *Histoire des vrays tesmoins* (1570), p. 25 recto.
104 Crespin, *Histoire des vrays tesmoins* (1570), pp. 25 recto, verso.
105 Crespin, *Histoire des vrays tesmoins* (1570), p. 25 verso.
106 Spinka, *Hus at the Council*, p. 203 n.
107 Crespin, *Histoire des vrays tesmoins* (1570), p. 25 verso.
108 Crespin, *Histoire des vrays tesmoins* (1570), p. 25 verso.

The Hussites and Protestant history   63

109 Spinka, *Hus at the Council*, pp. 209–10. Crespin, *Histoire des vrays tesmoins* (1570), p. 25 verso.
110 Crespin, *Histoire des vrays tesmoins* (1570), p. 25 verso.
111 Spinka, *Hus at the Council*, pp. 211–12. Crespin, *Histoire des vrays tesmoins* (1570), p. 26 recto.
112 Crespin, *Histoire des vrays tesmoins* (1570), p. 26 recto.
113 Spinka, *Hus at the Council*, p. 226. Crespin, *Histoire des vrays tesmoins* (1570), p. 28 verso.
114 Spinka, *Hus at the Council*, p. 226.
115 Crespin, *Histoire des vrays tesmoins* (1570), p. 28 verso.
116 Crespin, *Histoire des vrays tesmoins* (1570), p. 28 verso. Spinka, *Hus at the Council*, p. 227.
117 Crespin, *Histoire des vrays tesmoins* (1570), p. 19 verso.
118 Fudge, *The Magnificent Ride*, p. 131.
119 Fudge, *The Magnificent Ride*, p. 131.
120 Spinka, *Hus at the Council*, p. 232.
121 Crespin, *Histoire des vrays tesmoins* (1570), p. 30 recto.
122 Spinka, *Hus at the Council*, p. 232. Crespin, *Histoire des vrays tesmoins* (1570), p. 30 recto.
123 Crespin, *Histoire des vrays tesmoins* (1570), p. 30 verso.
124 Spinka, *Hus at the Council*, p. 234.
125 Crespin, *Histoire des vrays tesmoins* (1570), p. 30 verso.
126 Crespin, *Histoire des vrays tesmoins* (1570), p. 27 verso.
127 Crespin, *Recueil de plusieurs personnes* (1554), p. 95. Crespin, *Histoire des vrays tesmoins* (1570), p. 30 verso.
128 Crespin, *Recueil de plusieurs personnes* (1554), p. 96. Crespin, *Histoire des vrays tesmoins* (1570), p. 27 verso.
129 This letter can be found at Crespin, *Histoire des vrays tesmoins* (1570), pp. 35 verso–36 recto.
130 Crespin, *Histoire des vrays tesmoins* (1570), pp. 31 verso, 32 verso.
131 Crespin, *Histoire des vrays tesmoins* (1570), pp. 32 recto–verso.
132 Spinka, *Letters of John Hus* (Manchester: Manchester University Press, 1972), p. 183.
133 Crespin, *Histoire des vrays tesmoins* (1570), p. 34 verso.
134 Crespin, *Histoire des vrays tesmoins* (1570), p. 34 verso.
135 Crespin, *Histoire des vrays tesmoins* (1570), p. 32 verso.
136 Crespin, *Histoire des vrays tesmoins* (1570), p. 33 recto.
137 Howard Kaminsky, *A History of the Hussite Revolution* (Berkeley: University of California Press, 1967), p. 163.
138 Crespin, *Recueil de plusieurs personnes* (1554), pp. 139–40.
139 Francis Lutzow, *The Life and Times of Master John Hus* (London: J.M. Dent & Sons, 1921), p. 299.
140 R.R. Betts, *Essays in Czech History* (London: Athlone Press, 1969), p. 51.
141 Lutzow, p. 300 says 1398; Betts, p. 53, argues for 1399 or 1400.
142 Betts, p. 54.
143 Betts, p. 54. Spinka, *Biography*, pp. 59, 82.
144 Watkins, 'The Death of Jerome of Prague: Divergent Views', *Speculum* 42:1 (1967), p. 112.
145 Watkins, p. 112.
146 Kaminsky, *A History of the Hussite Revolution*, p. 143.
147 Kaminsky, *A History of the Hussite Revolution*, p. 144.
148 Spinka, *Biography*, p. 292.
149 Watkins, p. 120.
150 Crespin, *Recueil de plusieurs personnes* (1554), p. 129.

64 *The Hussites and Protestant history*

151 Crespin, *Recueil de plusieurs personnes* (1554), pp. 138–39.
152 Crespin, *Recueil de plusieurs personnes* (1554), p. 132.
153 Crespin, *Recueil de plusieurs personnes* (1554), p. 132.
154 Crespin, *Recueil de plusieurs personnes* (1554), pp. 133–34.
155 Crespin, *Recueil de plusieurs personnes* (1554), p. 135.
156 Crespin, *Recueil de plusieurs personnes* (1554), p. 137.
157 Crespin, *Recueil de plusieurs personnes* (1554), p. 138.
158 Watkins, p. 120.
159 David Watson points this out in *The Martyrology of Jean Crespin*, p. 150.
160 Crespin, *Recueil de plusieurs personnes* (1555), p. 130.
161 Crespin, *Recueil de plusieurs personnes* (1555), p. 130.
162 Crespin, *Recueil de plusieurs personnes* (1555), p. 130.
163 Foxe, *Commentarii rerum*, pp. *80 recto–*81 verso. Adriaen van Haemstede, *De Geschiedenisse ende den doodt der vromer Martelaren …* ([Emden], 1559), pp. 56–57.
164 Foxe, *Rerum in ecclesia gestarum* (Basle: Brylinger & Oporinus, 1559), p. 71.
165 Compare Crespin, *Recueil de plusieurs personnes* (1555), Vol. 1, p. 184, with Crespin, *Histoire des vrays tesmoins* (1570), p. 22 recto.
166 Crespin, *Recueil de plusieurs personnes* (1555), Vol. I, p. 133.
167 Crespin, *Recueil de plusieurs personnes* (1555), Vol. I, p. 133.
168 Crespin, *Recueil de plusieurs personnes* (1555), Vol. I, p. 133.
169 Crespin, *Recueil de plusieurs personnes* (1555), Vol. I, p. 133.
170 Crespin, *Recueil de plusieurs personnes* (1555), Vol. I, p. 135.
171 Crespin, *Actes des Martyrs* (1565), p. 62.
172 Crespin, *Actes des Martyrs* (1565), p. 64. Betts suggests that this information was drawn from an eyewitness at the council, possibly Mladonovice.
173 Crespin, *Actes des Martyrs* (1565), pp. 63–64. Calculation my own.
174 Crespin, *Actes des Martyrs* (1565), p. 65.
175 Crespin, *Actes des Martyrs* (1565), p. 65.
176 Crespin, *Actes des Martyrs* (1565), p. 64.
177 Crespin, *Actes des Martyrs* (1565), p. 68.
178 Crespin, *Recueil de plusieurs personnes* (1554), pp. 139–40.
179 Canons of Bishop Zelezny of Litomysl, cited in Kaminsky, *A History of the Hussite Revolution*, p. 163.
180 Crespin, *Recueil de plusieurs personnes* (1554), p. 140.
181 Aeneas Sylvius, *Historia Bohemica* (Rome: Oppenhym and Shurener de Bopardia, 1475), p. 38 verso.
182 Aeneas Sylvius, *Historia Bohemica*, p. 38 verso.
183 Crespin, *Recueil de plusieurs personnes* (1554), p. 141.
184 Crespin, *Recueil de plusieurs personnes* (1554), p. 168.
185 Crespin, *Recueil de plusieurs personnes* (1554), p. 141.
186 Aeneas Sylvius, *Historia Bohemica*, p. 30.
187 Crespin, *Recueil de plusieurs personnes* (1554), p. 142. Coranda was in fact based in Pilsen, where he was joined by Zizka, according to Frederick Heymann, *John Zizka and the Hussite Revolution* (Princeton, NJ: Princeton University Press, 1955), p. 88.
188 Crespin, *Recueil de plusieurs personnes* (1554), pp. 142–43. Kaminsky, *A History of the Hussite Revolution*, p. 277.
189 Aeneas Sylvius, *Historia Bohemica*, p. 30 verso.
190 Crespin, *Recueil de plusieurs personnes* (1554), p. 143.
191 Kaminsky, *A History of the Hussite Revolution*, p. 277, gives us this dating.
192 Crespin, *Recueil de plusieurs personnes* (1555), p. CXXX.
193 Crespin, *Recueil de plusieurs personnes* (1555), p. CXXX.
194 Crespin, *Recueil de plusieurs personnes* (1555), p. CXXX.

The Hussites and Protestant history 65

195 Haberkern, p. 189.
196 Crespin, *Recueil de plusieurs personnes* (1555), p. CXXXI.
197 Crespin, *Recueil de plusieurs personnes* (1555), p. CXXXI.
198 Crespin, *Histoire des vrays tesmoins* (1570), p. 42 verso. In 1555's version, Crespin only notes that Aeneas was a mortal enemy, and neglects to mention the fact that he eventually became Pope.
199 See Heymann, pp. 25–32 for Zizka's exploits in Poland against the Teutonic Order.
200 Crespin, *Recueil de plusieurs personnes* (1555), Vol. I, p. CXXXI–CXXXII.
201 Heymann, p. 448.
202 Crespin, *Recueil de plusieurs personnes* (1555), Vol. I, p. CXXXII.
203 Crespin, *Recueil de plusieurs personnes* (1555), Vol. I, p. CXXXII.
204 Fudge, *The Crusades Against Heretics in Bohemia, 1418–1437* (Aldershot: Ashgate, 2002), p. 38 n.
205 Heymann, p. 138 n.
206 Crespin, *Recueil de plusieurs personnes* (1555), Vol. I, p. CXXXIII.
207 Crespin, *Recueil de plusieurs personnes* (1555), Vol. I, p. CXXXIII.
208 Heymann, p. 79.
209 Heymann, p. 96.
210 Crespin, *Recueil de plusieurs personnes* (1555), Vol. I, p. CXXXIIII. This is cited, accurately, as coming from Aeneas Sylvius, though rejected as historical fact by Heymann, p. 433.
211 Crespin, *Recueil de plusieurs personnes* (1555), Vol. I, p. CXXXIIII. This detail, again rejected by Heymann, also comes from Aeneas Sylvius.
212 Kaminsky, 'Pius Aeneas', p. 301.
213 Crespin, *Actes des Martyrs* (1565), p. 81.
214 Crespin, *Histoire des vrays tesmoins* (1570), p. 41 recto.
215 Crespin, *Histoire des vrays tesmoins* (1570), p. 41 verso.
216 Compare Crespin, *Histoire des vrays tesmoins* (1570), p. 41 verso with František Palacký (ed.), *Documenta mag. Joannis Hus vitam ...* (Prague: Tempsky, 1869), p. 583.
217 Crespin, *Histoire des vrays tesmoins* (1570), p. 41 verso.
218 Kaminsky, *A History of the Hussite Revolution*, p. 144. The original letter was dated 2 September; Crespin's is dated from the Feast of St Wenceslaus, which would have fallen later in the month. The discrepancy is explained by Crespin's copying of a version which was signed later by a different group of nobles (see below).

2 'What little true light they had'
The Vaudois in history and martyrology

From the first edition of the *Livre des Martyrs*, Crespin paid particular attention to the situation of the Vaudois, first in France and in later editions also in the Alps and parts of Italy. A heretical group, based particularly in the Alpine valleys of France and Savoy, the Vaudois had expanded into Provence and parts of Italy in the fifteenth century. While the Vaudois heresy of the fifteenth century might have brought them to the attention of Protestant martyrologists and historians in any event, it was their contact with the Reformed Church in the 1530s that made them an integral part of Crespin's project. In the 1540s and 1550s Geneva was in regular contact with the Vaudois, and sending ministers to their congregations; the degree to which this represents a formal union between the groups has been the subject of intense historiographical discussion in the last thirty years.[1] The Vaudois contribution to Olivétan's vernacular bible at Geneva in the mid-1530s, for example, was clearly a significant gesture between the two groups, but Euan Cameron has questioned whether it represents the close union that some historians have suggested.[2]

Because of these existing links, it appears that the Vaudois had a different status from the other groups of martyrs that Crespin discussed. In his first comments on them, introducing an account of a series of massacres in Provence, he felt compelled to defend his decision to include them, arguing that: 'the history of those of Cabrières and Mérindol is not a question of two or three who have endured death, but of a people and an infinity of people'.[3] Before the advent of the *Récit d'Histoire* format in the editions published in 1563 and 1564, writing the story of a massacre was a technically difficult task. The usual sources, such as trial records, personal letters, or eyewitness accounts, were unavailable. Writing the 'history of a people' required the tools of history, not martyrology. Similarly, Crespin's conception of genre placed massacre victims outside of the scope of the *Livre des Martyrs*, a challenge that he initially met by including them in separate works of history, as well as the martyrology.

Further complicating Crespin's task were the numerous problems which the Vaudois posed to his conception of what a martyr should be. Crespin held to the Augustinian maxim that a martyr was made by his faith, but

The Vaudois in history and martyrology 67

the Vaudois held doctrines which set them apart from his Genevan orthodoxy. The best way to prove that someone had died for his faith was for him to have been condemned for such by a magistrate or a court, but the most notable actions against the Vaudois he depicted were large-scale, even military in nature.[4] Any suspicion that someone had been punished for actions against established authority would invalidate them as a martyr, and the Vaudois had a reputation for vigorous self-defence which verged on rebellion.[5] In the years before the 1545 massacres, the Vaudois raided a monastery before retreating behind their fortifications.[6]

The Vaudois people presented a real challenge to Crespin's conception of his project, yet he persisted in including them in his martyrology. In the case of the Provinçal Vaudois, he did so by stressing their doctrinal purity, by denying the authority of those who had moved against them, by focussing on individual cases which more closely resembled his other martyrdoms, and by heightening the parallels between the ordeal of the Vaudois and the more usual narrative of a single martyr. In the other major Vaudois narrative, which described the struggles of the Piedmontese community against Savoy in 1560–61, Crespin presented the Vaudois in an historical section, which allowed him to avoid the question of their qualifications as martyrs, focussing instead on their success in defending themselves and their faith.[7]

Crespin's work was an early entry in Reformed literature on the subject of the Vaudois. For the section that represents the largest portion of his discussion of the group, the history of Cabrières and Mérindol, he seems to have been the first to publish most of his material. Unlike some of his sources, who took an approach that often emphasised the faults of the Vaudois, and their divergences from the Reformed mainstream, Crespin's approach was aimed at incorporating them into the wider canon of Protestant martyrs.[8] He stressed their ancient roots and their long-standing opposition to the 'innovations' of the Papacy, and when they were discussed alongside the reformers of the early sixteenth century, Crespin largely emphasised their points of agreement. This approach, which emphasised the Calvinist elements in their creeds, and held them as long-standing opponents of the excesses of the Catholic Church, was to prove influential – large passages of Crespin appear to have been copied into the *Histoire Ecclésiastique*, and Foxe's martyrology. From there, they entered into the standard narrative of the French Reformed Church.[9] The Vaudois were not only a group well-known for their sufferings at the hands of Catholic authorities, but they also represented an answer to the old question of Protestant origins.[10]

A Vaudois history that reached back to the twelfth century, or perhaps even as far as antiquity – as Crespin suggested it did in one edition – would provide some counter to the 'spiritual lineage' of the Papacy.[11] What is more, they provided specifically French roots for reform, in Lyon and Provence, an appeal which may help to explain the French protestant interest

68 *The Vaudois in history and martyrology*

in the Cathars, or Albigensians, slightly later.[12] As enshrined in the leading Genevan martyrology, and later in the definitive history of the Reformed Church, Crespin's stance would have a reach and authority within the French Protestant community that no other work on the Vaudois could match. Certainly, in the decades after Crespin's first publication on them, the Vaudois found their reputation amongst the Reformed much improved.

The Vaudois have been the subject of increasing study in the last few decades, including monographs by both Euan Cameron and Gabriel Audisio. Almost all of this work has drawn, to some degree, on Crespin for information about the events of the mid-sixteenth century. This period is often treated as an endpoint of Vaudois history, as the Vaudois merged into the wider Reformed Church after three centuries of independence; several histories end in the mid-sixteenth century.[13] Cameron's *The Reformation of the Heretics*, a study of the interactions between the early Reformation and the Vaudois, similarly suggests that some Vaudois identity was lost in the merger. Cameron has argued that existing studies have traditionally overstated the speed and degree with which the two groups merged. His critique has met with strong resistance from French scholars in the field, including Audisio and Gilmont.[14] Much of the debate has centred on Cameron's doubts as to the importance, or decisiveness of the 1532 Synod of Chanforan, which the traditional historiography has usually regarded as the moment in which the Vaudois leadership decided to join the Reformed Church.[15] Amongst many other points, Cameron has suggested that the ecclesiastical leadership of the Vaudois was simply not centralised enough, and powerful enough, to quickly enact such changes amongst the community at large. Certainly it took continued missionary efforts of the 1550s and 1560s for serious change in doctrine and behaviour to take place.

As one of very few sources available for this time and place, Crespin's material on the Vaudois has often been used in regard to this question. Both Cameron and Audisio have had occasion to draw upon the martyrology; both cite the 1565 state of his 1564 *Actes des Martyrs*, for example. There have been fewer studies of the Vaudois that use the earlier editions of Crespin, however; Jean-François Gilmont's detailed comparison of sources for the Vaudois is an obvious exception, although not one that has been built upon to a great extent.[16] As a result, some of the material that Crespin cited in his works of 1554 and 1555, for example, and which was excluded from later works, has not been examined as thoroughly as that which was published in the editions from the 1560s. This is particularly important with reference to a confession of faith printed in the 1555 edition of the *Histoire memorable*, before being heavily reduced in 1556, and replaced altogether in 1564 and afterwards. Although, as discussed below, this is a problematic document with an uncertain provenance, this confession has only been discussed infrequently in studies of Vaudois belief during this period.

The Vaudois in history and martyrology 69

While the Vaudois conversion may have proceeded more slowly than sometimes claimed, it is clear that leading reformers took an interest in the conversion of the Vaudois, and were invested in the success of the project. In 1530, two preachers, Georges Morel and Pierre Masson, were sent to make contact with the reformers, eventually meeting with Oecolampadius and with Bucer.[17]

Through the 1530s and into the 1540s Calvin and Farel corresponded on the subject, and tried to intervene with various governments on their behalf. Farel and Viret attempted to rally support for the Vaudois amongst the Swiss Protestant cantons in 1535, and Calvin seems to have tried to build opposition to the French attack on the Vaudois in the 1540s, a tactic he repeated in 1555–56, when a renewed campaign of persecution was planned for Piedmont.[18] In a letter to Bullinger of 1544, Calvin wrote that: 'There are brethren in Provence, for whom you are aware that we have always taken much pains. Nor were they in any way undeserving that we should do so ...'[19] He praised their high standard of conduct (a compliment often paid to the Vaudois, even by their enemies), and emphasised that there was a duty to try and protect them.[20]

However, the reformers were sometimes cautious of the Vaudois, or their reputation, often choosing to avoid the terms 'Vaudois' or 'Waldensian' in favour of 'our friends' or 'the Provençals'.[21] They seem to have had suspicions about the habits the Vaudois had developed; their secrecy of worship earned them a rebuke from Oecolampadius, who regarded it as tantamount to Nicodemism.[22] The Vaudois themselves had expressed concerns about some aspects of Protestant theology, especially around the question of predestination; Morel and Masson's letter to Bucer reveals an attachment to the idea of good works, and Audisio suggests that debate over these questions was likely to have been one of the major stumbling blocks to joining the Protestant movement.[23]

It was only in the 1550s that enough Genevan-trained ministers began to enter Piedmont to reassure the nervous that reliably Protestant doctrine was being preached there. Church buildings were constructed, and parishes established; some of whom were represented at the 1559 national synod in Paris.[24] Indeed, these missions were very closely supervised by Genevan authorities, and took an often aggressive approach to reforming and leading their communities.[25] These arrivals often corresponded with renewed persecution from the local authorities, probably because of the definitive break from the Catholic parish that this entailed.

The Reformed orthodoxy of the Vaudois was an important issue in Crespin's coverage of them, essential not only to how he wrote about them, but to whether he wrote about them at all, and their 'conversion' was still a work in progress during the years that Crespin was active. Crespin used the term 'Vaudois' throughout his works, though many of the documents which he cited used phrases like 'those of Mérindol' or 'those of the Vallees'; Crespin usually made it clear to his readers that the

70 *The Vaudois in history and martyrology*

reference was to the Vaudois. He did, however, allow doubts about the Vaudois claims to true Christian knowledge to enter his martyrology at several points, offering direct commentary on their imperfection, and editing away some of their more striking divergences from Genevan orthodoxy. Although Geneva led the way in sending missions to the Vaudois, and agitating for political support, Calvin's attitude was such that Cameron has described him as being: 'consistent, and consistently patronizing. He would take the heretics' side as long as they followed him in doctrine.'[26] While the Vaudois might have had a long and honourable tradition of dissent, discussion of doctrine with Geneva was one-way. This attitude informed the *Livre des Martyrs*, which is occasionally dismissive of Vaudois doctrine, and seems to regard the Reformed Church as the only coherent opposition to the Catholic Church.

The Vaudois themselves had deep roots, and seem to have poorly understood their own origins. The most commonly accepted origin for them lies with a twelfth-century Lyonnais merchant by the name of Waldo, Valdes, or Valdensius, who took up a life of mendicant poverty, and who had portions of the Bible and the Church Fathers translated into the vernacular for his own purposes.[27] He developed a community around him, whom the ecclesiastical authorities granted some rights of public preaching. In this they resembled many of the other preaching groups, heretical and orthodox to emerge in the same era, such as the Petrobrusians to the Dominicans. Indeed, like the Dominicans, much of their early energy was devoted towards anti-Cathar activity. By 1184 their privileges had been withdrawn over a series of disagreements, possibly including female preachers, although they were not fully excommunicated from the Church until 1215.[28]

Later versions of the story, current in the fourteenth century, assigned Waldo the Christian name Peter, and sometimes placed his separation from the Catholic Church as far back as the fourth century, and the supposed Donation of Constantine.[29] Waldo's role in this theory was as a twelfth-century restorer of the movement.[30] These earlier origins framed the Vaudois as early critics of the established church, and as preserving in themselves a link to the pre-Constantinian church. Later theories would argue that their origin was associated with the ninth-century Bishop of Turin, Claudius, whose attacks on ritual and authority made him an attractive figure to co-opt. Euan Cameron has associated this theory with Protestant historiography above all.[31] Crespin, in different editions, subscribed to both the fourth- and twelfth-century theories of the Vaudois origins.

In the following centuries, the Vaudois spread across large parts of Europe, gaining large followings in the South of France, the Danube valley, Bohemia and Moravia, and as far as the Baltic.[32] Another group crossed the Alps into Piedmont in the thirteenth century, and in the fourteenth established a few small settlements as far away as Calabria and Apulia, wherein they were able to practice relatively freely in remote areas.[33]

The Vaudois in history and martyrology   71

Vaudois habitation spread across both sides of the Alps, with large settlements in both Provence and in Piedmont, as well as the Dauphiné. In the fifteenth century, some Vaudois seem to have made contact with the Hussite movement of Bohemia, probably with the more radical Taborite faction; there may have been some discussion of cooperation, though it came to nothing.[34] These links may have contributed to the suspicion with which they were regarded by others, however: a 'crusade' was launched against the Vaudois of the Dauphiné in 1487, following a major revolt earlier in the decade.[35]

The beliefs of the Vaudois before the Reformation are not fully understood, and much of what we do know is taken from hostile or otherwise unrepresentative sources; with no central bodies, they probably varied from region to region and over time. They often participated in the services of the established Church, while at the same time maintaining some distinctive doctrines. They were less inclined to establish perpetual masses for the dead than was usual, for they rejected the Catholic conception of Purgatory; instead they placed more emphasis on bequests for the poor.[36] They do not seem to have mixed much within communities, instead forming their own villages when they immigrated into an area (as they did in Provence or Calabria) and travelling to other Vaudois settlements in order to marry within their own group.[37] As a result, distinctive Vaudois family names can be identified, and their partial rejection of the Catholic cult can be traced in notarial records. There are places where they have left their name on the landscape to this day, as in the two towns in Calabria, San Sisto dei Valdesi, and Guardia Piemontese, which feature in Crespin. There exists some debate on whether this insular community represents a 'sect', which sought to 'un-church' the Catholic majority, or whether the Vaudois were content to co-exist with the Church; whether, in Peter Biller's phrase, the Vaudois were a religious order or a church. In Audisio's view, though Protestant historians have sought to emphasise the rupture between the Vaudois and Catholics, we still must regard the Vaudois as a sect, a group that separates itself from the world, and society, and is in many ways exclusive and independent.[38] This would place them necessarily in opposition to the Catholic Church. Cameron, for his part, argues that the Vaudois of the late fifteenth and early sixteenth centuries did not 'un-church' Catholics, and did not believe that only they, the Vaudois were saved.[39] They remained, to some degree, in affiliation with the institutional clergy, reliant on them for the application of sacraments, while criticising their morals and practice.[40] This view would place the Vaudois closer to their original reforming mission. The two views are, of course, not mutually exclusive – it is possible to imagine an insular Vaudois sect that still maintained some ties with the Catholic Church, despite the claims of later Protestant writers.

Like many minority groups of the period, most of our knowledge of the Vaudois comes to us from hostile sources like inquisition records, and

72 *The Vaudois in history and martyrology*

this remains true up to the period of the Reformation. Many of the documents Crespin presents, such as his longer version of the 1541 Vaudois Confession of Faith, cannot be found in any place or form before he published them, which makes his account both important and hard to verify.[41] Similarly, there exists a good deal of scholarly debate on the basic elements of Vaudois history in the sixteenth century, as evidenced in the debate over Chanforan, and over the place of what documents we do possess.[42]

The Vaudois were included in the *Livre des Martyrs* from the first edition, although just barely. At the very end of the first edition, out of the general chronology, Crespin included ten pages describing massacres at the Vaudois settlements of Mérindol and Cabrières in Provence in 1545. This information was repeated, better integrated, in the 1555 edition. The same basic narrative was found, separated into its own section, the *Histoire memorable de la persecution ... de Mérindol et Cabrières*, in 1555's sextodecimo-format martyrology.[43] Jean Calvin sent the German historian Johann Sleidan (several of whose works Crespin published in translation) an account of the massacres that closely fits that given in the 1554 *Livre des Martyrs*, in response to a series of letters of 1553 asking for information.[44]

The Vaudois' importance to Crespin seems to have been growing, even as its relationship to the rest of the martyrology remained ambiguous. 1555 also saw him publish a much longer treatment of the same events, separate from the martyrology. The *Histoire memorable de la Persecution & saccagement du peuple de Mérindol & Cabrières & Autres circonvoisins, appelez Vaudois*, to give it its full title, is a self-contained book independent of the *Livre des Martyrs*. Crespin had hinted at such a publication in the Vaudois section of 1554's *Livre des Martyrs*, writing that the current section contained 'The most necessary for the instruction of the faithful, until the whole story is composed more fully in writing.'[45] The *Histoire memorable* was clearly on his mind even as he was completing the first edition of the martyrology. Indeed, in some examples, a first edition of the history was bound with the martyrology to create a portmanteau book, reinforcing the status of the *Histoire memorable* as a companion to the *Livre des Martyrs*.

The *Histoire memorable* was reprinted the next year, in 1556, and cut by approximately 4,000 words, or 10 per cent of the earlier edition.[46] These cuts were made, as we shall see, to some of the most doctrinally sensitive portions of the text. Having produced a martyrological and an historical account of the massacres in Provence, Crespin did not update this text for several editions. The Latin editions of the martyrology, published in 1556 and 1560, effectively translated what had been previously published in French, though the 1560 edition also included one new document.[47] Later editions of the martyrology, as part of a trend towards including historical narrative, brought together both of Crespin's Vaudois

The massacre of hundreds of Vaudois in the villages of Mérindol and Cabrières, the topic of the *Histoire memorable*, in 1545 was the first and most important appearance of the Vaudois in the *Livre des Martyrs*. The Edict, or *Arrest*, of Mérindol was passed by the Parlement of Aix in 1540, condemning the village of Mérindol (which was, as we have seen, an important location for the Vaudois of the region) to be destroyed.[48] After much delay, this was enforced in 1545, leading to the destruction not only of Mérindol, but of the neighbouring settlement of Cabrières, in the papal enclave of the Comtat Venaissin. It was estimated that 2,700 people were killed, and many more were sentenced to the galleys; many of the survivors emigrated to Geneva.

texts, adding many of the documents of the *Histoire memorable* to the framework and introduction of the early editions of the *Livre des Martyrs*. Even after the inclusion of a great deal of the material from the *Histoire memorable*, it is notable that it was the martyrology's interpretation that prevailed in the 1564 and 1570 editions.

The massacres in Provence

The massacre of hundreds of Vaudois in the villages of Mérindol and Cabrières, the topic of the *Histoire memorable*, in 1545 was the first and most important appearance of the Vaudois in the *Livre des Martyrs*. The Edict, or *Arrest*, of Mérindol was passed by the Parlement of Aix in 1540, condemning the village of Mérindol (which was, as we have seen, an important location for the Vaudois of the region) to be destroyed.[48] After much delay, this was enforced in 1545, leading to the destruction not only of Mérindol, but of the neighbouring settlement of Cabrières, in the papal enclave of the Comtat Venaissin. It was estimated that 2,700 people were killed, and many more were sentenced to the galleys; many of the survivors emigrated to Geneva.

Crespin included a short description of these events at the end of the first edition of the martyrology in 1554, which appears to have been added late in the production process. The publication of the much-longer *Histoire memorable* the next year allowed Crespin more opportunity to discuss historical topics than the martyrology did at that stage of its development. The migration of material from the *Histoire memorable* to the *Livre des Martyrs* in 1564 marked a major step in the evolution of Crespin's approach to the writing of history, as the martyrology absorbed some of the information and function of the historical work. The tensions between his desire to include the Provençal Vaudois in the *Livre des Martyrs* and his difficulty in doing so are evident from the beginning, and this prompted major changes in the material from edition to edition.

Crespin's narratives of the massacres began with introductory passages; evidently it was not certain that the reader could be expected to have a firm knowledge of the Vaudois. In these introductions, Crespin tried to make clear his conception of who the Vaudois were, and how they fitted into the pattern of his wider work. It was in the introductions that he had to make the case for his subjects' inclusion alongside more traditional martyrs, and so he begins by trying to establish their Reformed (or at least anti-Catholic) credentials. The section in 1554 was introduced by a paragraph where Crespin defends his inclusion of the Vaudois, and explains their placement so late in the volume. Because:

It is not a question of two or of three who have endured death, but of a people and of an infinity of persons, as much men as women and children, who have endured all cruelties and all manner of death for

74 *The Vaudois in history and martyrology*

this same doctrine: we have here reserved for the end of this first volume, to touch, as in passing, what is at present the most necessary for the instruction of the faithful ...[49]

Crespin thus prepares his readers to expect the forthcoming *Histoire memorable*, explaining the unusual nature of the inclusion of the Vaudois massacre; in this case, the story simply needed to be told. The account would work to justify the inclusion of the Vaudois in other ways, as well, by portraying them as worthy martyrs, as well as notable victims.

The first two pages are dedicated to introducing the Vaudois to an audience not already familiar with them, claiming that: 'most people of the country of Provence had given always to [the Vaudois] this praise and testimony: that they were men of great work, and that around 200 years ago, they had left Piedmont to live in Provence', and subsequently, despite many setbacks, made their new home 'abundant in wheat, wines, oils, honey, almonds and great livestock, in which the entire country was greatly eased'.[50]

Crespin describes the Vaudois being dispersed, 'forced to live amongst wild beasts' due to the scorn that the world held for them.[51] In France, Crespin tells us, they were called the Poor of Lyons, in Poland and Livonia the same group were called Lollards; in Flanders and Artois, Turrelupins; in the Dauphiné, 'with extreme contempt, "Chaignars"'.[52] In the compendium editions, this section is annotated in the margin: 'The tower of Lollards in London.'[53] The *Livre des Martyrs* here is emphasising the geographic spread of the Vaudois (as we have seen above, they were indeed widely dispersed), and also bringing several pre-Reformation dissident groups under the umbrella of the Vaudois. Having given space to the Hussites, and later the Lollards in the martyrology, Crespin gave structure to the world of pre-Lutheran opposition to the Catholic Church.

He next associates the Vaudois (and all of their other guises, therefore) with the Reformation: 'The most vulgar name of Vaudois remained theirs, until the name of Lutheran came forward, which surpassed in horror all other injuries and shame.'[54] This association of the Vaudois with a wide, apparently 'proto-Reformation' movement was used by a succession of Protestant historians hoping to give their faith deeper historical roots.[55]

Distinguished by such integrity that 'their life preached, and their conversation was admirable', the Vaudois demonstrated that faith in God was strong among them.[56] Crespin did not wish to claim they were perfect, however. Having established the basic worthiness of the Vaudois, the *Livre des Martyrs* moved to denigrate their inherited creed: 'what little of the true light they had they strove to increase day by day'.[57] Although Crespin is careful not to claim that the doctrines of earlier Vaudois were correct, his general praise of their rustic virtues, and pre-Lutheran opposition to the Catholic Church echoes the view of the Vaudois put forward in 1535 by Farel and Viret, in a letter to German Protestants.[58]

The Vaudois in history and martyrology 75

Crespin then gives his own description of the relationship between the Vaudois and the Reformation, relating that at a 1530 synod in Mérindol, the Vaudois heard that the Word was being preached in Germany and Switzerland, they sent two envoys (Morel and Masson) to ask questions of Oecolampadius, Capito, Bucer, and Haller. The two men returned enlightened, saying: 'that in many ways and fashions they erred greatly, & that their old ministers (which they called Barbes, or Uncles), had surveyed the correct path'.[59] Thus, the Vaudois took the decision to join the Reformed Church, according to Crespin (he does not mention that this decision was taken at the 1532 synod in Chanforan, as traditional historiography has held).

This section, which remained only slightly altered in the martyrology until 1570, served the purpose of introducing the reader not only to the Vaudois of Provence, in this section, but the Vaudois in total – none of the other Vaudois entries, including those for Piedmont, would discuss the history or the doctrines of the group in any sort of detail. A different version of these events was, however, published in Crespin's non-martyrological *Histoire memorable*.

It seems likely that Crespin already had the raw material that would make up the much longer *Histoire memorable* at the time he compiled the second edition of his martyrology, as the two books were published within months of one another.[60] The 1555 edition of the martyrology, however, presented an identical text to that of 1554, changing only the headline and sub-headline. In 1554 these read: 'Touching the martyrs of Jesus Christ executed in large numbers on the day of the destruction of Mérindol and Cabrières, and other parts of the country of Provence.'[61] In 1555, this was changed to 'those of Mérindol & Cabrières, called the Vaudois', with the smaller italic text below reading: 'a very memorable history, occurring the year 1545'.[62] This phrasing abandons the characterisation of the Vaudois as 'martyrs' (and indeed, 'of Jesus Christ') as they appeared in the first volume. Crespin uses the word 'executed', which evokes judicial killing, and complements the case for Vaudois martyrdom.

The introduction to 1555's *Histoire memorable* has similar priorities to that of the martyrology's treatment, but uses very different material. This version was quickly abandoned, and the subsequent editions of the history and the martyrology used the first formula. Crespin again begins his discussion of the Vaudois with an account of their origins. It does not, however, touch on the Vaudois links to other heterodox groups like the Lollards. Instead, the narrative starts with the poor condition of the Church, which since the days of the primitive Church had slipped into pagan idolatry and such disgraceful 'foolishness' as applauding a particularly good sermon.[63] Having rehearsed the decline of the church to this time, Crespin continues by highlighting Vualdo's story:

> God raised up a character, which was touched by another spirit than these Caphards, that showed the ingratitude and rebellion of men,

76   *The Vaudois in history and martyrology*

against the divine visitation & the wages of those who were working to advance the truth, to the salvation & benefit of the Church. This person was named Vualdo, a very rich merchant of Lyon.[64]

Vualdo had scripture and then the church doctors translated, and began to remake the form of the religion. His followers built a good reputation, which in turn led to more people joining the sect. Crespin writes in broad strokes here, emphasising only doctrinal points that are clearly in line with Genevan teaching, and excluding those which retained elements of the Catholic cult, or the common practice of what Calvin would call Nicodemism.[65]

The new movement attracted the attention of the papacy, which was actively hostile, and was forced to go underground, which led to the instituting of the *barbes*:

> some children of good spirit, who would afterwards serve them as Ministers: which above all things they learned by heard the Gospel according to St Matthew, and the first Letter of Paul to Timothy. The Gospel, to instruct the people, and the Letter to know how they must behave in their duty.[66]

In comparison to the slighting references in the martyrology, this account stresses their attempts to retain their separate practices and biblical knowledge. A history of persecution and violence against the Vaudois is mentioned. They met in secret:

> as the Christians in the primitive Church had done, which also met in secret. They have been considered vulgar, incestuous, sorcerers, enchanters, and of all dedicated to devils.... See how the servants of Christ are defamed. See how the world informs itself of the truth, calling the light darkness, and the darkness light.[67]

In this comparison to the slanders against the early Church, Crespin provides an early example of a Protestant defence against many such accusations.[68] Crespin then defends their behaviour through reference to outside authorities who might be considered hostile, and thus credible: 'amongst others one may well receive the testimony of Master Claude de Seisel, Archbishop of Turin, a man of great knowledge, for his time, who wrote a tract against their beliefs in 1520, but admitted their good conduct'.[69] This information bolsters our sense of the Vaudois as an independent community, identifiable to outsiders, as Audisio's work has suggested.

The 1556 edition of the *Histoire memorable* was somewhat cut down from the previous edition: Gilmont estimates it as being 36,000 words in total, as opposed to the 40,000 of the 1555 edition.[70] This is despite the book actually having more pages (152 to 135) than the previous edition – the 1556 *Histoire memorable* appears to have been printed on paper slightly narrower than would be normal for the octavo format.[71] The most significant changes were made to the introduction, and in the Confession of Faith; in both cases there were more cuts than additions.

Much of the introduction, complaining of the state of the Church before Vualdo, was cut, and in another place inserts the section from the martyrology about the Lollards, 'Turrelupins', and 'Saramatiques'. This restored the link between the Vaudois and wider opposition to the established Church, although it did not go so far as to repeat the negative comment about the Lutherans.[72] Crespin also abandoned the claim that the massacres were committed against the wishes of the King, which had appeared in the earlier edition.

In 1554 and 1555, Crespin had presented two separate views of the history of the Vaudois. The first one, which discussed their spread, and their persecution, was ultimately chosen over the later version, which gave a more detailed account of the man and his history.[73]

With the creation of the compendium edition in 1564, Crespin was also able to incorporate the information from the writing of the *Histoire memorable* into the text of his main martyrology, although he did not do so verbatim. This section runs to thirty-two pages in folio, as opposed to the ten octavo pages in the 1554 and 1555 editions of the *Livre des Martyrs*, and the 135 pages of octavo in 1555's *Histoire memorable*. The title of this section in 1564 is: 'The persecution and sacking of Mérindol & Cabrières, and those faithful people of Provence', with a sub-headline that begins: 'This history is as memorable as anything which has happened for a long time'.[74] The sub-headline continues by repeating the opening sentence of 1554's introduction, to the effect that: 'it is not a question of two or three' – though here Crespin inserts the word 'Martyrs' – 'who have endured death'.[75] There is another difference in this sentence, besides the re-introduction of the word 'Martyr' into the equation. The phrase '... for this same doctrine' which appeared in the 1555 edition, has been cut, and the sub-headline ends with the claim that

> there is need for demonstration by judicial acts, for they serve for the instruction not only in particular to all of the faithful: but also in general to the peoples and republics who have received the Gospel of our Lord,

which does echo the similar claims for the importance of this work as teaching aid seen in the first paragraph of the two previous editions.[76] With the advent of the *Récit d'Histoire* format, Crespin could have published this account of the Vaudois with a stronger disclaimer than before, as he was to do with three martyrs of the Peasants' War, and include them without any implied approval. Instead, he went the other way, emphasising the right of the Vaudois to be included on their own merit by terming them 'martyrs'.

78 *The Vaudois in history and martyrology*

The body of the 1564 introduction summarises the earlier edition. With 1554's first paragraph having been subsumed into the sub-headline, 1564 starts: 'the world has held the Vaudois (a people of a religion somewhat more clear and pure than the common) in such horror, that all absurdity of infamy is placed upon them'.[77] The section about being dispersed among wild beasts, and bearing a variety of names from Lollard to Lutheran, survives, as does Crespin's claim that 'their life preaches', and demonstrates their love of God. Surviving also is the remark about 'what little of the true light they had', and the Vaudois translation of scripture.[78] Indeed, the only substantive update Crespin has made to this portion of his introduction is to make reference to the martyrdom of Martin Gonin on his mission to connect the Vaudois and the Reformed communities, which will be discussed below.

In terms of introducing the Vaudois people to the reader, Crespin seems to have found little need to improve upon his efforts of 1554, despite his work on the much larger introduction to the (better-sourced) *Histoire memorable*. The interpretations and narrative of his first treatment of the Vaudois in the *Livre des Martyrs* held until his last edition, in spite of the work that was done on the separate volume. Crespin did not let all the hard work that had gone into the *Histoire memorable* go to waste, however: its copies of documents would be used extensively in the later editions of the *Livre des Martyrs*. The portion of the 1554 and 1555 *Livre des Martyrs* devoted to the actual massacre at Mérindol and Cabrières had previously been rather slim, and could now be expanded.

Narrative

It was in the narrative sections of the martyrology, describing the massacres and their context, that saw the most significant changes. Crespin collected a mass of documents for the *Histoire memorable*, most of which were later used to expand the martyrology. In the 1554 and 1555 editions of the *Livre des Martyrs*, the Vaudois experience immediately after their contact with Oecolampadius and other reformers is one of persecution. As would happen in parts of Italy, Vaudois contact with Reformed missions seems to have brought them to the attention of the local authorities: 'the thing was done in such a way that the commotion came to the notice of the Parlement'.[79] From 1530, in order to: 'inform and bodily seize all those who were suspected of being of the Vaudois and Lutheran sect', Jean de Roma, a 'cruel brigand, of the Jacopin [Dominican] faction' was appointed as the inquisitor in Provence.[80]

From 1532, de Roma persecuted the Vaudois, capturing at least one of their *barbes*.[81] His cruelty, which includes torture, was so severe that the Vaudois petitioned the King, who in turn ordered the man imprisoned for his abuses.[82] Crespin relates that after he had returned to Avignon, de Roma soon died of 'a malady so horrible and so strange' that it caused his flesh to become 'all ulcerated and full of vermin', the condition becoming

The Vaudois in history and martyrology 79

bad enough that he tried to kill himself, lacking only the strength.[83] On the same page, Crespin outlines the illness and death of another persecutor, by the name of Meirani, again by a terrible illness.[84] These two incidents, so close together, suggest the intervention of divine providence, although this is not actually stated.

This short account of the events between the first meetings, of the Reformed and Vaudois in the 1520s and 1530s, and the military persecution of 1540 appeared again, unchanged, in the 1555 edition. In the later editions, the narrative moves directly from the introduction to the discussion and text of the *Arrest de Mérindol*.[85] The events of the 1530s were largely excluded; this meant passing over the gradual merger of the two groups, and milestones like the Vaudois subscription to publish the Olivetan Bible, a book whose publication caused a stir in Geneva and had some claim to be the first mass-produced French vernacular Bible. It also means that the Synod of Chanforan, so controversial in Vaudois historiography, is omitted, and with it, detailed discussion of the Vaudois union with the Reformed Church.[86]

Just as Crespin's accounts frequently say little about the actual martyrdoms of their subjects, compared to the focus given to their beliefs, the massacres themselves occupy a relatively small proportion of the text – four of the ten pages in 1554 and 1555, and just over two of the more than thirty pages in 1564 and 1570. Crespin had little in the way of eyewitness accounts from Mérindol and Cabrières, and had to rely on official documents for the bulk of his narrative.

Crespin describes how, with the men of Mérindol hiding in the woods to avoid arrest, 'All the goods that these poor people had saved were put to pillage, the women and girls stripped, some violated, beaten and outraged, the others sold and exposed to all disgrace.'[87] Also included was an incident which would later have a strong impact on the later repercussions of the massacre – the capture and killing, by firing squad, of a young apprentice, who died piously, and indeed was: 'martyrised'.[88] This death, seen as particularly notable, and cruel, among many others, seems to have had an especial impact: in the aftermath of the massacres, each of the three Commissioners involved in the expedition tried to excuse it; both they and Crespin seem to have seen its potential to discredit the Parlement.[89]

Cabrières, which was fortified, put up more of a struggle, but here, too, atrocities were committed:

> around 40 women, among whom there were several pregnant, & they shut them in a barn, and then set fire to the four corners. And when any escaped to flee the fire, they were pushed into the fire with great blows of pikes and halberds.[90]

Although brief compared to the rest of the account, this description is unusually graphic for the martyrology.

80 The Vaudois in history and martyrology

Crespin presented many martyrdoms without this level of gory detail. In this case, it probably helped to make the case for the exceptionality of the events promised in the first lines of the notice, that this was something worthy of recording.

In the *Histoire memorable*, the large tranche of new documents to be absorbed meant that the massacre was described even later in the volume: d'Oppède's troops do not move on Mérindol until page 94 of the 135-page book. The description of the sacking of Mérindol is this time, even shorter, receiving only one page's attention, and losing most of what detail the martyrology had possessed: 'they entered into houses, & put all to death, without sparing the sick, nor the elderly, nor the little children'.[91] Again, we hear of the young man executed in the orchard, but this time he is not referred to as a 'martyr'; clearly even outside the *Livre des Martyrs*, the ban on that term held.[92] The assault on Cabrières is similarly brief, and though new layers are added to the depiction of d'Oppède's treachery, the account is almost exactly the same as before. In this case, the recounting of the massacres themselves only takes five pages, of the book's 135 in total.

From 1564 onwards, the narration is refined: the young man executed by firing squad is placed first, and named as Maurizi Blanc, but the massacre at Mérindol itself is described simply: 'Mérindol, taken, was pillaged, burned, sacked & razed by the pioneers.'[93] The reader is no longer told of the men fleeing to the woods, or the extreme violence against the women. When d'Oppède moves against Cabrières, the emphasis is on the trickery he employs to convince the Vaudois to surrender, before slaughtering many of them. This section has in fact been added to Crespin editorialising ironically on d'Oppède's 'wild courage': 'a man of ill will he had neither truth nor honesty; thus this captain showed by treason his fury'.[94] The twenty-five or thirty men described in 1554 as being 'dismembered' are here: 'killed and hacked in pieces', while the burning alive of the women, and the massacre at the church (an *église* this time, instead of the previous *temple*) are both retained with few changes.[95]

The edict

If Crespin's discussions of the massacres in Provence were unusual in the attention which they paid to the carrying out of the sentence passed against the Vaudois by the court, they did not neglect the sentence itself, either. As with the martyrdom of a single person, the sentence, in this case the Edict of Mérindol passed by the Parlement in Aix, provided evidence that the deaths were committed by the authorities, for religious reasons. In the years before Crespin's inclusion of other massacres, the documentation around Mérindol and Cabrières helped to demonstrate the reasons why those in Provence deserved to be included.

The Vaudois in history and martyrology 81

In the first editions of the martyrology, the contents of the 'arrêt', the Edict of Mérindol, delivered against the Vaudois in 1540 are discussed briskly:

> by which all the inhabitants of the said Mérindol were sentenced to be burned, as much men as women & children: the houses battered and burned, all the trees cut down, olives as well as others, to 500 paces around.[96]

It would seem from this summary that Crespin was working from a report of some sort, rather than from an original copy of the text. Certainly he did not attempt to reproduce the text at this time, and some of the details vary from those in the version he was to publish later. The most egregious and destructive elements of the edict are stressed, while clauses explaining the charges and the judgement are omitted. It is only with the *Histoire memorable* that we see a proper reproduction of the Edict of Mérindol, which would be reproduced in later editions of the martyrology.

The *arrêt* and other primary documents were transferred to the later editions of the *Livre des martyrs* from the *Histoire memorable*, in a way that the introduction, for example, was not. In the 1564 edition, this takes slightly more than a sheet of folio paper. From the beginning it is clear that this is an arrest warrant, listing more than twenty people on the charge of 'lèse majesté divine and human', many of them the spouses and children of the named accused.[97] They had recently, by force of arms, helped a condemned man to escape his death by burning. This was the rescue of a man named Colin Pellenc, otherwise unnamed by Crespin, a reformer of the Mérindol churches who was in contact with Calvin during this period.[98] For good measure, the Vaudois also burned a mill belonging to Pellenc's principal accuser.[99] In the same year a group of up to 500 men from Mérindol and Cabrières raided and pillaged the monastery of St-Hilaire de Menerbes and a church at Lioux.[100] This was open and violent resistance to authority, and hardly a philosophical acceptance of martyrdom. It certainly changed the perception of the Vaudois; Calvin expressed 'consternation' to Farel on hearing that they were to be charged not with heresy, but with sedition and tumult.[101] While Crespin may not have mentioned this action in his own narrative of the events, he retained the accusation as part of the edict; a rebuttal was offered in the confession of faith which appeared in the 1564 edition of the martyrology. In addition to the destruction of the town and its orchards for being 'Retreat, cave, refuge and strength of the people holding such damned and reprobate sect', the surrounding area as well was to be made inhospitable for fugitives.[102]

The *arrêt* goes on to condemn the villagers for: 'Holding Vaudois and Lutheran sects, reproved & contrary to the holy faith and Christian religion.'[103] Indeed, the entire place is a: 'School of errors and false doctrines of these sects, people who dogmatise these said errors and false doctrines,

82 *The Vaudois in history and martyrology*

and booksellers who have printed and sold books full of such false doctrines.'[104] The confiscation of goods, and the destruction of the houses and trees (to 200 paces, as opposed to the 500 Crespin claimed in 1554) are all present, added at the end of the edict.[105] There is no mention of Cabrières, which was, of course, in the papally controlled Comtat Venaissin, and thus outside the jurisdiction of the French authorities.

We should also consider representations of the edict within the context of the criteria to be considered a martyr. The importance of the cause, rather than the suffering, for martyr status made this edict central to consideration of the Vaudois as martyrs. Although not specifically ordering the massacre, the edict is a legal document, full of harsh language, which condemns the town to destruction for reasons of heresy. The role of the Parlement's leaders in the enforcement of the arret can only have reinforced the perception that the massacre was a piece of policy. The edict, although controversial, was used by Crespin as though it were a mass death-sentence for heresy. It is a state document that commands collective punishments for religious reasons, and as for Crespin and his readers, would provide some confirmation that the massacres were martyrdoms by the letter of the law.

Beginning with the *Histoire memorable*, Crespin included much of the political activity that succeeded in delaying the enforcement of the Edict for five years. In 1554, a few lines had been devoted to the efforts of the Sieur de Langers (Langey), who was Lieutenant at Turin, to obtain letters patent from the King and thereby delay execution of the edict.[106] This was in fact Guillaume du Bellay, the humanist courtier and diplomat, and brother of the Bishop of Paris, though Crespin never names this powerful ally of the Vaudois. These delays held until Jean Meynier, Sieur d'Oppède, took over as President of the Parlement, and was able to cause the edict to be enforced. In the later versions, the stalling tactics are provided in more detail. Six pages of 1564's edition are devoted to these wranglings, starting with the protests of landowners whose lands the Vaudois had made more valuable, rebutted in turn by local bishops. Much of it is presented as a debate at a banquet, with various landowners (such as the Sieur d'Alene, 'a man who feared God'), expressing their misgivings at the prospect.[107] The first concern seems simply to be that the edict is disproportionate, and it: 'would be an unreasonable thing, and that the Turks, and the most cruel men in the world would judge it to be too inhumane and detestable'.[108] The main defence of the Vaudois' doctrines on religious grounds comes from a nobleman who argues that: 'you call Lutherans, those who preach the doctrine of the Bible'.[109] Many are unconvinced by the defences, asking: 'Do you call the blood of the damned of Mérindol, innocent blood? ... do you call the execution of Lutherans, the effusion of innocent blood?', but the argument primarily centres around the cruelty of the edict.[110] In later discussion, President Chassane notes that: 'the said arrest was given more to hold the Lutherans in fear, who are in great numbers in Provence, than

The Vaudois in history and martyrology   83

to perform the action contained in it'.[111] Crespin follows this scene by showing the ecclesiastical hierarchy, including the Archbishop of Arles, the Bishop of Aix, his Prevost and canons, and several Abbots and Priors gathering together to plot the enforcing of the edict of Mérindol. This scene is another that was absent from the first two editions of the *Livre des Martyrs*, and was first published as part of the *Histoire memorable* in 1555. As depicted by Crespin, they are most concerned with the potential loss of their benefices posed by the growth of heresy, and to: 'tear and destroy, to lose and subvert all that is raised against the church', though they also make time for carousing with the young ladies of Avignon.[112] In the *Histoire memorable* and the two compendium editions of the *Livre des Martyrs*, Crespin inserts here the martyrdom of a bookseller, executed in Avignon while this ecclesiastical plotting is taking place.[113]

This material, focussing on the political lead-up to the execution of the judgement against the Vaudois, took up more space than the description of the massacres themselves in most editions of the *Livre des Martyrs*. It appears to have been more concerned with defining the Catholic authorities than with describing the Vaudois and their beliefs, although the setting of the Parlement in Aix provided Crespin with an opportunity to do that in his later editions.

The confessions of faith (1541)

Crespin included a number of documents from this period of official indecision, ranging from reports by a royal commissioner, to royal letters delaying the implementation of the edict, and supplications by the villagers themselves.[114] The bulk of the documents that he included in the martyrology were generated during this period of petitions and counter-claims during the early 1540s. None of them were collected in the first two editions of the *Livre des Martyrs*; instead, almost all of them first appeared in 1555, in the *Histoire memorable*. Crespin quotes official reports, for example, that the Vaudois: 'are peaceable folk, loved by all their neighbours, & men of good morals, keep well their promises, in paying their debts ... they say their prayers without images ... and also do not adore the relics of Saints'.[115] Other passages outline legal processes, and political struggles between factions at the Parlement in Aix.

Probably the most important of these documents is what is claimed to be a Vaudois confession of faith of 1541. In the first two editions of the *Livre des Martyrs*, Crespin is only able to say that the Vaudois: 'presented their Confession of Faith: such that by impediments that God raised to give relief to his family, the said execution was deferred'.[116] In the *Histoire memorable*, Crespin included the text of this confession, apparently in full, which filled twenty-five quarto pages of that volume. 1556's *Histoire memorable* included a much-reduced version of the same document, a change which accounted for some of that edition's shorter length. In 1564 and

84 *The Vaudois in history and martyrology*

1570, he included an entirely different version of the 1541 confession which took up merely one folio page in the 1564 edition (perhaps only 10 per cent of the length of the first version he had printed).[117]

The differences between the confessions, one of which belonged to Crespin's historical writing, and was not reprinted after 1556, and the other to his increasingly popular martyrology, might suggest a change of mind between the printings or a difference of purpose between the two works and the two genres, as well as the possibility that the new, shorter confession seen after 1564 had become available in the intervening period. While Jean-François Gilmont has identified the successive versions of the confession, their content has not been fully explored.[118]

The confession that was included in both editions of the *Histoire memorable* is introduced as being that presented to Cardinal Sadoleto, the moderate author of the Letter to the Genevans. The *Histoire memorable* narrates that the Vaudois brought the confession to the Cardinal himself, encouraging him to examine it and to correct any errors.[119] Sadoleto does indeed seem to have received a document of this nature from the Vaudois, and promised to take it to Rome.[120] The reaction that the Vaudois expected from Sadoleto is one that mirrored an earlier event in their history, when Vladislaus the second of Bohemia and Hungary was said to have read an earlier such confession, and to have challenged his courtiers to find fault with it.[121] Later in the narrative, a reply from Sadoleto was printed, suggesting that the Vaudois had been falsely accused in some matters, and later he is said to have 'communicated their articles and Confession to the Cardinals'.[122]

The confession itself is phrased as a long series of articles, each beginning with the formula 'We believe and confess ...'. In many formal respects, this 'Sadoleto' Confession runs parallel to 1536's First Helvetic Confession: both begin with articles concerning the divine inspiration of Holy Scripture, and the Holy Spirit's role in prophecy, before addressing the nature of God and His relationship to Man.[123] This is done in a series of articles that derive from the Ten Commandments, the Nicene Creed, and the Apostles' Creed, expressing basic tenets such as belief in Christ who was conceived of the Holy Spirit, and 'suffered under Pontius Pilate, was crucified, died, and buried for our sins' and a belief in the 'Holy Catholic Church'.[124] Euan Cameron has argued that this very traditional format was part of an established campaign of placation by the Vaudois:

> For the protestant churches a confession was normally used to define a faith in distinction, either from Catholicism, or from another protestant creed. The Waldenses used a confession to show, for the benefit of persecutors or possible allies, that they were respectable and credible Christians, not disreputable heretics with scandalous ideas. Their confessions were eirenicons rather than rallying points.[125]

The Vaudois in history and martyrology   85

This desire to placate the Catholic authorities is rather different from the openly defiant confessions which are more usual amongst Crespin's martyrs, and which would be more familiar to his readers. It appears to reflect the instincts of a group trying to survive, rather than overthrow, their opposition, and may share its origins with the sort of Nicodemite tendencies that Oecolampadius noted.[126]

This, then, was not a conventionally Catholic or Reformed confession. Exclusionary attitudes are displayed which raise the question of the Vaudois relationship with the Catholic Church – they contrast a large church 'called the congregation of the good and the wicked' with: 'the Church which we believe in, which is called holy'.[127] Their church has no space for tyrants, Judas, Cain, or the *mauvais riche* and is compared to a: 'beautiful confraternity, in which are registered all the true Christians'.[128] This 'visible church', containing only the saved (like the Vaudois), by necessity excludes the majority of society, and is destined to remain a sect. This runs directly contrary to Calvin's teaching that the earthly Church must include many who are unworthy to be there, for it is often impossible to sort the wheat from the chaff. By this thinking, only God knows who is truly saved, and truly part of the 'invisible church'.[129] This confession would seem to strengthen Audisio's view of the Vaudois as a sect, conscious of their differences with the institutional Catholic Church. Nor does it contradict the view of the Vaudois as reliant on the Catholic Church while holding themselves in some way above it; this phrasing may condemn the quality of some of the members of the Catholic Church (as the Vaudois had always done), but it does not 'un-church' them.

The confession does contain several crucially Protestant doctrines. Any past Vaudois uncertainties about saints had now been resolved, and in this document they proclaim that only the Son intervenes with the Father.[130] That the Vaudois put faith in only two sacraments, which Crespin had mentioned earlier, is here confirmed, and their sacramental theology appears robustly Calvinist, with mention of spiritual eating: 'one who eats the flesh and drinks the blood of the Lord, & in fact participates, contemplates the coming together of the invisible things and the spiritual food'.[131] Criticism of those who believe that Christ can be brought down to earth by the serving of the Eucharist as against the word of God rejected not just the Catholic Church, but the Lutheran teachings on the subject as well.[132] This was a common formulation in Crespin, and seems to have been a commonplace in the Calvinist confessions included in Crespin.

The second half of the confession is devoted to a long explanation of each of the Ten Commandments, enumerated in the Reformed fashion. Cameron's argument for eirenic confessions says that the Ten Commandments were often used by the Vaudois, as another uncontroversial element.[133] Certainly the Provençal Vaudois had used them in previous documents. In 1533, the Vaudois of Cabrières had sent to the inquisitor de Roma a statement of faith which had insisted 'we believe all of the

86   *The Vaudois in history and martyrology*

commandments of God'.[134] While their inclusion may be a Vaudois tradition, these articles appear to be largely Reformed in content. The discussion of the Second Commandment (in the Reformed estimate), forbidding false idols, sees a strong attack on images:

> Oh, what dishonour is done to the majesty of God, in the greater part of Christendom, by infinite idolatries, & superstitions, & carnal services. What scandal could be greater? In what greater mockery could Christianity be exposed? ... Is this the means to convert and bring to the true religion the Jews and the Turks?[135]

The Third Commandment's discussion of blasphemy indicates the degree of Reformed influence upon the confession's authors; the issue of whether it was lawful for a Christian to swear oaths had been an item of debate during the very first contact between Vaudois leaders and Reformers, suggesting that the swearing of oaths was not a settled practice amongst the Vaudois.[136] The confession agrees that swearing on God's name in support of legal cases is permissible, and indeed that it is forbidden to swear using other formulae.[137]

Other commandments similarly reflect Reformed perspectives. The Fifth Commandment, for example, suggests that honouring one's father and mother ought to include, more widely, respect for the magistrates and princes of this world, as well.[138] The Seventh Commandment, after decrying the sin of adultery, attacks the:

> false judgements of the judges, who condemn the priests to death for being married, and permit the public lewdness of the priests, and commit innumerable ordures and defilements. God condemns the bawds, and they absolve them; God approves priests to marry, and they condemn them to death.[139]

This reflects, of course, Protestant sensibilities; the Vaudois had required their *barbes* to swear an oath of chastity.[140]

Once the credal elements and the exposition of the Ten Commandments had been expounded, the confession dealt with a few other matters. One article stressed justification by faith alone, attaching no importance to 'les oeuvres de la loy'.[141] Sobriety and temperance are praised, while the Old Testament dietary laws are rejected, for Christians are delivered from servitude to the Law by Jesus Christ.[142]

This confession adheres to the customary interest in the Creeds and Commandments that Cameron leads us to expect, but surely this document is anything but eirenic. It is robustly Reformed on most issues, and on some points goes out of its way to attack Catholic doctrine, as in the discussion of the Second Commandment.

The next year, with the 1556 edition of the *Histoire memorable*, Crespin oversaw some alterations to this text, reducing its length by about

The confession in 1564's *Livre des Martyrs*, which is placed within the narrative in a similar manner to that in the *Histoire memorable*, is much shorter than that in either version of the *Histoire memorable*. Attached to a remonstrance, the confession itself stretches to only one folio page in 1564, compared to twenty-five octavo pages in the first *Histoire memorable* (the difference being approximately 700 as compared to 7,000 words).[144] This confession is in fact a completely separate document.

While the longer version in the *Histoire memorable* was said to have been presented to Cardinal Sadoleto, this claims to be a version submitted to the Parlement in Aix, and to François I in 1541 through his reader and librarian Castellanus (Pierre du Chastel).[145] The fact that this new confession entered the *Livre des Martyrs* alongside two other important documents from the Parlement (the letter from Henri II, and the full text of the edict of Mérindol), suggests that Crespin may have gained access to important official documents, although these may well have been publically available.[146]

In an open acknowledgement of the changes that he had made, Crespin told the reader that: 'the other, fuller, confession of these articles, which was taken to the Cardinal Sadolet ... we have inserted into the history printed separately, in 1556'.[147]

The compendium editions attach to the confession a remonstrance, sent in April 1541 by the Vaudois which complains about their treatment at the hands of the Inquisition (specifically de Roma), denies any seditious motivations, and rejects accusations of disobedience to the law by arguing that were they only treated as well as Turks in Venice, or Jews in Avignon, they would certainly obey the commands of the law.[148] To the specific charge of retiring behind fortified walls, they insist they have but rarely fled to caves and woods to escape: 'the anger of men ... the furor of the people, who were so inflamed against us', and they flatly deny having engaged the assistance of mercenary gendarmes.[149] Above all, they insist that: 'all the indignities and persecutions which have been made against us, have come for the cause of religion'.[150] As a result, they want to make public an account of what they believe (this formulation allows them to fit into the Augustinian formulation of martyrdom, though the term is not mentioned). The confession ends with several appeals to the 'King our lord',

88 *The Vaudois in history and martyrology*

enjoining him to 'human pity and Christian charity', and hoping for letters of pardon and remission, which did play a role in forestalling the execution another four years. They conclude by hoping that:

> the father of Mercy, that he ensure that the truth was known, and that he change the heart of his enemies, and we wish all to unite in one faith, in one law, and in one Baptism: and to recognize and confess one God, and one saviour, Jesus Christ.[151]

These claims of loyalty and injustice are not followed, however, by a confession which could be described as eirenic, or placatory. The longer confession's opinions on the sacraments and on the place of the magistrate are still present, but the lengthy citation of the Creeds has been removed. The Ten Commandments, removed in 1556's *Histoire memorable*, are no longer even referred to. What remains is a briefer confession, much closer in content, and in form to other, Reformed confessions. Cut, too, are most of the insistences on orthodoxy phrased in terms of the Creeds.[152]

Crespin also altered a note about the antiquity of Vaudois doctrine, claiming ancient foundations for the group, claiming: 'the doctrine which they have professed, as from father to son, truly the same since the year twelve hundred years after the birth of our Lord Jesus Christ ...', which in 1555's *Histoire memorable*, had been: 'since the year two hundred years after the birth of our Lord Jesus Christ'.[153]

It is not clear that the earlier phrasing had been a simple error, for Vaudois claims to effectively predate the Catholic Church were not unknown. A founding date of c.AD 200 would place the Vaudois tradition in direct contact with the ancient Church, before the corruption of Constantine took hold, and would have avoided the question of a Vaudois break with Rome at some point in the middle ages. Instead, a parallel true church would have existed since the earliest time, made up of Foxe's 'secret multitude of true professors'.[154] Whether it had been a mistake or not, this early date also manifested itself in the *Histoire Ecclésiastique*, which, otherwise following the content of the compendium edition, reads: 'The doctrine they professed, as from father to son, truly since the year 120 after the birth of our Lord Jesus Christ ...'[155]

The doctrinal content of the confession was presented in a series of short declarative points. As in the *Histoire memorable*, it insists that: 'in the sentence & opinion of the Christian Church and religion we agree totally'.[156] Their only rule is the Scripture contained in the Old and New Testaments, and they insist that they do not subscribe to any heresies condemned by the ancient Church.[157] Their third point moves onto more combative ground: they claim that it is only by the grace and bounty of God that the elect can be saved from Original Sin – a distinctly Protestant conception of salvation – good works are sanctification afterwards. As before, dietary laws are specifically rejected, suggesting that this point was of

The confession asserts that Christ alone is mediator between man and God, rejecting the power of saints and priests, and specifically the 'adoration of images, pilgrimages & such similar things' as part of a rejection of the traditional cult practices of the Catholic Church.[159] Baptism and the Eucharist are the only two sacraments of which they approve.[160] As regards the power of the State, the Vaudois claim that they believe Magistrates to be ordained by God, and 'would be obedient to their laws & constitutions which concern goods and people, promising obedience in all things that are not contrary to God'.[161] This continues the string of insistence on paying to Caesar what is Caesar's present in each of the successive confessions.

Whatever the reason for the diverging confessions, Crespin elected to keep them separate, choosing the shorter, more straightforwardly Calvinist version to be included in his martyrology. The longer, more nuanced and, perhaps, more traditionally Vaudois confession was chosen for the *Histoire memorable*, and was heavily edited the next year. It never appeared again. It may have been that Crespin discovered the shorter confession between 1556 and 1564, and used it to replace the other one, and it may have been that the shorter confession, for some or all of the reasons above, was thought to be more suited for the martyrology. It certainly seems that Crespin drew a distinction between his historical and his martyrological work, and deployed the confessions accordingly. That, in the martyrology, he refers his readers to the longer version in the history (when he does not seem to have been pressed for space), but does not reproduce it, suggests that Crespin did not want to ignore the shorter version entirely, or to expunge it, but instead decided that it was the wrong confession for that particular work. The shorter confession, which is more clearly Calvinist, in form and in content, is the one which Crespin decided to place in the *Livre des Martyrs*. If we accept the argument that the martyrology, by its nature, had very little room for unorthodox opinion, then the division between the *Histoire memorable* and the *Livre des Martyrs* (centred on the confessions of faith, due to the overwhelming overlap in material elsewhere) becomes clear. The history could contain such opinions, but the martyrology had an educational purpose, and had to be careful about what it taught its readership.

Certainly, Calvin was personally impressed by one of the confessions, although we cannot know which version he saw. In the same 1544 letter to Bullinger in which he had praised the Vaudois generally, he wrote that: 'It is now three years bypast since they were so far advanced as to have presented to the Parliament of Aix a confession of faith, pure and simple as we could have set it forth ourselves.'[162] He felt that they had become full

90   *The Vaudois in history and martyrology*

members of the Reformed community: 'In one little town they have thoroughly cleansed the parish church from all its defilements, and there they celebrate the Supper and Baptism in the same manner we do.'[163]

Other documents

The *Histoire memorable* ends with a letter quoted at length, from King Henri II, calling members of the Provençal Parlement to be held to account by the Parlement of Paris, denouncing what he had heard of the massacre as being: 'against all right and reason'.[164] The ensuing trial, of members of the Parlement of Provence by the Parlement of Paris, was an unprecedented attack on a Parlement's privileges, and was also a denunciation of d'Oppede's actions, providing some hope to the survivors that Royal authority might be on their side after all.[165] Crespin tells us that: 'by these letters each one understood, that the King would unravel the deeds of these tyrants, as exploited to the annoyance & great regret of his late father François'.[166] What Crespin did not include, but which his readers might have known in 1555, was that the trial ended in 1553 with d'Oppède's acquittal.[167]

From the 1564 edition of the *Livre des Martyrs* onwards, this royal response is treated differently. A paragraph of only a few lines mentions Henri's 1549 intervention. Crespin himself expresses the hope that the King will do justice for the great cruelty practised, but Henri's letter, which in earlier editions had seemed to promise exactly that, has been moved.[168] At the beginning of Book Three of the 1570 edition of the *Livre des Martyrs*, outside of the section devoted to Mérindol and Cabrières, the King's letter is the first document to be presented after the introduction of his accession.[169] It had been moved from the story of the Vaudois, to which it provided a conclusion, to the wider story of France, where it is used to introduce the new King.

There are practical reasons for this change to have been made, for it places Henri's letter within the chronology of the late 1540s rather than placing it in 1545 along with the rest of the section on Mérindol and Cabrières. As in the *Histoire memorable*, it is reproduced apparently in full.[170] This paragraph is slightly longer, and entirely different in its details to the earlier versions: we finally learn that despite a lengthy trial, President Menier 'escaped in the end the hand of men, but not that of God'.[171]

From the 1555 *Histoire memorable* onwards, Crespin included in his notices of the Provencal massacres a document which purports to be a record of a meeting of Vaudois elders who survived the assault. This section appears immediately after the narration of the massacre itself. The four elders quoted strike a consolatory tone, reassuring each other and making the case for carrying on in the face of terrible opposition, providing a sort of conclusion to the episode. In the course of this, they restate their unwavering belief in the basic creeds of the Christian faith, and the

The Vaudois in history and martyrology 91

importance of fidelity to them: 'the principal and greatest fear that moves us, is that by torments and by infirmity, we do not waver in the confession of our Lord Jesus Christ & his holy Gospel'.[172] The strongest emphasis is on remaining true to their beliefs, even to the extremity of death – for what good is it to gain the world if you should lose your soul? – and to that end they pray repeatedly for divine aid.[173] But the overwhelming idea expressed is that they should be obedient to God's will, no matter how hard, for everything that happens is part of God's plan: 'the Lord does not permit a single hair of our head to fall on the ground without his will'.[174] The mood is one of resignation and determination; one in which comparison to the suffering of the Israelites is made.[175] Indeed, the idea of themselves as a group being tested by God underlies the entire argument for perseverance, as they reassure themselves that: 'the Lord will give good issue to all of this persecution'.[176] One of the few direct biblical references made in this section is to the Book of Judith (a book regarded as uncanonical by the Reformed Church); the lesson drawn, that: 'it is said that all the faithful who have pled to God, are thus passed through many tribulations', is a notably passive selection from a book whose most famous episode was the assassination of Holofernes.[177]

Another coda to the affair was the acquittal of d'Oppède and the other officers of the Parlement, information that though occurring in 1553, first appeared in the 1564 edition, and was retained in 1570. It is in these editions that Crespin moved the letter by Henri II away from the rest of the Vaudois section, with the effect that the history of Mérindol and Cabrières ends with an appeal to divine justice, not a promise of royal justice. That promise, and the failure of the resulting trial to convict d'Oppède, are reserved for a separate *Récit d'Histoire*. Crespin added to the King's letter a paragraph saying that d'Oppède had: 'finally escaped the hand of man, but not that of God', while the advocate Guerin was hanged in Paris.[178] His death of a painful illness, like that of the earlier tormenter Jean de Roma, is outlined as God's final judgement upon him (Crespin notes in the margin, again, that 'Menier escaped man, fell into the hands of God').[179]

Crespin was cautious about assigning blame for the massacres, choosing to emphasise the resistance to persecution that existed in several institutions. Like any of his martyrs, it was important that the Vaudois appear to have been loyal subjects, as any trace of sedition would have justified the action against them. To that end, the emphasis can be seen to be on the good relations between the monarchy and the Vaudois, in contrast to the aggression of the local authorities. The persecutors, who were primarily associated with the Catholic Church (the leaders of the 1545 expedition included Antoine Trivulee, a Papal vice-legate; President d'Oppède was made a Compte Palatin the year after the massacres) were forced to subvert almost every established civil power in order to enforce the edict and march on the towns.[180] The local seigneurs, and indeed some members of the Parlement, stood on custom and their established rights to oppose

92   *The Vaudois in history and martyrology*

passage of the edict, concerned with constitutional limits, with rents, and with property values.[181] While they did not seem to be receptive to Vaudois doctrine, neither did they accept the sweeping claims made by the bishops. The Crown, by contrast, emerges as a potential fount of justice, a power to which appeal may be made, and the references to Vlaudislaus of Hungary show the desire, and perhaps expectation among the Vaudois for such royal benevolence. François did grant letters of pardon, halting the persecution for the time being, and took serious action against the abuses of the Inquisitor de Roma.[182] His actions are presented as being in favour of keeping the peace, and of moderation, even if they were frequently undermined by his own officials (a clerk's greed rendered a royal grant of tolerance useless in the 1540s).[183] This is despite the fact that François Ier approved the actions of the Parlement of Aix in their early stages, and approved them after the fact on 18 August 1545.[184] He does not seem to have immediately regretted the decision, either – it was not until 1547, with a new monarch in Paris, that any reconsideration of the events in Provence was taken, and it was 1551 before these had any concrete results.[185] The unusual, military, actions of the Parlement had caused Crespin many problems of format and content; not the least of them was the question of whether the Vaudois had invited military force against themselves with their own actions in 1540.[186]

The *Livre des Martyrs* presents a rather triumphalist view of the early interactions between the Vaudois and the Reformed Church. Despite being depicted as chronologically the forerunners of the Protestant movement, and their literal link to the past, the Vaudois are placed later in the martyrologies, in accordance with the 1545 date of the massacres. They are also shown as accepting, rather than imparting, theological wisdom. The Vaudois are shown as eager for Reformed leadership, and in real need of it. In the sections on the events of the 1540s, the Vaudois have joined the Reformed congregation, and begun to rectify some of their past errors. This move towards Reformed orthodoxy was emphasised by the more conventional confessions of faith that appeared in the later editions of the *Livre des Martyrs*, the content of which helps to demonstrate the suitability of the Vaudois to be included. That the Vaudois could be shown to have suffered on behalf of that belief helped to demonstrate their eligibility for inclusion in both the church and in the martyrology. As will be discussed in the next chapter, Crespin's later discussions of the Vaudois, in Piedmont and elsewhere, appear to be more comfortable treating them as full members of the Reformed Church.

Aside from the questions of doctrine and obedience, for which Crespin eventually found a satisfactory form, the accounts of the massacres at Mérindol and Cabrières were marked by the early use of the narrative format to bring a massacre into a genre usually marked by solitary examples. Developed before the widespread use of the *Récit d'Histoire* format, the narrative of the massacres of 1545, as seen in the *Histoire memorable,*

The *Vaudois in history and martyrology* 93

acquired attributes of martyrology when it was added to the *Livre des Martyrs*. In its final form, the account included an accusation, a trial of sorts, a confession of faith, official condemnation, terrible cruelty and suffering, and concluded with the taking of both quiet solace and providential justice.

As Crespin himself acknowledged, the story of the Vaudois was an imperfect fit in the *Livre des Martyrs*, largely for reasons of genre. His attempts to separate them out into narrative histories were quickly abandoned, however, and by 1563, events featuring the Vaudois of Piedmont and Savoy, as well as a number of Genevan ministers, led to a new series of Vaudois-affiliated martyrs being included in the martyrology.

Notes

1 Jean-François Gilmont, 'Les Vaudois des Alpes: mythes et réalités', *Revue d'histoire ecclésiastique* 83 (1988), p. 73.
2 Euan Cameron, *The Reformation of the Heretics: The Waldenses of the Alps, 1480–1580* (Oxford: Clarendon Press, 1982), p. 133.
3 Jean Crespin, *Recueil de plusieurs personnes qui ont constamment enduré la mort pour la nom pour la nom de N.S. Jesus Christ* ([Geneva: J. Crespin], 1554), p. 656.
4 David El Kenz, *Les bûchers du roi: la culture protestante des martyrs (1523–1572)* (Paris: Seyssel, 1997), pp. 127–28.
5 Cameron, *Reformation of the Heretics*, p. 22.
6 Marc Venard, *Réforme protestante, Réforme catholique dans la provence d'Avignon au XVIe siècle* (Paris: Cerf, 1993), p. 316.
7 Jean Crespin, *Cinquieme partie du recueil des martyrs* ([Geneva]: Jean Crespin, 1564 [1563]), p. 31. Jean Crespin, *Actes des Martyrs* ([Geneva]: Jean Crespin, 1565), p. 870. Both sections are titled *Touchant l'église des fidèles in Piedmont*. The pages were headed *Histoire de l'église en Piedmont*.
8 Cameron, *Reformation of the Heretics*, p. 232.
9 Theódore De Bèze, *Histoire Ecclésiastique*, Vol. I. Baum and Cunitz (eds) (Nieuwkoop: De Graaf, 1974), pp. 1, 30–45.
10 Yves Krumenacker, 'La geneologie imaginaire de la Reforme protestante', *Revue Historique* 638 (2006), p. 263.
11 S.J. Barnett, 'Where was your Church Before Luther? Claims for the Antiquity of Protestantism Examined', *Church History* 68:1 (1999), p. 24.
12 Krumenacker, p. 260. Luc Racaut, *Hatred in Print, Catholic Propaganda and Protestant Identity During the French Wars of Religion* (Aldershot: Ashgate, 2002), p. 117.
13 The chapter in Audisio's *Les Vaudois* which covers the sixteenth century is titled *Mourir: une solution d'avenir*.
14 Gabriel Audisio, *Les Vaudois: Histoire d'une dissidence XIIe–XVIe siècle* (Paris: Fayard, 1998), p. 241. Gilmont, 'Les Vaudois des Alpes', pp. 69–89.
15 Cameron, *Reformation of the Heretics*, pp. 138–44. Gilmont, 'Les Vaudois des Alpes', p. 74.
16 Jean-François Gilmont, 'Aux origines de l'historiographie vaudoise du XVIe siècle: Jean Crespin, Étienne Noël et Scipione Lentolo', in *Collana della Societa di Studi Valdesi, 9: I Valdesi e l'Europa* (Torre Pellice: Claudiana, 1982), p. 193.
17 Gabriel Audisio, *The Waldensian Dissent: Persecution and Survival c.1170–c.1570* (Cambridge: Cambridge University Press, 1999), p. 165.

94   *The Vaudois in history and martyrology*

18 Charles Schmidt, 'Aktenstucke besonders zur Geschicte der Waldenser', *Zeitschrift fur die historische Theologie* 22 (1852), pp. 252–56. Cameron, *Reformation of the Heretics*, p. 190.

19 Calvin to Bullinger, 25 November 1544. Jules Bonnet (ed.), *Letters of John Calvin*, Vol. I (Philadelphia: Presbyterian Board of Publication [1858]), p. 430.

20 Calvin to Bullinger, p. 432.

21 Cameron, *Reformation of the Heretics*, p. 187.

22 Cameron, *Reformation of the Heretics*, p. 203.

23 Audisio, *The Waldensian Dissent*, p. 169.

24 Audisio, *The Waldensian Dissent*, p. 183.

25 Cameron, *Reformation of the Heretics*, p. 193.

26 Cameron, *Reformation of the Heretics*, p. 191.

27 Audisio, *Les Vaudois*, pp. 20–26.

28 Audisio, *The Waldensian Dissent*, p. 14.

29 Audisio, *The Waldensian Dissent*, p. 8.

30 Malcolm Lambert, *Medieval Heresy: Popular Movements from the Gregorian Reform to the Reformation* (Oxford: Blackwell, 1992), p. 157. Schmidt, pp. 239–42.

31 Euan Cameron, *Waldenses: Rejections of Holy Church in Medieval Europe* (Oxford: Blackwell, 2000), p. 11.

32 Cameron, *Waldenses*, pp. 98, 17.

33 Cameron, *Waldenses*, p. 204.

34 Audisio, *Les Vaudois*, pp. 112–22.

35 Cameron, *Reformation of the Heretics*, p. 31.

36 Gabriel Audisio, 'How to Detect a Clandestine Minority: The Example of the Waldensians', *Sixteenth Century Journal XXI* (1990), p. 214.

37 Audisio, 'How to Detect a Clandestine Minority', p. 212.

38 Audisio, *Les Vaudois*, p. 304.

39 Cameron, *Reformation of the Heretics*, p. 75.

40 Cameron, *Waldenses*, p. 189.

41 Lentolo's history, for example, derives much from Crespin. Cf. Cameron, *Reformation of the Heretics*, p. 231.

42 The attitudes of Vaudois scholars to the varying confessions of 1541 being the most germane example. See below.

43 Gilmont, 'Aux origins de l'historiographie', p. 193.

44 Gilmont, *Jean Crespin*, p. 149 n.

45 Crespin, *Recueil de plusieurs personnes* (1554), p. 656.

46 Gilmont, 'Aux origins de l'historiographie', p. 193.

47 Gilmont, 'Aux origins de l'historiographie', p. 194.

48 Audisio, *Les Vaudois*, p. 191.

49 Crespin, *Recueil de plusieurs personnes* (1554), p. 656.

50 Crespin, *Recueil de plusieurs personnes* (1554), p. 656.

51 Crespin, *Recueil de plusieurs personnes* (1554), p. 657.

52 Crespin, *Recueil de plusieurs personnes* (1554), p. 657. While Crespin may be exaggerating the degree, there was some co-operation between the Vaudois and the Hussites in the fifteenth century. See Audisio, *Les Vaudois*, pp. 118–21.

53 Jean Crespin, *Actes des Martyrs* ([Geneva]: Jean Crespin, 1565), p. 189.

54 Crespin, *Recueil de plusieurs personnes* (1554), p. 657.

55 Barnett, p. 21.

56 Crespin, *Recueil de plusieurs personnes* (1554), p. 657.

57 Crespin, *Recueil de plusieurs personnes* (1554), p. 657.

58 Schmidt, p. 250.

The Vaudois in history and martyrology 95

59 Crespin, *Recueil de plusieurs personnes* (1554), p. 658.
60 Gilmont, *Bibliographie des Éditions de Jean Crespin (1550–1572)* (Verviers: Gason, 1981), pp. 57–59.
61 Crespin, *Recueil de plusieurs personnes* (1554), p. 656 (mislabelled 956).
62 Jean Crespin, *Recueil de plusieurs personnes qui ont constamment enduré la mort pour la nom pour la nom de Nostre Seigneur* ([Geneva]: Jean Crespin, 1555), p. 239.
63 Crespin, *Histoire memorable de la persecution de Merindol et Cabrieres* ([Geneva], 1555), sig. iii recto.
64 Crespin, *Histoire memorable ...* (1555), sig. iii verso.
65 Cameron, *Reformation of the Heretics*, pp. 71, 93.
66 Crespin, *Histoire memorable ...* (1555), sig. iiii recto.
67 Cameron, *Reformation of the Heretics*, p. 34. Crespin, *Histoire memorable ...* (1555), sig. iiii verso.
68 Racaut, *Hatred in Print*, pp. 61–64.
69 Jean Crespin, *Histoire memorable ...* (1555), sig. iiii verso. Cameron, *Reformation of the Heretics*, p. 77.
70 Gilmont, 'Aux origins de l'historiographie', p. 194.
71 The British Library example measures 89 mm across, compared to 97 mm for an example of the 1556 Latin martyrology. This very rough metric fails to take into account the size of margins, font, and other factors which could and did vary considerably.
72 Jean Crespin, *Histoire memorable de la persecuton de Merindol et Cabrieres* ([Geneva]: Jean Crespin, 1556), p. 3.
73 Crespin, *Histoire memorable ...* (1556), p. 3.
74 Crespin, *Actes des Martyrs* (1565), p. 189.
75 Crespin, *Actes des Martyrs* (1565), p. 189.
76 Crespin, *Actes des Martyrs* (1565), pp. 239, 189.
77 Crespin, *Actes des Martyrs* (1565), p. 189.
78 Crespin, *Actes des Martyrs* (1565), p. 189.
79 Crespin, *Recueil de plusieurs personnes* (1554), p. 658.
80 Crespin, *Recueil de plusieurs personnes* (1554), p. 659. William Monter, *Judging the French Reformation: Heresy Trial by Sixteenth-Century Parlements* (London: Harvard University Press, 1999), p. 76.
81 Monter, p. 76.
82 Crespin, *Recueil de plusieurs personnes* (1554), p. 659. Monter, p. 78.
83 Crespin, *Recueil de plusieurs personnes* (1554), p. 660.
84 Crespin, *Recueil de plusieurs personnes* (1554), pp. 660–61.
85 Crespin, *Actes des Martyrs* (1565), p. 190; Jean Crespin, *Histoire des vrays tesmoins de la verité de l'Evangile* ([Geneva: Jean Crespin]), p. 115.
86 Cameron, *Reformation of the Heretics*, pp. 264–67.
87 Crespin, *Recueil de plusieurs personnes* (1554), p. 663.
88 Crespin, *Recueil de plusieurs personnes* (1554), p. 663.
89 Monter, p. 99.
90 Crespin, *Recueil de plusieurs personnes* (1554), p. 664.
91 Crespin, *Histoire memorable ...* (1555), p. 94.
92 Crespin, *Histoire memorable ...* (1555), p. 94.
93 Crespin, *Actes des Martyrs* (1565), pp. 213–14.
94 Crespin, *Actes des Martyrs* (1565), p. 214.
95 Crespin, *Actes des Martyrs* (1565).
96 Crespin, *Recueil de plusieurs personnes* (1554), p. 661.
97 Crespin, *Actes des Martyrs* (1565), p. 190.
98 Venard, p. 316.
99 Venard, p. 316.

96 *The Vaudois in history and martyrology*

100 Venard, p. 316.
101 Calvin to Farel, 19 February 1541. In A.-L. Herminjard, *Correspondance des Réformateurs dans les pays de Langue Française*, Vol. VII (Nieuwkoop: De Graaf, 1965), pp. 25–28.
102 Crespin, *Actes des Martyrs* (1565), p. 191.
103 Crespin, *Actes des Martyrs* (1565), p. 190.
104 Crespin, *Actes des Martyrs* (1565), p. 190.
105 Crespin, *Actes des Martyrs* (1565), p. 190.
106 Crespin, *Recueil de plusieurs personnes* (1554), p. 661. Monter, p. 95.
107 Crespin, *Actes des Martyrs* (1565), p. 192.
108 Crespin, *Actes des Martyrs* (1565), p. 192.
109 Crespin, *Actes des Martyrs* (1565), p. 192.
110 Crespin, *Actes des Martyrs* (1565), p. 192.
111 Crespin, *Actes des Martyrs* (1565), p. 197.
112 Crespin, *Actes des Martyrs* (1565), p. 194.
113 Crespin, *Actes des Martyrs* (1565), p. 196.
114 Crespin, *Histoire memorable* ... (1555), pp. 29–31.
115 Crespin, *Histoire memorable* ... (1555), pp. 29–30.
116 Crespin, *Recueil de plusieurs personnes* (1554), p. 661.
117 Crespin, *Actes des Martyrs* (1565), pp. 202–05.
118 Gilmont, 'Aux origines de l'historiographie', p. 195.
119 Crespin, *Histoire memorable* ... (1555), p. 66.
120 Venard, p. 336.
121 Crespin, *Histoire memorable* ... (1555), p. 41.
122 Crespin, *Histoire memorable* ... (1555), p. 68.
123 Crespin, *Histoire memorable* ... (1555), p. 42. First Helvetic Confession in: *Reformed Confessions of the Sixteenth Century*, ed. Arthur Cochrane, (London, 1966), p. 100.
124 Crespin, *Histoire memorable* ... (1555), pp. 46–47.
125 Cameron, *Reformation of the Heretics*, p. 210.
126 Oecolampadius, 1530, cited in: Gabriel Audisio, *Preachers by Night: The Waldensian Barbes (15th–16th centuries)* (Leiden: Brill, 2007), p. 130.
127 Crespin, *Histoire memorable* ... (1555), p. 47.
128 Crespin, *Histoire memorable* ... (1555), p. 47. The damned rich may well be a reference to the Lazarus parable in Luke 16, and thus not be a simple attack on the wealthy, though we should remember the Waldensian ideal of poverty.
129 Calvin, *Institutes*, IV, 1, p. 288.
130 Cameron, *Reformation of the Heretics*, pp. 70, 73.
131 Crespin, *Histoire memorable* ... (1555), p. 51.
132 Crespin, *Histoire memorable* ... (1555), p. 52.
133 Cameron, *Reformation of the Heretics*, p. 212.
134 'Les Vaudois de Cabrières a Jean de Roma, 3 February 1533'. In Herminjard, Vol. VII, pp. 466–68.
135 Crespin, *Histoire memorable* ... (1555), p. 55.
136 Cameron, *Waldenses*, p. 235.
137 Crespin, *Histoire memorable* ... (1555), p. 56.
138 Crespin, *Histoire memorable* ... (1555), p. 59.
139 Crespin, *Histoire memorable* ... (1555), pp. 60–61.
140 Audisio, *Les Vaudois*, p. 170.
141 Crespin, *Histoire memorable* ... (1555), p. 63.
142 Crespin, *Histoire memorable* ... (1555), p. 63.
143 Crespin, *Histoire memorable* ... (1556), p. 67.
144 The document in total is about 4.5 folio pages long.
145 Crespin, *Actes des Martyrs* (1565), p. 202.

The Vaudois in history and martyrology 97

146 Gilmont, 'Aux origines de l'historiographie', p. 201.
147 Crespin, *Actes des Martyrs* (1565), p. 202.
148 Crespin, *Actes des Martyrs* (1565), p. 203.
149 Crespin, *Actes des Martyrs* (1565), p. 204.
150 Crespin, *Actes des Martyrs* (1565), p. 202.
151 Crespin, *Actes des Martyrs* (1565), p. 205.
152 Cameron, *Reformation of the Heretics*, pp. 212, 231.
153 Crespin, *Histoire memorable* ... (1555), p. 40. Crespin, *Histoire des vrays tesmoins de la verité de l'Evangile* ([Geneva: Jean Crespin], 1570), p. 120 verso.
154 John Foxe, *The Unabridged Acts and Monuments Online* (1570 edition) (HRI Online Publications, Sheffield, 2011). www.johnfoxe.org, p. 987. [Accessed 27 August 2011].
155 de Bèze, p. 57.
156 Crespin, *Actes des Martyrs* (1565), p. 202.
157 Crespin, *Actes des Martyrs* (1565), p. 202. Crespin, *Histoire des vrays tesmoins* (1570), p. 121.
158 Crespin, *Histoire memorable* ... (1555), pp. 63–64.
159 Crespin, *Actes des Martyrs* (1565), p. 202.
160 Crespin, *Actes des Martyrs* (1565), p. 203.
161 Crespin, *Actes des Martyrs* (1565), p. 203.
162 Calvin to Bullinger, 25 November 1544. In Bonnet (ed.), *Letters of John Calvin*, Vol. 1, p. 431.
163 Calvin to Bullinger, p. 432.
164 Crespin, *Histoire memorable* ... (1555), p. 122.
165 Monter, p. 120.
166 Crespin, *Histoire memorable* ... (1555), p. 134.
167 Monter, p. 122.
168 Crespin, *Histoire des vrays tesmoins* (1570), p. 131 recto.
169 Crespin, *Histoire des vrays tesmoins* (1570), p. 175 verso.
170 Crespin, *Histoire des vrays tesmoins* (1570), p. 176 recto.
171 Crespin, *Histoire des vrays tesmoins* (1570), p. 176 recto.
172 Crespin, *Actes des Martyrs* (1565), p. 215.
173 Crespin, *Actes des Martyrs* (1565), p. 216.
174 Crespin, *Actes des Martyrs* (1565), p. 216.
175 Crespin, *Actes des Martyrs* (1565), p. 217.
176 Crespin, *Actes des Martyrs* (1565), p. 216.
177 Crespin, *Actes des Martyrs* (1565), p. 216.
178 Crespin, *Histoire des vrays tesmoins* (1570), pp. 176 recto–verso.
179 Crespin, *Histoire des vrays tesmoins* (1570), p. 176 verso.
180 Daniela Boccassini, 'Le massacre des Vaudois de Provence', *Archiv für Reformationsgeschichte*, 82 (1991), p. 257.
181 Crespin, *Histoire memorable* ... (1555), p. 5.
182 Crespin, *Histoire memorable* ... (1555), p. 41. Fredric Baumgartner, *France in the Sixteenth Century* (London: Palgrave Macmillan, 1995), p. 144.
183 Crespin, *Histoire des vrays tesmoins* (1570), p. 120 recto.
184 Boccassini, p. 260.
185 Crespin, *Histoire memorable* ... (1555), p. 261. Crespin, *Histoire des vrays tesmoins* (1570), p. 174 verso.
186 Venard, p. 316.

3 The alpine Vaudois in the 1550s and 1560s

While the massacres in Provence were the only mention of the Vaudois in the first edition of the *Livre des Martyrs* (the *Histoire memorable*, of course, was concerned entirely with those events), later editions brought other Vaudois settlements into discussion. The Vaudois had always had a strong presence in the Alpine valleys (Crespin had noted in his introduction to the massacres in Provence that the Vaudois had travelled to there from Piedmont), and had farther-flung branches as well, notably in Calabria.[1] From the 1550s, Geneva sent ministers to some of these communities, bringing them increased attention both from Protestant writers and Catholic authorities. Indeed, the first formal mission to the Piedmontese Vaudois, of Jean Vernou and Jean Lauvergeat, was featured in Crespin from 1556 onward.[2] The process of integrating Vaudois beliefs and structures into Reformed patterns was a slow one, but by the late 1550s the efforts of the missionaries and the Vaudois leadership was bearing fruit. The establishment of distinctively Reformed churches and practices was visible in areas like the Luberon, but it is clear that this had been a slow process.[3]

Protestant narratives of the Vaudois were often derived from the accounts of those Genevans who had been sent to make official contact with them, men like Jean Vernou or Scipione Lentolo. These accounts tended to emphasise the difficulties the ministers faced in teaching doctrine, and in winning obedience with few resources from a community with its own traditions and interests. Lentolo's work underlined the need for missions like his, stressing the relative backwardness of the Vaudois, and their weakness in doctrine.[4] Crespin's early discussions of the Vaudois, particularly in Provence during the 1540s, make repeated reference to deficiencies in their doctrine, and his later work on the alpine communities of the 1550s and 1560s, directly contributed to and borrowed from Lentolo and others, as Gilmont and Balmas have shown.[5]

Crespin's writing on the Vaudois in Italy, both in the North and South, appears to treat these communities as a more integral part of the Reformed Church than those in Provence. The narrative passages refer to them as the 'church in Piedmont', suggesting a full membership in the Reformed Church, and indeed, they are rarely referred to as Vaudois at all outside of

The alpine Vaudois in the 1550s and 1560s   99

the introductions and other paratext. Similarly, the martyrdoms associated with the Italian Vaudois have a structure and content identical to those of French martyrs, with orthodox Calvinist positions expounded at length, and with some skill. The relative conformity of the Italian Vaudois with Genevan standards means that in some cases it is only through his introduction or titling that we know that an individual has any Vaudois links at all, and in other cases we have to rely on outside sources for that information. Later editions of Crespin generally presented more context for these martyrs, and thus make the reader more aware of the links with the Vaudois.

The earliest of these individual Vaudois martyrdoms to be added to the *Livre des Martyrs* was that of Martin Gonin. Gonin occupies an important place in the historiography of Vaudois union with the Reformed Church, as he is believed to have been one of the envoys sent to Guillaume Farel in the 1520s.[6] Gonin was certainly in contact with Farel in 1536, and may have been an envoy to the Provençal Vaudois at this time.[7] Though Euan Cameron urges caution identifying this figure with the martyr of the 1530s, it appears that Gonin was one of the principal figures linking the two groups.[8] As a visitor to Geneva and a correspondent of some of its religious leaders, Gonin was a natural choice for Crespin to include. He represented a middle ground where Vaudois and Reformed could meet, and was a figure on whom it would have been possible to gather information.

In 1536, Gonin had been arrested on the road from Geneva, where he had been to ask Farel: 'to take charge of reforming their churches: those in Dauphinié, Provence, & Piedmont, as well as those in Apulia and Calabria' by those communities of Vaudois who felt that their own customs were inferior.[9] On their return, he and his companion were arrested, and taken to Grenoble, where the letters they were carrying betrayed them; Gonin was strangled and his body consigned to the river.

This account of Gonin's martyrdom first appeared in the 1555 edition of the *Livre des Martyrs*, at the very end of the first book – only a single paragraph devoted to Estienne Brun was placed after him. This placement breaks the rough chronology of the book, as it follows a series of accounts which run to 1552, which suggests it was made as a late addition, while the printing of the edition was actually under way.[10] Given that 1555 was also the year in which Crespin published the stand-alone edition of the *Histoire memorable*, it is therefore possible that it was in the process of producing that work that Martin Gonin's case was discovered, although this must remain supposition.

It is a relatively short piece, and spends little time on theology or doctrine, grappling instead with self-identity. In his interrogation, Gonin insists that he is not a Lutheran, for: 'Luther did not die for me, but Jesus Christ, whose name I wear'.[11] The interrogators decry Farel and Viret as: 'the biggest Lutherans in the world', and again Gonin is prepared to deny

100 *The alpine Vaudois in the 1550s and 1560s*

the term, insisting that the two are 'true servants of God'.[12] Gonin, in turn, decries the Pope as Antichrist, and the Catholic Church as 'the Church of the evil', using apocalyptic language, and offers to defend his stances if given a Bible from which to work.[13] Further rejecting identification with a denomination, Gonin says that he rests his faith on the Creeds, and insists that if he is a heretic, then so too must be the Apostles, Saints, and even Christ.[14] As in so many other interrogations, Gonin's reached a peak when he was questioned on the subject of the Mass, which he vehemently denied the value of, for it repeats Christ's sacrifice, when once was enough to save all souls.[15]

His captors were apparently impressed, for they decided 'it would be best to throw him by night into the river, from fear that the world would hear him speaking, for he spoke well'.[16] Gonin's death is recounted in relatively great detail, taking roughly a third of the length of his account.

Later editions added a short passage to the beginning of Gonin's account, which introduces the Vaudois people to the reader, and explains the nature of his mission to Geneva. It stresses, more than the actual account does, the connection of Gonin and the Angrogna valley to the Vaudois. In 1555, Gonin is introduced as being the:

> native of a small valley in Piedmont, called Angruene (Angrogna), where those of the place nearly always had knowledge of abuses and human traditions, came to be minister of those who were called Vaudois. And because the Vaudois (some of whom were men of means, and very affectionate to the word of God) understood by the clarity of the Gospel, which they began to read, that their Churches were badly ruled in many things, & rusted by the ignorance and darkness of the earlier times. They sent the said Martin with Jean Girard to Geneva to ask Master Guillaume Farel, who was then preaching in the said city, to take charge of reforming their churches, those in Dauphinié, Provence, & Piedmont, as well as those in Puglia and Calabria.[17]

From 1564 onwards, Gonin was introduced with the sub-headline: 'this history shows how those of the Angrogna valley by long succession, and as from father to son, had followed some purity of doctrine ... called Vaudois'.[18] Crespin's introduction then moves on to a much broader discussion of the Piedmontese valleys, a traditional home of Vaudois belief:

> For fuller knowledge of the narration of this martyr of the Lord, we need to know that there is a certain valley in Piedmont near Mount Vesulus, of five or six leagues in extent or thereabouts, which has taken its name from the city of Lucerne, called for that reason Val-Lucerne. This contains in itself another small valley which was called that of Angrogna, because of a small stream of that name which

The alpine Vaudois in the 1550s and 1560s   101

passed by it. There are also two other valleys adjoining the first; know that of Peruse, which thus was named for the town of the same name: the other is the valley of St. Martin. Many settlements and villages are in the said valleys. The locals make profession of the Gospel, and have nearly always held in horror the abuses & traditions of the Roman seat. Those who frequent these valleys estimate that the number of habitants may well be nearly 8,000 people. M. Martin Gonin, a God-fearing man, was in these times the Minister in the said valley of Angrogna: the locals of which, having heard that many cities in the lands of Germany, Switzerland, and Savoy had for some time held the true doctrine & reformation of the Gospel, decided, in their fashion, to reform their churches. Thus being strongly fond of the word of God, having long desired to have it: & aware enough that their churches were badly ruled in many thing, & rusted by ignorance & the darkness of earlier times.[19]

From this point the narrative follows that of the 1555 edition cited above. Much of this new, descriptive, material was drawn from Scipione Lentolo's *Narratio* which had been published since the last version of Gonin's martyrdom had been published. Lentolo's account, which itself drew on earlier editions of the martyrology, was frequently critical of the Vaudois, and testified to the slow process of assimilation then in progress.[20] As a result, and as had been done in the discussion of Mérindol and Cabrières, the flaws of the pre-Reform Vaudois are openly discussed, and framed as being in real need of guidance from Geneva. These passages introducing the Piedmontese Vaudois serve to attune the reader to some signifiers of Vaudois identity: references to the Angrogne valley, as can also be found in the case of Geoffroy Varagle, are to be read as marks of Vaudois connection. In the *Livre des Martyrs* as in life, early *barbes* like Gonin and Varagle acted as a link between the Reformed and their Vaudois allies.

In the 1570 edition, the *Arguments des 8 Livres*, effectively the table of contents, repeated the connection made in 1564 between Gonin and the Vaudois of the Angrogne, with their hereditary faith.[21]

Despite these descriptions in the paratext, the account itself focuses squarely on Gonin, rather than the wider Vaudois community. Gonin is thus the first Vaudois individual to be featured outside the self-contained section on Mérindol and Cabrières, and the first one to be tested against Crespin's criteria for martyrhood. When, in the compendium editions, he was placed with other martyrs of the 1530s, Gonin was used as a sort of introduction to the Vaudois, establishing their place in the history of the Reformed movement, and their willingness to suffer martyrdom, an appropriate function perhaps, given his role in bringing the two denominations together.

102 *The alpine Vaudois in the 1550s and 1560s*

Estienne Brun

From the life and death of Martin Gonin, Crespin moved on to that of Estienne Brun, who first appeared in the second, 1555, edition of the *Livre des Martyrs*. The two accounts were placed together in the final pages of that version, seemingly as late additions. Brun's entry in 1555 was initially very short, at less than a page long, and made no mention of Brun being of Vaudois origin, though it perhaps hints at it: his origins are: 'of the diocese of Aumbrun in Dauphiné', an area with some well-known Vaudois connections.[22] He was taken prisoner 'for the word of God', and died with 'such constancy, that the enemies of the truth did cry to the sound of a trumpet, that people must not talk of the death of Estienne Brun, on pain of being declared a heretic and burned like him'.[23] This is a straightforward account, and only circumstantial things, such as Brun's placement next to Gonin, and his links to the Dauphinie, give the reader any suggestion of a Vaudois connection at all. Later scholars, however, have been unanimous in labelling Brun a member of the group.[24]

In the 1564 edition, Brun's story was given a page in folio, and provided with a brief sub-headline telling the reader that they might: 'Know the gifts and graces that God gives to rural people, without observing human methods'; Brun 'is the first after' Jean Cornon, another rustic martyr with surprising depths of knowledge, who had been the 'patron and mirror of the men of the fields'.[25] Cornon seems to have served as a version of the German type, *Karsthans*, the eloquent and disputatious peasant who can best the Church sophists on their own terms.[26] Now given a date, of 1540, this version stresses Brun's rural life, and his ability to: 'surmount all the craft and finesse of the grandest of Dauphiné'.[27] Though triumphing in French debate, he is tricked into signing an abjuration in Latin, which he cannot read. As in the earlier version, Brun harangues his interrogators and judges, insisting that they are condemning him not to death but to eternal life; the judges ban the people from discussing his case (thus the headline to the notice).[28] 1564's other addition to this narrative is a strong wind that keeps Brun's pyre from being lit, though this is never explicitly attributed to an act of God.[29] The 1570 iteration of Brun's story follows 1564's, aside from the sub-headline. Reading in 1564: 'who is given as patron and mirror to the labourers on the land', the word 'patron' does not appear in 1570's version; perhaps giving Brun status as something more than an exemplar.[30]

The Chambéry Five

Amongst the very earliest ministers sent out from Geneva to the Vaudois of Piedmont was Jean Vernou, originally from Poitiers.[31] His letters to Geneva, some of which were included in his entry in the *Livre des Martyrs*, discuss some practical problems of ministering to Vaudois communities,

The alpine Vaudois in the 1550s and 1560s   103

arguing that their leadership placed themselves in danger by preaching so openly.[32] Later in 1555, he and a number of companions were arrested, tried, and executed by the French Parlement in Chambéry.

Crespin included the story of the 'Five of Chambéry' in 1556's *Troisieme Partie* of the martyrology, placing a particular emphasis on Vernou and four of his companions, Antoine Laborie, Jean Trigalet, Guyraud Tauran, and Bertrand Bataille.[33] All of these were French immigrants to Geneva, though not all were ordained ministers, or theologically trained. This section of their account consisted of a series of letters written jointly and individually, taking up more than 110 pages of the octavo edition.

The section describes Geneva's role in spreading reform: 'the city of Geneva, having now maintained its own space for more than twenty years, did send as though from their park many valiant champions, to show to men the truth'.[34] Crespin relates that: the five men had been *en route* from Geneva when they were arrested crossing through Savoy. They were interrogated, and eventually tried, where their deportment and constancy were admired.[35] The rest of the notice was made of trial documents and letters both individual and collective. Vernou's letters are addressed to several recipients, including his cousin, his sister, a 'Sieur de B.', and the Ministers of Geneva; one of the communal letters was addressed to Calvin himself.[36]

These personal letters centre around themes of consolation, and reinforcement of faith. The letter to the Ministers subtly discusses martyrological themes of testimony and battles against Satan before engaging in some description of the hearings, where Vernou particularly seems to have done everything in his power to confound the Catholic sensibilities of his judges.[37] He denounced a crucifix belonging to the President of the Parlement as an idolatrous image, the Pope as Antichrist, and the mass as idolatry.[38]

The focus is entirely on the events of their captivity in Chambéry; little is written about their mission or their past experiences. Vernou's first letter does include a brief narrative of the arrest of his group, but that adds nothing to what had already been included in the introduction.[39] Although the reader of the *Livre des Martyrs* received a full account of the trial and execution of these five men, they were deprived of some of Vernou's other correspondence to Geneva, on the subject of the Vaudois.[40]

For example, in a 1555 letter to Calvin, only a few months before his capture, Vernou had described his hard voyage into the mountain valleys of Fenestella and Angrogne to make contact with the Vaudois. Although they seemed receptive to his message, he appeared to be concerned by their insistence on public preaching, rather than secret worship, and the letter as a whole gives an insight into the work and the challenges of the Genevan missionaries to the Vaudois communities.[41] Given that other letters which Vernou had sent to Calvin, and Geneva, appeared in the *Livre des Martyrs*, it seems possible that this one was excluded as it did not directly illuminate

104 *The alpine Vaudois in the 1550s and 1560s*

the discussion of Vernou's trial and execution. This omission, whatever its reason, downplays the links between the Vaudois and a major cluster of entirely orthodox Genevan martyrs, and so has the effect of isolating the Vaudois from the Reformed mainstream.

Barthelemy Hector

Another martyr with connections to the Alpine communities was Barthelemy Hector, who died at Turin (then the seat of a French Parlement), in 1556, arrested while smuggling Genevan books into the Alpine valleys. He first appeared in the 1563 *Cinquieme Partie*, of the martyrology, the first full edition after his death (the *Quatrieme Partie* was largely concerned with translations from Foxe's English martyrology).[42] Gilmont has suggested that this account was taken from the official records of the Turin administration.[43] As with the Chambéry Five, the records reproduced do not make specific mention of the Vaudois. However, unlike that case, Crespin makes the Vaudois connection clear.

He introduces the section by noting that when people refer to the residents of the Angrogne valley, they mean Vaudois.[44] The trial records that Crespin reproduces confirm this connection, when Hector confirms that alongside the minister M. Estienne, worked an elected minister known as Barbe Paul; Crespin notes in the margin that: 'in Piedmont the ministers are named "Barbes", that is to say "Uncles", or elders'.[45]

Hector's account thus gives us a view into the period when Genevan-trained ministers, such as M. Estienne, were replacing the old Vaudois order which Barbe Paul represented. As a *colporteur*, Hector had been smuggling Protestant works to sell in the Vaudois valleys, and Crespin names some of them: Bibles, Calvin's *Institutes*, collections of Psalms, a book titled *Instructions pour les petits enfants*, and several others, which are not named.[46] This gives some sense of the sort of effort to make the Vaudois into better Protestants that must still have been ongoing during the 1550s, and perhaps Crespin's own involvement with Barthelemy Hector, who may well have been carrying some of Crespin's wares.

By the time of Hector's death, Crespin had printed several Bibles, several books of psalms, and Fabri's *Familiere instruction des petis enfans*. He had also printed many editions of Calvin, though not an *Institutes*.[47] Given the competition and overlap between Genevan printers during the period, there is no way to be sure that it was Crespin's books which Hector was selling in the valleys, or even to know if the two men would have been known to each other. However, the Genevan network of booksellers, publishers, and printers was not that large in the 1550s. If there was any personal contact between martyrologist and martyr, Crespin did not make use of it: Hector's account seems to be entirely based on the trial records. The account of Hector's arrest and death remained basically unchanged through 1570.

Geoffrey Varagle

Another Piedmontese martyr who first appeared in the *Cinquieme Partie* was Geoffroy Varagle, or Giafredo Varaglia. He was executed in Turin in late 1557, having been arrested in the town of 'Busque' (Busca), Piedmont, on his return from a preaching tour of the Angrogne valley. As such, he represents a record of the Reformed mission to the Vaudois which was slowly supplanting the *barbes*. As with Jean Vernou, there is no specific mention of the Vaudois in this account. Instead, Crespin describes the mission using the formula that Varagle was chosen by Calvin and other Genevan ministers to preach to 'those of Angrogne'.[48] He was selected to do this alongside Martin Taschart, the two sent by the Company of Pastors in response to a letter in the spring of 1557 from Piedmont, asking for more preachers in the wake of Vernou's martyrdom.[49]

He was arrested in November of the same year.[50] Crespin claims that some of the information that we possess about Varagle's interrogation comes from the records of the Parlement of Turin, as Barthelemy Hector's may have done, including the description of his execution.[51] Crespin also includes a letter written to Varagle by Jean Calvin, which stresses to the condemned man the good his death will do to the cause, though we do not know if its source is the Parlement's records, or the archives of Calvin himself.[52] Like most martyrs in Crespin, Varagle's account in the *Livre des Martyrs* is primarily comprised of his confession of faith, which is Reformed in every respect. A former monk, with ties to Bernardino Ochino, Varagle's answers are relatively sophisticated, and aggressively attack the ideas of purgatory, the treasury of merit, and transubstantiation.[53] Varagle's denunciation of images contains a line of attack unique to Crespin, arguing that they had been rejected from Christian worship until their implementation around the year 800 by Theodora Irena (the Byzantine Empress had indeed endorsed the veneration of icons at the end of the iconoclastic struggle in or around 843), and were thus to be eliminated by any return to the forms of the Apostolic Church.[54]

Varagle also presents to us a few tantalising pieces of information: amongst the books which he had contact with in the Angrogne valley were the *Alcoranum Franciscanorum* (presumably Erasmus Alber's *Alcoranus Franciscanus*, an attack on the cult of St Francis), *De fatti de veri successori de Jesus Christo & des Apostati*, and the *Unio Hermanni Bodi*.[55] The account of Varagle's burning also contains the ancient trope wherein a white dove was seen to fly around the smoke as his body was burned, though Crespin advised on the principle of being cautious of being curious about such unusual events.[56]

106 *The alpine Vaudois in the 1550s and 1560s*

The Vaudois in Southern Italy

In 1554, in the introduction to his first account of Mérindol and Cabrières, Crespin had written about the Vaudois presence in Italy, particularly Apulia and Calabria, far to the South. This group seems to have migrated to there from the Alps at the same time other Vaudois were moving into Provence, in the thirteenth or fourteenth centuries.[57] They had by the sixteenth century established a strong community there, confident enough, at least, to be able to preach semi-publicly.[58]

In 1563's edition of the martyrology, Crespin presented his first proper account of the communities there. Crespin illustrated the persecution of the Vaudois of Calabria through the individual martyrdom of the Genevan-trained minister Jean-Louis Pascal (Gianluigi Paschale), rather than through a *Récit d'Histoire* or description of the whole community. This is another of Crespin's synecdoches, giving the reader the history of the Calabrian Vaudois within the scope of a single martyrdom tale.

As with several other Italian groups of Vaudois, Pascal first appeared in Crespin as part of the 1563 *Cinquieme partie*, given a substantial part of the book amounting to up eighty quarto pages, or perhaps 22,000 words.[59] However, the account is largely made up of Pascal's own correspondence. Crespin claims in his introduction that this is the story of more than just one man, describing: 'the persecution of the land of Calabria, and other cities of the Kingdom of Naples ... Jean Louys Pascal, Piedmontais'.[60] The sub-headline describes him as a minister bringing the Word to the faithful of Calabria, when he 'fell into the hands of the Roman Pope'.[61] In the *Cinquieme Partie*, the sub-headline strikes an apocalyptic note: 'and thus in these latter times all the forces of the great of this world were deployed to inhibit the progress & preaching of the Gospel'.[62] This was not repeated in the later editions. Instead, 1564's sub-headline emphasises instead that he died in Rome: 'before the leading and principal enemies of the truth of the Lord'.[63]

Crespin does not depict Pascal as having had any Vaudois background, though he was from Cuneo, in Piedmont, and relatively close to the Angrogne valley.[64] Instead, Pascal had converted to Protestantism while serving as a soldier in Nice, and moved to Geneva to join the Italian Church there, which in turn elected him to serve as a minister in Calabria.[65] His arrival to minister to the existing churches of Sainct-Sixte and la Guardia (which are to this day named San Sisto dei Valdesi, and Guardia Piemontese) immediately stirred up angry resentment in the area, attracting attention amongst the locals, who began to: 'murmur, some grinding their teeth, others crying that he should be exterminated with all of his followers' and the local lord soon took Pascal into custody.[66] As had happened in Provence, it was the arrival of an emissary ('a Lutheran') from Geneva that appears to have been the catalyst for local Catholic reaction against the Vaudois, a sequence which underlined the compromises the

The alpine Vaudois in the 1550s and 1560s 107

Vaudois had taken in order to avoid persecution in centuries past, and which runs contrary to Vernou's earlier concerns about the Vaudois exposing themselves to needless risk.[67]

After this introduction, the remainder of the account is made up of Pascal's letters to his fellow Protestants, in Italy and in Geneva, and to his wife, who had stayed in Geneva. Another is by his brother, Barthelemy, who relates the final events of Jean Louis' life. These letters are largely conventional epistles from prison, reassuring his former congregation, recounting his interrogations, and telling his friends and family of his readiness to suffer and to die for his faith. The main themes that arise from his clashes with his captors are the usual points of contention between Reformed and Catholic: the status of the Eucharist, the power of the Papacy, the existence of Purgatory, and the intercession of the Virgin and the Saints.[68] Pascal is depicted in these letters as defending Reformed doctrine capably and at length in a manner entirely in line with other educated prisoners elsewhere in the *Livre des Martyrs*.

There is very little in his letters to connect Jean Louis Pascal to any tradition other than the purely Genevan one, other than a single reference to his erstwhile congregation in Calabria. In this, sent to: 'my most dear and honoured brothers of San Sisto and la Guardia', Pascal warns them of the dangers of complacency, reminding them:

> your brothers in Piedmont and Provence have suffered battle for the preaching of the Gospel, which is the scepter of Jesus Christ, & what constancy they have shown, remaining linked & joined in a holy union, which Satan has assailed to exterminate them.[69]

The 'your' here is perhaps important; Pascal was not one of their number. Crespin added, in the margin: 'he meant those of Mérindol & Cabrières, of which the history is rehearsed above'.[70] This is the only reference, by either Pascal or by Crespin, to the Calabrians having Vaudois connections. Pascal, for his part, is very clear about his Genevan connections and education.[71]

Crespin later added some context about the Calabrians to whom Pascal was sent to minister. The 1570 edition of the martyrology adds a few lines to the beginning of the description of Pascal, emphasising the Protestant, or at least anti-Catholic, credentials of the communities there: 'as they had long had some knowledge of the true Religion, and had also been threatened by persecution'.[72] In no edition does Crespin mention that the year after Pascal's arrest and execution, his congregation at San Sisto and La Guardia were attacked and massacred by Neapolitan forces.[73] Given his reliance on the papers of Pascal, it is at least possible, if unlikely, that he was unaware of this incident which so closely mirrored events in the Luberon.

108 *The alpine Vaudois in the 1550s and 1560s*

The Vaudois in Piedmont

Crespin's more general narrative account of the Vaudois of Piedmont first appeared in 1563's *Cinquieme Partie*, and was included, with major alterations, in each of the editions of the *Livre des Martyrs* which followed. It was based upon at least three histories which had been published early in the 1560s.[74] The principal of these was a 1561 work called the *Histoire memorable*, attributed to Scipione Lentolo, a Genevan pastor and author active in the Vaudois territories.[75] The second was the 1562 *Histoire des Persecutions*, which Gilmont attributes to the minister Etienne Noel, and which would itself become one of the major histories of the 'Church of the Valleys'.[76] We do not know the third source, which is inferred from the presence of information not present in any known publication.[77]

Crespin was describing a series of moves against the Vaudois in Savoy which had followed the influx of Genevan ministers in the mid-1550s. The first of these was an investigation launched at the end of 1555; in the spring of the following year members of the Parlement of Turin toured the valleys and ordered an end to Protestant services.[78] International pressure, orchestrated from Geneva, helped relieve the pressure on the Vaudois in the short term.[79]

The second, and more serious incident, came after Savoy had returned to the control of Duke Emmanuel-Philibert in 1559 from French hands. From 1560, Savoyard forces, led by the Count della Trinita, moved into the valleys and (after a period of hesitation) were resisted by the Vaudois with force.[80] Their success, and evident religious devotion, in the years before the French tensions broke into open conflict, became well-known.[81] A number of refugees arrived in Geneva, and helped to provide the material for the books that Crespin would use as his source material.[82] In 1561, the Treaty of Cavour between the Vaudois and the Duke of Savoy was agreed, providing an early example of negotiated tolerance for a religious minority. Given the prominence of the Vaudois resistance, and their success, these events played a major role in later editions of the *Livre des Martyrs*.

Like Crespin's work on Mérindol and Cabrières, this narrative was the story of the community as a whole, rather than a single martyr, though with a very different outcome. Where the Provençal account had wrestled with the confessions of faith and the question of Vaudois doctrine, the Piedmontese one raised questions about the use of force, and resistance to established authority. The pugnacious reputation of the alpine Vaudois concerned Calvin himself: in 1556 he had written about their willingness to use force to defend themselves against Savoyard invasion.[83] Crespin's challenge was to present their actions in a positive light, a task made easier both by their success, and the outbreak of war in France itself in 1562. In the years since Calvin had voiced his concerns, the debate had changed dramatically, and Protestants in France had taken up arms against Royal

The alpine Vaudois in the 1550s and 1560s 109

authority. The battles in Piedmont no longer distinguished the Vaudois so sharply from the mainstream of the Reformed church, and this may account for Crespin's willingness to include these conflicts in 1563.

Therefore, in the *Cinquieme Partie*, along with the Piedmont-linked martyrs Hector, Pascal, and Varagle, Crespin included a narrative section titled *On the church of the faithful in Piedmont*, of slightly more than two quarto pages long, dealing with incursions launched by the Parlement of Turin against the Vaudois heartlands of Piedmont in 1555.[84] He reprinted it in 1564, virtually unchanged aside from the headings. It began by identifying the residents of Angrogne, Lucerne, St Martin, and other valleys from which: 'came the Vaudois people, (who had once retired, due to persecution, to the deserts and high mountains of Piedmont)'.[85] As with the discussion of Barthelemy Hector, this underlined the association between Piedmont and the Vaudois, and did so outside of the confines of a martyr's account.

In 1564 Crespin changed this section to include:

the poor peasants of the valleys of Piedmont all had recourse to God, not seeking aid elsewhere, they have experienced in their great need that the Lord is the address of the simple who rest in him & protector of his churches, gathered in his name, enemy of their enemies, as he has always been.[86]

Crespin makes it clear that at the time they were attacked, these people were faithfully preaching the Gospel in: 'true purity and sincerity of doctrine'.[87] The status of the alpine Vaudois as an integral part of the Reformed Church did not appear to be a matter of controversy.

In explaining his choices in this section, Crespin made reference to the fact that he was selecting incidents and events, telling the reader that: 'memorable things are cited in the history of the persecutions and wars conducted since the year 1555 against such peoples as deserve to be raised and understood'.[88] Amongst these is an incident where the Minister of Angrogne had his nose slashed by a local man while preaching and was attacked by a wolf which ate his nose, in turn ('An admirable and notable judgement of God', Crespin opines in the margin).[89] This fantastic story is couched in terms of hear-say: 'this is notoriously known by all the land'.[90]

Reminding us that the example of Barthelemy Hector shows us the lengths to which the Parlement of Turin would go to fight Protestantism, Crespin details the travels of two Commissioners of the Parlement into the valleys to question the inhabitants about their links to Protestantism. Though one simple farmer admits he has had his son baptised at Angrogne, because: 'Baptism is administered there as follows the rule of Jesus Christ.'[91] He is saved from punishment when, in a providential example of, as Crespin noted in the margin: 'God gave voice to poor idiots to confound the great and wise of the world.'[92] This farmer thereby gains the

110   *The alpine Vaudois in the 1550s and 1560s*

inspiration to challenge the judge's authority to enact summary judgement on him. Instead he argues that the president of the court: 'Wrote and signed with his hand how he discharged such a sin, & that he took it on himself and on those close to him', and astonishes the commissioner into freeing him.[93] Meanwhile, the Parlement's Commission carries on its

> goal that the people of the said valleys would be reduced to obedience to the Pope on pain of confiscation of persons and possessions. But the effect of this constancy would be by order hereafter demonstrated in the death of certain martyrs of the people executed for the same cause.[94]

In 1564, this mention of further martyrdoms is no longer there. Instead, the further efforts of the Commission are met with appeals to the Royal Court, and a year of delay during which the Vaudois of the area were able to live in peace, as: 'the Mass then ceased in all of Angrogne and in many other places', and preaching began to take place openly.[95] Although the monks and priests kept plotting to bring the Parlement's repression back to the valleys: 'God did well overthrow the councils and plots of his enemies, for the mass for that time ceased in Angrogna & in many other places'.[96] Here, as in Mérindol and Cabrières, the monarchy is only able to delay persecution, while divine providence in invoked to explain the successes of the Vaudois.

The same section was included in the 1570 edition of the *Livre des Martyrs* as well, and Crespin did not alter it greatly from what he had presented in 1564. The sub-headline has been changed to remove the word 'poor': we are now simply discussing the 'peasants of the Piedmont valleys', while Crespin has changed a closing description of the community from: 'the Vaudois people' to 'the people called Vaudois', an example of the distinctive term Vaudois fading from emphasis in these later works.[97] The tale of Jean Martin Trombau (now named) losing his nose to the wolf is presented in italics this time, perhaps furthering Crespin's attempt to distance his book from a slightly outlandish tale, while still allowing it to be retained.[98]

Crespin continued the story of the Piedmontese Vaudois in the conclusion to the 1564 edition of the martyrology, suggesting by its placement that it may have been a late addition. Indeed, later in the conclusion Crespin mentions the latest of possible additions: the martyrdom of a certain Augustine Marlorat, who had been executed in February 1564.[99] The Vaudois portion takes two paragraphs of the nearly two folio pages that make up the general conclusion.

After a discussion of the themes of the book as a whole, Crespin moves onto the events of 1560–61 in Piedmont, which were 'of fresh memory'.[100] Crespin gives the group their Vaudois identity, referring to the community as: 'the poor Vaudois people of Lucerne and Boby'.[101] The bulk of the first of two paragraphs dealing with the Vaudois in the conclusion centres on the unusual death of the labourer Odoul Gemet in the Lucerne Tower rather than the Savoyard incursion into the valleys. Torn apart by beasts, Gemet's death is notable primarily for its savagery, rather than for any fortitude he himself showed, and Crespin includes a citation: 'these things, so barbarous & inhumane, have been revealed by some of the same soldiers: & since attested by worthy men of faith'.[102]

The second paragraph on the Vaudois briefly describes an early crisis of faith amongst them because of the persecutions. They were: 'marvellously distressed', and 'they had not preached as per their custom'.[103] But the sacrifice of Gemet and others gave courage to them to: 'restart the sermons, but secretly and quietly', in order to keep out of trouble with the Duke and with the soldiers until their emissaries returned from Verceil, at which point they intended to preach openly once more – an example of the Vaudois instinct to hide their faith under a bushel which was such a divide between them and the Genevans.[104] The conclusion then moves on to other topics, and we hear no more of the Vaudois until the next edition of the *Livre des Martyrs*.

1570 saw Crespin expand upon these events in Piedmont, increasing what had been two paragraphs to five and a half folio pages. As he had in 1564, Crespin described the Vaudois as a Church and a community, rather than through the story of one exemplary martyr. It was a group which was becoming increasingly visible, and in conflict with the state of Savoy. By 1560 the Vaudois were receiving Reformed ministers trained in Geneva; they famously mounted armed resistance to a Savoyard expedition against them, and duly won concessions and rights in the Capitulation of Cavour.[105]

The account of the fighting in Piedmont, and the Treaty of Cavour in the 1570 martyrology begins on page 573 verso, closely after Pascal's martyrdom, which ends on page 556 verso. Between the two was placed an account of the Conspiracy of Amboise. The juxtaposition of the Vaudois' struggle with Savoy, and the Protestant situation in France, is suggestive of the questions about the use of resistance to authority then current, and presents an example of necessary and successful armed resistance to one's ruler.

Crespin's narrative begins by introducing the Capitulation: 'an accord was made in these times, on the subject of religion, between the Duke of Savoy and those of the valleys of Piedmont, called Vaudois, which was the 5th of June, 1561'.[106] Crespin then goes on to relate the good state of relations between the Duke of Savoy and 'those of the valleys of Piedmont, called Vaudois'. Indeed, he had: 'no subjects more faithful & obedient, that these, though they follow a different religion to him'.[107] Eventually, Satan: 'by rumours, ruses, and wickedness irritated the Duke against his own subjects'.[108] In practical terms, this meant that the Papal Legate: 'employed all of his means to convince him that it was his duty to

112 The alpine Vaudois in the 1550s and 1560s

exterminate all of the Vaudois, who did not hold the religion of the Pope'.[109] The Vaudois resist this gathering persecution by arguing before the Duke that they are being persecuted solely for the sake of their religion, a point which again carries with it the implication that this was unusual or unexpected, and which again clearly echoes the Augustinian definition of martyrdom.[110] Reported conversations between the Duke's representatives and the Ambassadors of the valleys also emphasise that the Vaudois were willing to submit in all things, save their faith.[111] Throughout this passage the text refers consistently to 'the Vaudois' and 'the Vaudois Churches'; later in the same section he prefers the term 'those of the Valleys' or similar formulations. The use of Vaudois more often appears in the introductions and conclusions of sections, which were written by Crespin, as opposed to the body of the text, which was very often taken verbatim from elsewhere. Thus it seems that the use of the term 'Vaudois' was preferred by Crespin to the more circumlocutory labels used by some of his sources.

Before the Savoyard forces get under way, the narrative describes a period of persecutions and executions. Crespin mentions by name a couple named Mathurin and Jeanne, alongside a Jean de Carquignan, who fell into the hands of the Duke's forces, though they are not given separate accounts of their own. The constancy and resolve of de Carquignan, who had already been imprisoned many times 'for the cause of the Religion' as he met his death are mentioned, but few details are given.[112] At the same time, we are told, monks at Pignerol raised a mob of peasants to march against the minister of S. Germain, M. Jean, and had him tortured by roasting over a deliberately low fire to increase his torment.[113] Carrying echoes of the capture and execution of Heindrichs van Zutphen in 1524 at the instigation of the local clergy, this suborning of the peasantry by monks may have been the easiest way to explain a popular assault on a Protestant minister.

These small snapshots of extra-judicial martyrdoms only occupy a few hundred words, while the primary focus of the account is on the Savoyard army assembled and sent against the valleys of Angrogne and Lucerne. Between 4,000 and 5,000 men were sent with a mission to 'putting all to fire and blood', but were opposed by small bands of the locals, who managed to stave them off with little loss.[114] After some fruitless negotiations, a second campaign led to the capture of fourteen prisoners, of whom a dozen were freed. Of the two who were taken into captivity, one was strangled almost immediately, while the other was Odoul Gemet, who was killed by wild animals, as described in the 1564 edition. In 1570, this story was reproduced almost verbatim from 1564 (under the name Odoul Gemel), but with two minor alterations – the reference to his having died 'invoking the name of the Lord' was removed, and the truth-claim which previously rested on soldiers confirmed by 'worthy men of faith' now relies upon the soldiers only.[115] In the next passage, Crespin no longer refers to the man as having been a 'martyr' – indeed, in the 1570 edition, Gemet/

The alpine Vaudois in the 1550s and 1560s   113

Gemel's death is not said to have had any effect on his compatriots.[116] This death was clearly being reduced in status: Crespin appears to have questioned not only the man's faith, but the very accuracy of the account, and its impact on other Vaudois. Like the tale of the wolf biting off the man's nose, the death of Odoul Gemet was reduced almost to a piece of hearsay. As in the earlier telling, the people decide that: 'the word of God they have not preached as was usual'.[117] However, while 1564's version has the Vaudois deciding to covertly resume preaching until their messengers return, 1570's tells us that they used this time to: 'fortify some passages, and block some paths' and procure supplies for their defence, for they would rather die than accept the Mass.[118] Resistance is now portrayed without apology, and is considered to be preferable to secret worship and covert preaching, in direct contrast to the account of only six years previously.

The effectiveness and tenacity of that resistance is epitomised by a few paragraphs which depict the actions of Captain Truchet, who was one of the bravest Savoyard officers. This part is written as if it were taken from a laudatory document, for it is full of praise of the man, and consistently refers to the Vaudois simply as 'those of the said Valleys', which may suggest the authorship of an outsider. In any case, Truchet succumbs to the resistance of the seemingly outmatched locals and is killed by a large stone wielded by a youth. This incident prompts the vanguard of the invading force to carry huge wooden shields before them thereafter.[119] It is this sort of dogged resistance that led to the Savoyards relenting, and agreeing to sign the Capitulation of Cavour.

This is reproduced in full; it names each valley to which the treaty is to apply, and pardons the residents of each for acting against the Duke.[120] According to its provisions, the Vaudois ministers are allowed to visit the sick, and: 'exercise other things necessary to their religion', though preaching to an assembly is still banned, and indeed, ministers must be licenced.[121] A clutch of locales are allowed to have a single minister shared between them, and given exemption from attending Mass. The treaty was signed by a host of observers; the names Crespin reproduces are those of the Syndics and ambassadors of the valleys.[122] He also credits the Duchess of Savoy, François I's daughter Marguerite, who was sympathetic to Reformed beliefs, for helping to impose the deal. Indeed, her support was part of an important development for the Vaudois. As their connections with the wider Reformed Church grew in the 1550s and 1560s, they were increasingly able to draw on international support, particularly from the Swiss cities. Their Protestant credentials, as demonstrated in works like the *Livre des Martyrs*, made it much easier for these states to support them than it had been in earlier generations.[123]

This treaty was a major triumph for the Vaudois, an early example of a Catholic ruler giving up his power over religious affairs in his land, and granting toleration.[124] Crespin makes the most of this, proclaiming that

114   *The alpine Vaudois in the 1550s and 1560s*

God has shown: 'All things turn well for those who love and believe in him', and, in the margins: 'the profit of the sufferings of this world'[125] Crespin stresses the devotion of the people, particularly that they gave prayers before defending their land and after battle. In the conclusion, for the first time in this passage since the introduction, we find the word 'Vaudois', though only in a marginal note, the addition once again by Crespin.[126] This section on the valleys of Piedmont is focussed more on resisting an unjust ruler, and on the winning of tolerance and concessions through armed force, than it is on the beliefs and structures of the Vaudois. Crespin spent much of his writing on the Provençal massacres in justifying the faith and reactions of his subjects; in this instance the major document is the treaty of peace and toleration rather than a confession of faith. Some of the previous concerns appear again, however. As in Provence, the relationship between the Vaudois and their ruler had supposedly been easy until the Catholic Church somehow turned the secular forces against the dissenters; even after armed conflict there was no underlying conflict between prince and subjects. The position of Crespin as a Geneva-based author must be considered in these depictions of Savoy, whose relationship with Geneva during this period was frequently tense. Although there must have been some temptation to glory in a Reformed victory over the Duke of Savoy, and to depict him as a persecutor, Crespin deployed the same sort of caution as characterised in his depictions of France, and instead tried to shift any blame to others.

Conclusion

Crespin's concern with the Vaudois was both relatively slight, and extremely well-sourced. For both practical and doctrinal reasons, his concern was almost entirely with those sections of the Vaudois community who were in contact with the church in Geneva, and he did not spend a great deal of time discussing the history of the Vaudois before the year 1530. For the fifteenth century, the Lollards and the Hussites are much better represented, a circumstance that is likely the result of the available sources. Once contact had been made, however, Crespin had direct access to first-hand accounts, and was able to describe both martyrdoms and the armed resistance against the Duke of Savoy. While the earlier discussion (in the *Livre des Martyrs* and in the *Histoire memorable*) of the Vaudois origins and persecution of the 1540s centred on the Provençal communities, the passages on communities in Piedmont, Savoy, and in Calabria were current enough to require new updates with each new edition.

Outside of the Mérindol confession of faith discussed in the previous chapter, the bulk of the theological content in Crespin's depiction of the Vaudois came from the letters and personal statements of the martyrs themselves. These are almost entirely Genevan-educated men, such as Varagle, Pascal, or Hector, whose theological roots were in Calvin's

The alpine Vaudois in the 1550s and 1560s 115

writings, not Vaudois traditions. Of the individual martyrs, only Gonin represents an earlier tradition, and we are not given much about his beliefs, save that he was one of the leading figures in bringing the Vaudois into the Reformed fold. In both the account of Mérindol and Cabrières, and in the description of the Piedmontese valleys preceding Martin Gonin's notice, Crespin had included comments derogatory of the pre-reformation faith of the Vaudois. The arrival of the missionaries from Geneva provided the martyrology with material that could be cited without reservation, as it was both detailed and orthodox. As Euan Cameron has noted, this had important implications for gaining international support for the Vaudois at times of persecution; it would have had a similarly encouraging effect on the readers of the *Livre des Martyrs*.[127] Doctrinally and politically, the Vaudois in Savoy and Italy were becoming hard to distinguish from the mainstream Reformed Church, and the martyrology reflected a particularly optimistic version of this idea.

The other major topic of concern to Crespin seems to have been the relationship of the Vaudois to temporal power. His concerns seem to have been complex: he was concerned not to portray the Vaudois as seditious, or as violent (hence the omission of the military action taken by the men of Mérindol and Cabrières from his chronicle of the period 1540–45), while at the same time celebrating the armed resistance in Piedmont. Crespin seems to have been concerned to preserve respect for secular authority amongst his readers; at several points he excused secular leaders for their role in the persecution of the Vaudois, or at least mitigated their involvement.

In Calabria, it is Satan who begins raising suspicion against Jean-Louis Pascal.[128] The massacres in Provence are said to be driven by the plotting of ecclesiastical authorities at Avignon. The fighting in the Piedmontese valleys is caused by Satan disrupting the previously excellent relations between the Vaudois and the Duke of Savoy, and exacerbated by the plotting of monks and priests.[129] The mob which attacked the minister of St Germain was mustered and led by monks.[130] Not only do Crespin's martyrs do nothing to pique the anger of the authorities, so too any action by the authorities against the Vaudois is portrayed not as a legitimate and just action of government, but part of a scheme concocted by Satan, or the Catholic Church, or perhaps the two working in tandem. This dynamic also helps to explain why these communities, which had often lived peacefully for some time, suddenly found themselves under attack, though we might consider that increasing religious tensions after the 1530s, and the arrival of the Genevan ministers themselves, also played an instrumental role.

This is clearly related to the question of Nicodemism, or of the ability of the Vaudois to live in Catholic areas in relative anonymity. Just as the arrival of Reformed doctrine transformed the medieval pattern of Vaudois beliefs on Protestant principles, so too in Crespin the arrival of a Genevan

116 *The alpine Vaudois in the 1550s and 1560s*

minister clarified the religious situation in an area, and drew battle lines between Vaudois and Catholic. In Mérindol: 'after they were communicated to Basle with Oecolampadius, with Capito and Bucer at Strasbourg, & to Berne with Berthold Haller', the Vaudois began to reform their ways: 'in such a manner, that the noise came up to the notice of Parlement, the bishops, priests and monks'.[131] In Calabria, Jean-Louis Pascal had no sooner arrived in Italy than Satan created: 'a great noise through all the country, that a Lutheran had come from Geneva, who wastes all by his doctrine. Everyone murmured, some grinding their teeth, others crying that he should be exterminated with all of his followers.'[132] It was only after contact with the Reformers that Martin Gonin was taken prisoner and executed. In the absence of a minister, the reaction of the Vaudois appalled by the death of Odoul Gemet was first to abandon their preaching, and then to: 'restart the sermons, but secretly and quietly'.[133] Crespin mentioned the hardships and persecution faced by the Vaudois in the centuries before the Reformation, but in the *Livre des Martyrs* their suffering was largely a product of their contact with the Reformed Church.

Despite these major issues involving the Vaudois, Crespin continued to include them, and to include new notices involving them as well. The Vaudois were important to the Genevan Church, who sent their first mission of trained ministers to Piedmont, not France.[134] These were events, often on a large scale, happening relatively near to Geneva; until the outbreak of the Wars of Religion, it was the Vaudois who saw the most overt persecution, and the most militarised response. Crespin was willing to tinker with the attested beliefs of the Vaudois, and he seems to have been disingenuous about their supposed pacifism, but they were too important to him to exclude, perhaps because of their outsized role as victims of the 1540s and 1550s.

Notes

1 Jean Crespin, *Recueil de plusieurs personnes qui ont constamment endure la mort pour la nome de N. S. Jesus Christ* ([Geneva], 1554), p. 656.

2 Robert Kingdon, *Geneva and the Coming of the Wars of Religion to France, 1555–1563* (Geneva: Droz, 2007), p. 2.

3 Gabriel Audisio, *The Waldensian Dissent: Persecution and Survival, c.1170–c.1570* (Cambridge: Cambridge University Press, 2008), p. 185.

4 Euan Cameron, *The Reformation of the Heretics: The Waldenses of the Alps, 1480–1580* (Oxford: Clarendon Press, 1984), pp. 193–94.

5 Jean-François Gilmont, 'Aux origines de l'historiographie vaudoise du XVIe siècle: Jean Crespin, Étienne Noël et Scipione Lentolo', in *Collana della Societa di Studi Valdesi, 9: I Valdesi e l'Europa* (Torre Pellice: Claudiana, 1982), p. 193.

6 Cameron, *Reformation of the Heretics*, p. 132. Audisio, *The Waldensian Dissent*, p. 163.

7 Cameron, *Reformation of the Heretics*, p. 184.

8 Cameron, *Reformation of the Heretics*, p. 183.

The alpine Vaudois in the 1550s and 1560s 117

9 Jean Crespin, *Actes des Martyrs* ([Geneva]: Jean Crespin, 1565), pp. 138–39.
10 Jean Crespin, *Recueil de plusieurs personnes qui ont constamment enduré la mort pour le nom de Nostre Seigneur* ([Geneva]: Jean Crespin, 1555), Vol. I, pp. 394–400.
11 Crespin, *Recueil de plusieurs personnes* (1555), p. 395.
12 Crespin, *Recueil de plusieurs personnes* (1555), p. 395.
13 Crespin, *Recueil de plusieurs personnes* (1555), p. 396.
14 Crespin, *Recueil de plusieurs personnes* (1555), p. 396.
15 Crespin, *Recueil de plusieurs personnes* (1555), p. 397.
16 Crespin, *Recueil de plusieurs personnes* (1555), p. 398.
17 Crespin, *Recueil de plusieurs personnes* (1555), p. 394.
18 Crespin, *Actes des Martyrs* (1565), p. 138.
19 Crespin, *Actes des Martyrs* (1565), p. 138.
20 Gilmont, 'Aux origines de l'historiographie', p. 197. Cameron, *Reformation of the Heretics*, p. 2.
21 Jean Crespin, *Histoire des vrays tesmoins de la verité de l'Evangile* ([Geneva: Jean Crespin], 1570), sig. *a* [viii verso].
22 Crespin, *Recueil de plusieurs personnes* (1555), Vol. I, p. 400.
23 Crespin, *Recueil de plusieurs personnes* (1555), Vol. I, p. 400.
24 Cameron, *Reformation of the Heretics*, p. 145.
25 Crespin, *Actes des Martyrs* (1565), p. 154.
26 Robert Scribner, *Religion and Culture in Germany (1400–1800)* (Leiden: Brill, 2001), p. 245.
27 Crespin, *Actes des Martyrs* (1565), p. 154.
28 Crespin, *Actes des Martyrs* (1565), pp. 154–55.
29 Crespin, *Actes des Martyrs* (1565), p. 155.
30 Crespin, *Actes des Martyrs* (1565), p. 154. Crespin, *Histoire des vrays tesmoins* (1570), p. 94 verso.
31 Jean Crespin, *Troisieme Partie du recueil des martyrs* ([Geneva]: Jean Crespin, 1556), p. 142.
32 Kingdon, p. 56.
33 Kingdon, p. 56.
34 Crespin, *Troisieme Partie du recueil des martyrs* (1556), p. 142.
35 Crespin, *Troisieme Partie du recueil des martyrs* (1556), pp. 143–44.
36 Crespin, *Actes des Martyrs* (1565), p. 643. Many of the letters can be found in *Calvin Opera Omnia* XV, e.g. cols 689–91, 707–09, 805–09.
37 Crespin, *Troisieme Partie du recueil des martyrs* (1556), pp. 195–96.
38 Crespin, *Troisieme Partie du recueil des martyrs* (1556), p. 198.
39 Crespin, *Troisieme Partie du recueil des martyrs* (1556), pp. 144–45. Crespin, *Actes des Martyrs* (1565), p. 625.
40 Kingdon, p. 70.
41 CO, XV, col. 576. Kingdon, p. 56.
42 Jean Crespin, *Cinquieme partie du recueil des martyrs* ([Geneva: Jean Crespin], 1564 [1563]), pp. 12A–30A.
43 Gilmont, 'Aux origines de l'historiographie', p. 197.
44 Crespin, *Cinquieme partie du recueil des martyrs* (1563), p. 12A.
45 Crespin, *Cinquieme partie du recueil des martyrs* (1563), p. 16A.
46 Crespin, *Cinquieme partie du recueil des martyrs* (1563), p. 15A.
47 Gilmont, *Jean Crespin: Un éditeur réformé du XVIe siècle* (Geneva: Droz, 1981), pp. 246–48.
48 Crespin, *Cinquieme partie du recueil des martyrs* (1563), p. 402.
49 Crespin, *Cinquieme partie du recueil des martyrs* (1563), p. 402. Gilmont, 'Aux origines de l'historiographie', p. 187. Cameron, *Reformation of the Heretics*, p. 158. Robert Kingdon, Jean-Francois Bergier, and Alain Dufour (eds)

118 *The alpine Vaudois in the 1550s and 1560s*

Registres de la Compagnie de Genève au temps de Calvin, Vol. II (Geneva: Droz, 1962), p. 74.

50 Crespin, *Cinquieme partie du recueil des martyrs* (1563), p. 398.
51 Crespin, *Cinquieme partie du recueil des martyrs* (1563), p. 423.
52 Crespin, *Cinquieme partie du recueil des martyrs* (1563), pp. 413–15.
53 Crespin, *Cinquieme partie du recueil des martyrs* (1563), pp. 398, 402–11. Cameron, *Reformation of the Heretics*, p. 159.
54 Crespin, *Cinquieme partie du recueil des martyrs* (1563), p. 407.
55 Crespin, *Cinquieme partie du recueil des martyrs* (1563), p. 421.
56 Crespin, *Cinquieme partie du recueil des martyrs* (1563), p. 423.
57 Gabriel Audisio, *Les Vaudois: Histoire d'une dissidence XIIe–XVIe siècle* (Paris: Fayard, 1998), p. 272. Crespin, *Recueil de plusieurs personnes* (1554), p. 657. See Martin Gonin in Crespin, *Recueil de plusieurs personnes* (1555), p. 394.
58 Audisio, *Les Vaudois*, p. 272.
59 Jean Crespin, *Cinquieme partie du recueil des martyrs* ([Geneva]: Jean Crespin, 1564 [1563]), pp. 516–95. Gilmont, 'Aux origines de l'historiographie', p. 198.
60 Crespin, *Actes des Martyrs* (1565), p. 969.
61 Crespin, *Cinquieme partie du recueil des martyrs* (1563), p. 516.
62 Crespin, *Cinquieme partie du recueil des martyrs* (1563), p. 516.
63 Crespin, *Actes des Martyrs* (1565), p. 969.
64 Crespin, *Cinquieme partie du recueil des martyrs* (1563), p. 517.
65 Crespin, *Actes des Martyrs* (1565), pp. 969–70.
66 Crespin, *Actes des Martyrs* (1565), p. 970.
67 Crespin, *Cinquieme partie du recueil des martyrs* (1563), p. 519.
68 E.g. Crespin, *Cinquieme partie du recueil des martyrs* (1563), p. 529.
69 Crespin, *Actes des Martyrs* (1565), p. 982. This letter was published in the larger editions after 1564, something Crespin had promised in the 1563 edition.
70 Crespin, *Actes des Martyrs* (1565), p. 982.
71 Crespin, *Actes des Martyrs* (1565), p. 972.
72 Crespin, *Histoire des vrays tesmoins* (1570), p. 544 verso.
73 Crespin, *Actes des Martyrs* (1565), p. 870. Audisio, *Les Vaudois*, p. 273.
74 Gilmont, 'Aux origines de l'historiographie', pp. 198–99.
75 Gilmont, 'Aux origines de l'historiographie', pp. 198–99.
76 Gilmont, 'Aux origines de l'historiographie', p. 188.
77 Gilmont, 'Aux origines de l'historiographie', p. 199.
78 Cameron, *Reformation of the Heretics*, p. 160.
79 Cameron, *Reformation of the Heretics*.
80 Audisio, *The Waldensian Dissent*, p. 199.
81 Audisio, *The Waldensian Dissent*, p. 200.
82 Audisio, *The Waldensian Dissent*, p. 200.
83 CO XVI, cols. 102–04.
84 Audisio, *Les Vaudois*, pp. 92, 277.
85 Crespin, *Cinquieme partie du recueil des martyrs* (1563), p. 30.
86 Crespin, *Actes des Martyrs* (1565), p. 870.
87 Crespin, *Cinquieme partie du recueil des martyrs* (1563), p. 31.
88 Crespin, *Cinquieme partie du recueil des martyrs* (1563), p. 31.
89 Crespin, *Cinquieme partie du recueil des martyrs* (1563), p. 31.
90 Crespin, *Cinquieme partie du recueil des martyrs* (1563), p. 31.
91 Crespin, *Cinquieme partie du recueil des martyrs* (1563), p. 32.
92 Crespin, *Cinquieme partie du recueil des martyrs* (1563), p. 32.
93 Crespin, *Cinquieme partie du recueil des martyrs* (1563), p. 32.

The alpine Vaudois in the 1550s and 1560s   119

94 Crespin, *Cinquieme partie du recueil des martyrs* (1563), p. 32.
95 Crespin, *Actes des Martyrs* (1565), p. 871.
96 Crespin, *Actes des Martyrs* (1565), p. 871.
97 Crespin, *Histoire des vrays tesmoins* (1570), p. 457 verso.
98 Crespin, *Histoire des vrays tesmoins* (1570), p. 457 verso.
99 Crespin, *Actes des Martyrs* (1565), p. 1085.
100 Crespin, *Actes des Martyrs* (1565), p. 1085.
101 Crespin, *Actes des Martyrs* (1565), p. 1085.
102 Crespin, *Actes des Martyrs* (1565), p. 1085.
103 Crespin, *Actes des Martyrs* (1565), p. 1085.
104 Crespin, *Actes des Martyrs* (1565), p. 1085.
105 Audisio, *Les Vaudois*, p. 278.
106 Crespin, *Histoire des vrays tesmoins* (1570), p. 573 verso.
107 Crespin, *Histoire des vrays tesmoins* (1570), p. 573 verso.
108 Crespin, *Histoire des vrays tesmoins* (1570), p. 573 verso.
109 Crespin, *Histoire des vrays tesmoins* (1570), p. 573 verso.
110 Crespin, *Histoire des vrays tesmoins* (1570), p. 573 verso.
111 Crespin, *Histoire des vrays tesmoins* (1570), p. 574 verso.
112 Crespin, *Histoire des vrays tesmoins* (1570), p. 573 verso.
113 Crespin, *Histoire des vrays tesmoins* (1570), p. 574 recto.
114 Crespin, *Histoire des vrays tesmoins* (1570), p. 574 recto.
115 Crespin, *Actes des Martyr* (1565), p. 1085. Crespin, *Histoire des vrays tesmoins* (1570), p. 574 verso.
116 Crespin, *Histoire des vrays tesmoins* (1570), p. 574 verso.
117 Crespin, *Histoire des vrays tesmoins* (1570), p. 574 recto.
118 Crespin, *Histoire des vrays tesmoins* (1570), p. 574 recto.
119 Crespin, *Histoire des vrays tesmoins* (1570), p. 575 recto.
120 Crespin, *Histoire des vrays tesmoins* (1570), p. 575 recto.
121 Crespin, *Histoire des vrays tesmoins* (1570), pp. 575 verso, 576 recto.
122 Crespin, *Histoire des vrays tesmoins* (1570), p. 576.
123 Cameron, *Reformation of the Heretics*, p. 198.
124 Audisio, *Les Vaudois*, p. 279.
125 Crespin, *Histoire des vrays tesmoins* (1570), p. 576 verso.
126 Crespin, *Histoire des vrays tesmoins* (1570), p. 576 verso.
127 Cameron, *Reformation of the Heretics*, p. 198.
128 Crespin, *Actes des Martyrs* (1565), p. 970.
129 Crespin, *Histoire des vrays tesmoins* (1570), p. 573 verso. Crespin, *Actes des Martyrs* (1565), p. 871.
130 Crespin, *Histoire des vrays tesmoins* (1570), p. 574.
131 Crespin, *Recueil de plusieurs personnes* (1554), p. 658.
132 Crespin, *Actes des Martyrs* (1565), p. 970.
133 Crespin, *Actes des Martyrs* (1565), p. 1085.
134 Kingdon, p. 2.

4 'Luther n'est point mort pour moy'
Crespin and Lutheran martyrs

Unlike the Hussites or the Lollards, the Lutherans depicted in the *Livre des Martyrs* were contemporary with Reformed martyrs. The Lutherans and Reformed had an often overlapping tradition and membership, especially in Germany and the Low Countries. Crespin implicitly treated the Lutherans as being part of his own era, and used Luther as the dividing line between the 'old times' and the present age reform and of persecution. Although Crespin involved himself in several confessional disputes between the Reformed and Lutheran churches, and was very well informed about the issues at stake, he treated Lutherans in this context as part of the same movement. Within the martyrology, Crespin does not identify Lutheran martyrs as being in any way different from Reformed ones; there are none of the caveats that mark his description of Vaudois or Hussite beliefs. Indeed, as Brad Gregory has noted, he appears to have actively made changes to the text to create conformity on important issues.[1]

With the Lutherans, the *Livre des Martyrs* had reached a group who, despite some fundamental conflicts, were treated as essentially part of the same movement. This was an approach that closely followed Calvin's, who worked to maintain cooperation with the Lutherans while revealing his disagreement with their tenets, and his frustration with Luther himself.

Luther and Protestant history

In his later editions, Crespin used the coming of Luther to indicate the beginning of a new era in the history of the Church. However, this arrangement was slow in developing. In the first edition, 1554's *Recueil de plusieurs personnes* ... Luther is not mentioned. Instead, the Hussites are immediately followed by a Lutheran martyr, Heindrichs van Zutphen. This passage is also used to outline the growth of: 'the word of God in many places', and provide a connection to the earlier Hussite material.[2] In a short paragraph before van Zutphen's account, Crespin argued that with the resurgence of the gospel had come a resurgence in the travails of the Church: 'the persecutions of the primitive Church had begun again ... nevertheless it was required in these times to be sealed with the blood of

Crespin and Lutheran martyrs 121

these faithful martyrs, and by their deaths'.[3] The Lutherans are thus given an important position in this understanding of ecclesiastical history, as full members of the restored Church following directly from the Hussites, but concrete details are lacking of the early years of the movement, and Luther himself is not named. Just as Calvin himself played a very small part in the martyrology, these martyrs are not described as followers of any one figure, but members of the True Church. As one Vaudois martyr was to put it, they wished to be described as Christians, not Lutherans, for 'Luther did not die for me'.[4]

In 1555, the structure of this section had been changed by the rearrangement of the early martyrs, which added a number of Lollards executed during a: 'large persecution in England against the true and faithful servants of God'.[5] These additions were included, however, in a new quire, and the link to the Lutherans in the opening paragraph of van Zutphen's account remained unchanged. Luther was, however, mentioned by name for the first time, in the context of Jan Hus' supposed prophecy. As we have seen, Crespin reproduced Luther's own 1531 version of the Hussite prophecy, to the effect that:

> the great restorer of the Gospel, a man of holy memory, Martin Luther, had otherwise understood this remark: we put here his interpretation as it was written in his commentaries on Daniel. Saint Jan Hus (he said), has been the precursor or forerunner of the contempt of the Papacy, as he to them prophesised in spirit, saying: After one hundred years you will answer to God and to me ... surely, they have cooked the Goose (for in the Czech language, 'Hus' means 'Goose'), but they will not cook the Swan, who comes after me. And certainly that which has happened has verified and proved the prophecy. For [Hus] was burned in the year 1416, & in our times the difference and debate which had begun over the Pope's pardons [indulgences], started in the year 1517.[6]

The later octavo editions, up to the *Cinquieme Partie* of 1563, were primarily concerned with more recent events, and so presented Crespin with little opportunity to revisit the role played by Lutherans in this new age of the Church. It was with the collection of previously published work into the compendium edition of 1564 that Crespin had a chance to revisit this information, and to apply to it some historical context and background which had not been included in the past.

This was first achieved by discussing Luther in the introductory section to the book, the: 'Advertisement to all Christians, on the utility of returning to the reading of these Collections of Martyrs', which acted as a book-by-book summary and table of contents. In this, Luther is placed immediately after Savonarola within Book One through another reference to Hus' prophecy:

122 *Crespin and Lutheran martyrs*

EIGHTEEN years after the death of the aforesaid martyr [Savonarola], this light grew a few degrees stronger, being enlightened in many places by the Christian doctrine which is necessary to the Church. It was the year 1517 when Martin Luther began by asserting in articles, preaching, and public writings the truth of the Gospel: the hundred and first year after the death of Jan Hus, who is said to have predicted to the bishops who were at Constance in the year 1415, when he was put to death, 'After a hundred years you will answer to God and to me.'[7]

The other mention of this prophecy, in the context of the section on the Hussite Wars in 1564, remained almost as it had been in 1555, although the complementary language directed towards him was entirely removed. Despite the extra space and significance devoted to him, Luther was no longer described as 'the great restorer of the Gospel' or a 'man of holy memory', as he had been in 1555, instead he was simply 'Martin Luther'.[8] This passage was supplemented elsewhere: Luther did not yet merit (and the format could not provide him) his own entry in the martyrology, but he was featured in a couple of places before the first Lutheran martyrs, as a way of establishing some context for this era of ecclesiastical history, and new wave of persecutions.

The section ostensibly devoted to the fifteenth-century Florentine friar Savonarola, which appeared in the 1564 and 1570 editions of the martyrology was, primarily, a discussion of the history of the Church, and praise for Martin Luther. As we have seen, the two figures had been placed together in the 'Advertisement', as well. Crespin appears to have derived this passage from Philip Melencthon's biography of Luther, the *Vita Lutheri*, likely through the medium of John Foxe's martyrology, either in English or in Latin, which informed many sections of this edition of the *Livre des Martyrs*.[9] Crespin took a different approach to his source material, which, in Foxe, was fulsome in its praise of the German reformer, and which rehearsed a great many of Luther's early debates, such as against Eck, and against Karlstadt.[10] Where Foxe had suggested that Luther was: 'not only gouerned by humain diligence, but with a heavenly light, considering how constantly he abode within the limites of his offyce', was omitted. Instead, Crespin began his section at the point which suggests that God, above all, should be credited for the good works of Luther.[11] Otherwise, it followed in its plan, if not in every detail, the passage that had been printed in the *Actes and Monuments* the year previous. Thus the passage begins with a short introduction to Luther:

In these times the Lord brought forth Martin Luther to better show His truth to the world. And such was the virtue in this praiseworthy person, in so much as he used all of the gifts of God in all reverence. Notwithstanding, we must principally render grace to God, that

Crespin and Lutheran martyrs 123

through [Luther] gave to us the light of the Gospel, & we must guard and extend the memory of His doctrine.[12]

This was the beginning of a history of the Church which took nearly three-quarters of the space supposedly dedicated to Savonarola. Luther's emergence was followed with a robust defence of the 'doctrine of the Gospel against Epicurians and hypocrites'.[13] The passage next traces what a marginal note described as 'Four mutations since the Apostles': the heresies of Origen, of Pelagius, the age of the mendicant friars and Albertus Magnus, and that of Thomas Aquinas.[14] To combat these, 'God brought forth Saint Augustine' who: 'if he had judged the differences of today', would side with those

> who have since been named Lutherans. For about the free remission of sins, the justification of faith, the usage of the Sacraments, & other points of the Christian religion he agrees entirely with those who are of the side of truth.[15]

Despite the intervention of the apparently proto-Lutheran Augustine, innovation and decline continued within the Church. Wealth grew, most strikingly amongst the mendicant orders, which Crespin refers to as 'vermin'. Equally disturbing was the growth of the study of scholastic philosophy, which 'convert ecclesiastical doctrine into profane philosophy', especially that of Thomas Aquinas, who gave such: 'labyrinthe and false opinions, that theologians of good and pure judgement have always desired another manner of teaching, more familiar and pure'.[16] Scholasticism is held responsible for having allowed doctrines of idolotry, for denying 'free pardon' for sins, and all other manner of false doctrine.[17] The passage concludes by describing: 'dark times, of horrible things, and a confusion so pernicious, that when one thinks of it, all the body is in a trembling of horror & of fear'.[18] God, however, has willed that the

> muck and the fish be again cleansed in these times out of the Evangelical fountain, and has given us not only the true Doctors & Fathers, but also of these true Martyrs in witness and more ample confirmation of the true doctrine.[19]

According to this passage, Luther's emergence was a key part of God's plan. Like Augustine (and Peter Vualdo) before him, he was described as being 'raised by God'. The conformity of the Reformation with the Fathers of the Church was asserted, and the reader was assured that the great Doctor would surely have taken the Lutheran side were he alive in the sixteenth century. Where Foxe's version of this passage believed that St Augustine 'wold speake for vs, and defend our cause. Certenlye, as concerning free remissyon, iustification by faithe, the vse of the Sacramentes

124 *Crespin and Lutheran martyrs*

and indifferent thinges he consenteth wholy with us', Crespin's version of this was careful to specify Lutherans as the objects of Augustine's approval, as we have seen above.[20]

In 1570, the section on Savonarola was changed, supplemented with new information and stripped of the passages describing Luther and Church history. The references made to Luther elsewhere in the 1564 edition were largely retained: this edition's introductory *Dispositions et Argumens des VIII Livres* was largely unchanged from the previous version, although it omitted the reference to Luther's preaching.

The biggest change came shortly afterwards, when Luther was prominently, though not exclusively, featured as a subject of the 'Historical discourse on the horror of the times which preceded the coming of Martin Luther, and other faithful Doctors of the Gospel'.[21] This four-page section gave a history of Church controversy from the Council of Constance to the Ninety-five Theses, with the main focus being on the first decades of the sixteenth century. Although similar thematically to the history presented in the Savonarola section of 1564's edition, 1570's version of the events was entirely new. It focussed initially on Church councils, touching on the Council of Basel, where the Greek Orthodox delegation, pleading for help against the Turks, managed to fall out with the Catholic Church over transubstantiation, and on the Fifth Lateran Council, where the cardinals would 'confirm the old idolotries, the errors, abuses, superstitions, & the tyranny of the Pope'.[22] Further advancing the idea of a Church in decline was a disagreement between the Cordelier and the Jacopin (Dominican) orders about the birth of the Virgin Mary, which ended with a Dominican statue of the Virgin being created at Berne which seemed to weep and move miraculously, until the forgery was discovered and its creators sentenced to be burned in 1509.[23] It is in this context that Crespin places a passage about God '(by his infinite mercy)' bringing forth Luther.[24] In this edition, though, he has changed the description of the reformer:

> who was of the order of Augustinians. [Luther] was of a small but honest household, and without any credit in the world, a man remaining of good spirit & of singular knowledge. God gave him a marvellous courage, & armed him with an incredible constancy. By these means, and by using the word of God, he untangled all of the greatest difficulties with which the Popes had embroiled the poor world.[25]

Crespin once again made reference here to Hus' prophecy:

> There had already been five hundred years that the Popes had oppressed the Church by their tyrannies, and one hundred years had passed since the Council of Constance.... Jan Hus had predicted that there would be such changes in the Roman Church, that could not be diverted by fire nor any such cruelty.[26]

Crespin and Lutheran martyrs   125

The depiction of Luther here is highly complimentary, suggesting, again, that he was directly inspired by God, and had begun the process of saving the world. As a marginal note read: 'In what misery was the world when God gave life to Luther'.[27] Whilst 1564's edition had compared Luther to Augustine, indirectly, that of 1570 made mention of Christ himself:

> Luther began to war against the sale of indulgences, and chased from the Church of Jesus Christ a number of merchants, overturning their tables, stools, and stalls. That is to say he began to destroy, spiritually, the altars of idols, & by the word of God overturned all the fanfares of the hypocrites, who showed themselves with pretty lustre here & there in the temples.[28]

At another point Luther is described as: 'being touched by a true sentiment of the fear of God, established his positions which are found in the first volume of his works'.[29] Luther's battles with Tetzel, the aid of the Duke of Saxony, and his dispute with Erasmus are all recorded. Crespin even found a formula for describing Luther's stance on the Eucharist, a controversial subject with Calvinists, in positive terms:

> There followed the disputes about the difference of human and divine laws: of the execrable profanation of the Lord's Supper: of fairs and sales of masses, of the application of the Eucharist other uses for which it had not been instituted, as if it served others than those who received it ... Luther therefore wanted to better declare his doctrine, putting forward that which he must summarily hear of true penitence, of the remission of sins, of faith, of indulgences, and of several other points of the Lord's doctrine.[30]

As a result of this hard work, and the God-given assistance of Philip Melancthon, amongst others: 'Little by little the Church of the Lord tightened its grip, and the reign of the Pope fell into decadence.'[31] Crespin saw this moment as the distinct re-emergence of the Gospel: 'by which [we] recognise the great benefit of this Evangelical light regiven in this time, and thanks that it has pleased him to give the clear fountains of the Gospel after the swamp of monastic doctrine'.[32] He gives credit, however, to those who fought to keep it alive through the dark ages, comparing them to Moses, who never got to set foot in the Promised Land:

> And do not believe that it was any less a miracle to have maintained the Church against the tyranny of the Pope, and so much hatred, threats, & violence of the kings of all Europe than was the deliverance of the people of Israel from the servitude of Egypt. Believe also that restitution of the pure doctrine after such an abyss of so many superstitions and opinions of men, is as much or more miraculous than the

126 *Crespin and Lutheran martyrs*

deliverance & steering of the said people through the Red Sea and through the deserts, to the promised land.[33]

This passage puts into place more clearly than any other Crespin's conception of the history of the Church and the place of the Reformation, within it, especially Luther's role. He had described a dark age of 500 years, during which the Popes tyrannically oppressed the Church, which had to survive underground, like the tribes of Israel wandering in the desert, oppressed by the temporal powers of Europe. The miraculous maintenance of the Church through these years was due to the groups Crespin had just finished depicting – the Lollards and Hussites, as well as more isolated figures like Savonarola. The Vaudois had not yet been discussed at this point in the martyrology, but they too had played a role in this dark period. However, with the actions of Luther (and the 'other doctors', Wittenburg theologians like Caspar Creuziger, Justus Menius, and Justus Jonas, who are briefly named), this period had ended. Whatever else Crespin might write about Luther, he had played a decisive role in the restoration of the word of God, and this was a different achievement to that of the Vaudois, who held on to a faith that was imperfect, but better than that of the Catholics.

Conflict between denominations

This positive view of Luther is the more remarkable considering the tensions that existed between Lutherans and Reformed at the time that Crespin was compiling his martyrology. A key debate, and the one on which Crespin was most focussed, was one over the exact nature of the Eucharist. The Lutheran doctrine of consubstantiation still required the Real Presence of Christ in the bread and the wine of the Eucharist, an idea to which the Catholic Church held, but which the Zwinglian and Calvinist thinkers rejected.[34] Instead, Zwinglians held a commemorative view of the sacrament, and Calvinists subscribed to an idea of 'spiritual eating'. Their critique of the Mass often relied on biblical statements identifying Christ's place at the 'right hand of God', and thus served equally well to undermine the Lutheran belief in the Real Presence.[35]

There was a rift between those who believed that the celebration of the Eucharist required Christ to physically descend from heaven to be really present in the bread and wine, and those who argued that he remained at the right hand of God at all times until the day of judgement. When defined in these terms, Lutherans found themselves on the same side of the debate as the Catholic Church; as a result, many Reformed attacks on Catholic doctrine were also inherently critical of Lutheran positions.

The dispute had surfaced in 1524, when Luther denounced the Eucharistic views of Zwingli, Jud, and soon Oecolampadius, believing them to be derived from those of Karlstadt; his principal test being that of the Real

Crespin and Lutheran martyrs 127

Presence.[36] The derivation from Karlstadt placed the Swiss reformers in the company of Müntzer and the Zwickau prophets, and effectively beyond the pale.[37] This view shaped events at the Colloquy of Marburg, where Luther famously chalked 'hoc est corpus meum' (this is my body) on the table before Zwingli.[38] Later, in the seventeenth century, this debate would become central to the controversy between denominations over the rite of *fractio panis*, a Calvinist breaking of the bread which served to deny the Real Presence.[39] Calvin, in the *Institutes*, argued strongly against the idea of consubstantiation, which to his mind: 'admits that the bread of the Supper is truly the substance of an earthly and corruptible element, and cannot suffer any change in itself, but must have the body of Christ inserted under it'.[40] He attacked the Lutheran stance for its failure of comprehension: 'they cannot conceive any other participation of flesh and blood than that which consists either in local conjunction and contact, or in some gross method of enclosing'.[41] Indeed, 'they leave nothing for the secret operation of the Spirit, which unites Christ himself to us'.[42]

This was of course an extremely important issue. An entire section of Chapter XVII of Book IV of the *Institutes* was devoted to answering those who, like Luther, objected on the grounds of Christ's statement that: 'this is my body'. Above all, though, both doctrines of the Real Presence, the Catholic and the Lutheran, demanded a ubiquity of Christ: 'unless the body of Christ can be everywhere without any boundaries of space, it is impossible to believe that he is hid in the Supper under the bread'.[43] This, in Wandel's words, 'denied Christ the integrity of his person, as well as of his body'.[44] Calvin posited, instead, that

> though he withdrew his flesh from us, and with his body ascended to heaven, he, however, sits at the right hand of the Father; that is, he reigns in power and majesty, and the glory of the Father. This kingdom is not limited by any intervals of space, nor circumscribed by any dimensions. Christ can exert his energy wherever he pleases, in earth and in heaven, can manifest his presence by the exercise of his power, can always be present with his people, breathing into them his own life, can live in them, sustain, confirm, and invigorate them, and preserve them safe, just as if he were with them in the body; in fine can feed them with his own body, communion with which he transfuses into them. After his manner, the body and blood of Christ are exhibited to us in the sacrament.[45]

Echoes of this debate appears throughout the *Livre des Martyrs*, where under questioning martyrs would denounce the Catholic institution of the Eucharist on the grounds that Christ was at the right hand of God. Martyrs might instead mention that belief in an introductory phrase, a statement of Christology from which other conclusions could be drawn

128   *Crespin and Lutheran martyrs*

about their beliefs. They often mimic Calvin's own words from the *Institutes*, that: 'we deem it unlawful to draw him down from heaven'.[46] The notices of Pierre Bruly, Claude Monier, Pierre Escrivan, Charles Favre, Godefroy de Haemelle, Bernard Seguin, Pierre Naviheres, Denis Peloquin, Claude de Canestre, and Jean Rabec, amongst others, contained some variation on the declaration that: 'Christ is up in heaven and he is sitting at the right hand of God the Father'.

The argument had existed before Calvin, as well. The famous placards of 1534, as reproduced in Crespin, carried many of the same ideas, describing:

> public idolotry, when falsely one gives to understand, that under the kinds of bread and of wine, Jesus Christ is contained and covered, bodily, really, and personally, in flesh and in blood ... the holy scripture and our faith do not teach this, but is entirely contrary, for Jesis Christ after his resurrection ascended to heaven, and is seated at the right hand of God the Father almighty, and will come to judge the living and the dead.[47]

It was not necessary for the martyrs to have read the *Institutes* to have absorbed this lesson. Similar critiques appear in the French Confession of 1559, which has been attributed to Chandieu, and was based on a Genevan draft which was probably the work of Viret, Beza, and Calvin.[48] This stated that Christ:

> ... feeds and nourishes us truly with his flesh and blood, so that we may be one in him, and that our life may be in common. Although he be in heaven until he come again to judge all the earth, still we believe that by the secret and incomprehensible power of his Spirit he feeds and strengthens us with the substance of his body and of his blood. We hold that this is done spiritually ...[49]

This is much stronger language than that of the Genevan Confession of 1536, in which Calvin had also played a part. That document makes no mention of the whereabouts of the body of Christ, though it stresses that the Supper is a 'true spiritual communion'.[50] In 1541, Calvin's *Short Treatise on the Lord's Supper* argued that:

> It was a serious fault not to recognise that which is so well testified in the Scripture, touching the Ascension of Jesus Christ, that he had been received in his humanity to heaven, where he remains until he descends to judge the world.[51]

This document pointedly traced the history of the dispute between the denominations, as well. Calvin wrote:

Crespin and Lutheran martyrs 129

Luther thought [Zwingli and Oecolampadius] meant to leave nothing but the bare signs without their spiritual substance. Accordingly he began to resist them to the face, and call them heretics.... It was Luther's duty first to have given notice that it was not his intention to establish such a local presence as the Papists dream: secondly, to protest that he did not mean to have the sacrament adored instead of God ... after the debate was moved, he exceeded bounds as well in declaring his opinion, as in blaming other with too much sharpness of speech.[52]

In his private writings, Calvin had also expressed some ambivalence about Luther and his legacy. In a 1545 letter to Melanchthon, Calvin wrote of Luther: 'we must always be on our guard, lest we pay too much deference to men. For it is all over ... when a single individual, be he whosoever you please, has more authority than all the rest' before referring to his 'overbearing tyranny'.[53] Writing to Bullinger in November 1544, Calvin struck a balance between annoyance at Luther's attacks on Bullinger over sacramental matters, and respect for his achievements:

I do earnestly desire to put you in mind ... that you would consider how eminent a man Luther is, and the excellent endowments wherewith he is gifted, with what skill, with what efficiency and power of doctrinal statement, he hath hitherto devoted his whole energy to overthrow the reign of Antichrist, and at the same time to diffuse far and near the doctrine of salvation. Often I have been wont to declare, that even though he were to call me a devil, I should still not the less hold him in such honour that I must acknowledge him to be an illustrious servant of God. But while he is endued with rare and excellent virtues, he labours at the same time under serious faults ... I wish, moreover, that he had always bestowed the fruits of that vehemence of natural temperament upon the enemies of truth, and that he had not flashed his lightning sometimes also upon the servants of the Lord.[54]

Calvin concluded by warning Bullinger against exposing to their opponents any divisions: 'you will do yourself no good by quarrelling, except that you may afford some sport to the wicked, so that they may triumph not so much over us as over the Evangel'.[55] Calvin's attitude towards Luther was complex, therefore, reflecting annoyance with the German's fractiousness, and disagreement with his doctrine, while at the same time showing respect for the man and his achievements. Above all was a concern not to engage in open conflict with him, for the sake of the wider Protestant movement. Crespin seems to have been sensitive to Calvin's approach on this subject, for the *Livre des Martyrs* follows exactly this line, as one might expect from the printer and publisher of many of Calvin's works.

130   Crespin and Lutheran martyrs

In his *Short Tract on the Lord's Supper*, when trying to explain how the division between the denominations had arisen, Calvin felt that: 'Luther failed on his side ... it was Luther's duty first to have given notice that it was not his intention to establish such a local presence as the Papists dream'.[56] Yet Crespin equally admits that Zwingli and Oecolampadius were also at fault for the disagreement, for they had 'laboured more to pull down what was evil than build up what was good; for though they did not deny the truth, they did not teach it so clearly as they ought to have done'.[57]

These distinctions became complicated, as Protestants of all stripes were referred to as Lutherans by the authorities, a habit which seems to have been resented by several of the heretics in the *Livre des Martyrs*. Martin Gonin was depicted as objecting to the term in 1536 on the grounds that: 'I am not a Lutheran, nor would I be, for Luther did not die for me, as did Jesus Christ, whose name I do carry, and for whom I wish to live and die.'[58] This was not an objection to the idea of Lutheranism, so much as the use of a term which sought to depict the martyr as part of a small sect, rather than a true Christian. Godefroy de Haemelle elaborated on the idea, and objected less to the title, when requesting his interrogators not to refer to him as heretic or schismatic: 'But rather a poor sinning Christian, or Lutheran, if you would not like to call me otherwise: however I would not like to be called Lutheran nor heretic, but poor Christian sinner, if you please.'[59] To be referred to as Lutheran was part of the experience of martyrdom in France, up to the early 1560s.

Crespin was certainly aware of these differences and arguments. He was strongly involved in the printing of theological polemic – a quarter of his titles, making up 8 per cent of his total printed volume, were of this genre – and several of these engaged with the Lutherans.[60] In total, Crespin published twelve titles arguing against the Lutherans on the subject of the Eucharist, double the number he had published against Catholic doctrine on the same subject.[61] His authors included leaders of the Reformed Church like Calvin, Bullinger, and Beza, and lesser-known figures such as Pincier, Simone Simoni, and Eraste. These appeared in Latin and in French (in one case, in parallel editions in each language) against the Lutherans Westphal, Andrae, Flacius, and Schegk, amonst others.[62] These were mainly produced in the 1560s and 1570s, following an earlier burst of printing on the subject of Nicodemism in the first half of the 1550s.[63] Crespin also published works that engaged in other controversies against the Lutherans: in 1558, Crespin was denied permission by the council of Geneva to print a work by the Flemish reformer Jan Utenhove. The work in question complained at Utenhove's treatment at the hands of Danish and Northern German Lutherans, who, when he had fled Marian England, had turned him away for his 'heretical opinions'.[64] Calvin later explained to Utenhove that the printing ban had been made to 'calm the controversy between Lutherans and Calvinists'.[65] Controversy between the

Crespin and Lutheran martyrs 131

denominations, then, was significant enough to be of concern to the Genevan council, and Jean Crespin was involved as one of the more prolific publishers on the Reformed side. These divisions were of course well-known amongst Catholics, as well. Jean Vernou's letter to the Ministers of Geneva, printed in the *Troisieme Partie*, describes an interrogator who: 'knew well the differences of Luther, Zwingli, and Oecolampadius, & that he had seen the books of our Doctors'.[66]

Although a dedicated Calvinist, Jean Crespin was not a dedicated opponent of Luther's. The first work Crespin produced on his own, without the assistance of Claude Baudius, was an edition of Luther, and in the late 1550s Crespin translated and published five of Luther's biblical commentaries.[67] Luther even made it into Crespin's polemical publishing on other subjects: 1558's *Conseils et advis de plusieurs excellens personnages, sur le process des temporiseurs*, for example, used content taken from the German reformer.[68] Crespin also published more sensational works. His presses were responsible for the French edition of Luther and Melanchthon's work on the two miraculous monsters the 'Monk-Calf' and the 'Papal Ass'.[69] Crespin's activity translating Lutheran texts into French was influential enough that W.G. Moore suggested one could refer to the post-1550 era of Lutheran translation into French as that of Jean Crespin.[70]

This period of Lutheran printing was a relatively short one, however. Crespin did most of his printing of Lutheran works by the end of 1558, and almost all of his counter-Lutheran polemics were published after 1560. The Genevan Council seems to have similarly set itself against Luther at that time, refusing to license a 1559 reprinting of Melanchthon's *Commonplaces*, and then allowing a translation of the Magdeburg Centuries to be made on the condition that it was done without 'the doctrine of the Lutherans and Germans which they have collected'.[71]

The representation of Lutheranism in the *Livre des Martyrs* was shaped by the demands of the martyrological format, as the depictions of the Peasants' War, or the Vaudois, also were. In all of these examples, Crespin was happy to point his reader to a fuller, historical, account of events, often one he had published himself. The demands of martyrology were different, and driven above all by doctrinal concerns.

In so far as he was depicted at all, Luther was seen as a praiseworthy individual, with laudable personal characteristics, and a prime mover in the Reformation. He taught what was described as 'pure doctrine', and was compared to Moses, having been 'raised by God' to 'untangle all of the greatest difficulties with which the Popes had embroiled the poor world'.[72] The Reformation, for Crespin, seems to have started with Luther in 1517 in a way that the movements of the Hussites and the Vaudois could not match. Unlike those groups, there are no direct comments about the shortcomings of Lutheran doctrine.

The differences of opinion between Lutherans and the Reformed Church were generally effaced in the *Livre des Martyrs*, but in such a way as to

132 Crespin and Lutheran martyrs

give prominence only to the Genevan interpretation of such matters. On the most important, and thus most controversial issue, that of the Eucharist, the differences between the denominations were largely not explored. Instead, the Lutherans were depicted without expressing any views on the subject, while from the Reformed side martyr after martyr put forward his (and occasionally her) doctrine in a formula which implicitly denied the Lutheran stance as well as the Catholic. This was not a practice restricted to Crespin. On the other side of this confessional divide, Ludwig Rabus is known to have edited out a positive reference to the Genevan leadership when reproducing the account of the murder of Juan Diaz, and he avoided citing Crespin in the fifth volume of his *Historien der Martyrer*, despite drawing large amounts of the material in it from the French martyrology, decisions Robert Kolb attributes to confessional rivalry.[73]

There were relatively few Lutherans included in the *Livre des Martyrs*, most of them figures who were executed in the 1520s. As we have seen, Luther came to be portrayed as a key figure in the return of the true faith in Crespin's scheme. The Lutheran martyrs were of course part of that world-historical movement, but on a more prosaic level, they formed the spine of the martyrology's coverage of the events of the 1520s. Most of the major Lutheran martyrs Crespin presented were executed between 1523 and 1529, and there are very few from after 1534, as the number of Lutheran martyrs fell and the prosecution of heresy in France began in earnest.[74] These accounts were primarily added in the first three editions, from 1554 to 1556, and were mainly composed of information found in pamphlets published in the 1520s in Germany. Many of these martyrs were killed in relatively unofficial contexts, rather than in formal trials and executions. Some of the pamphlets were written, or contributed to, by major figures such as Luther himself; as a consequence most of Crespin's German martyrs were relatively well-known before he included them in the *Livre des Martyrs*. As the Vaudois and the Lollards connected the sixteenth-century reformation to the primitive Church, so on a much smaller scale the Lutherans of the 1520s provided a link between the Reformed Church and the more recent past.

Voez and Esch

Henry Voez and Jean Esch were considered by many to be the first Lutheran martyrs, executed in Brussels in 1523. Members of Antwerp's Augustinian community (as Luther had been) headed at one point by the future martyr Heindrichs van Zutphen, they were arrested along with the rest of their monastic community for their Lutheran preaching.[75] They and Lambert Thoren (or Thorn) were the only members who refused to recant, and were thus sentenced to death. They were included by Crespin in the first edition of the *Livre des Martyrs*. Their account seems to have been based on a number of contemporary pamphlets.[76] One of them was a work

Crespin and Lutheran martyrs 133

in German, which purported to have been composed only four days after the event.[77] This was reprinted at least sixteen times in the same year, and must be judged to have been a successful work.[78] Another was a longer (thirty-two page) pamphlet, the *Historia de Duobus Augustinensibus ...* written in Latin, which included a long discussion of the articles of faith professed by Henry Voez. Luther published a letter of consolation to his followers in the Low Countries on the occasion, which was included in a pamphlet alongside a dialogue purportedly between the martyrs and their accusers. This work saw at least two printings.[79] In addition, Luther himself wrote a ballad of the Brussels martyrs, entitled *Eyn newes lyed eyr heben an*; it was his first musical work.[80]

Crespin used the longer pamphlet, the *Historia de Duobus Augstinensibus* as the main source for his section on Voez and Esch. In the 1554 edition, Voez and Esch were introduced with their own title, proclaiming them to be 'De Deux martyrs executez a Bruxelles'.[81] In contrast, the account of Heindrichs van Zutphen, which preceded them, did not have its own title. Crespin did not shy away from describing them as members of the Augustinian order. No context or background is given, but the reader is told immediately that the two were: 'degraded & stripped of their habits as monks, and this at the pursuit of the inquisitor of faith and the theologians of Louvain, because they had not denied or retracted their opinion'.[82]

The two went to their deaths joyfully, proclaiming that they were dying as good and faithful Christians.[83] They made light of their burning, and 'these two servants of God received the crown of martyrdom'.[84] After this narration, Crespin returns to the question of their beliefs, though only in a short paragraph: 'Henry among others was interrogated, if Luther had not seduced him. Yes, he said, as Jesus Christ seduced the Apostles.'[85] He also protested that it was against divine right that clerics should be exempt from temporal jurisdiction, which attacked to some degree the very system which was then trying him.

In 1555, this account was moved earlier in the book, putting them in line with chronology.[86] Voez and Esch were now the first Lutheran martyrdom in the *Livre des Martyrs*. The first paragraphs, introducing the two martyrs and their defrocking, were unchanged. Partway into the second paragraph, however, the account has been expanded. The theological arguments of Voez and Esch were expanded for the 1555 edition. Where in 1554 they were depicted as protesting that they died as good Christians, in 1555 Crespin insisted that: 'they died for the glory of Christ, for the Evangelical doctrine, & for the Apostolic writings, as good and true Christians, and not as heretics or pagans'.[87] Their courageous behaviour at the stake is also given in more detail: now they are described as reciting the Symbol of Faith (Nicene Creed) 'to witness and confess their faith'.[88] This edition also showed Henry Voez explaining his high spirits to a nearby doctor who was puzzled by them. As throughout the rest of the 1555 edition, the references to 'martyrs' are removed. Instead of 'receiving the

134 *Crespin and Lutheran martyrs*

crown of martyrdom', the deaths of the two are now given in the rather more succinct form: 'they suffocated'.[89]

In 1564, the two were again included very early in the martyrdoms from the Reformation. This revision retained and added to the original narrative of the executions, including a series of supporting letters, confessions, and other documents. This expanded section was placed in the first book, shortly after the introduction of Martin Luther there. A short sub-headline gives new context, explaining that:

> all the Augustinians of the city of Antwerp were made prisoners at Villevord, a city renowned for the main prison of Brabant. There were three who for the profession of the truth were long detained. The martyrdom of two is here described.[90]

This is the first mention of a third prisoner, whom we know from the pamphlets to be Lambert Thoren.[91] The position of Voez and Esch as the first martyrs of the Lutheran era is recognised by the long paragraph of historical context which appears here for the first time in Crespin. This starts by placing them within the movement:

> When Luther had begun to publish his doctrine in printed books, they attracted many, and did well in their favour before their adversaries had readied a defence. The Augustinians of Antwerp were not the last: for all that Martin Luther was also from the order he was not suspected, but more quickly agreeable.[92]

Most of these monks were summoned to Brussels by the Bishop of Cambrai to give confessions of faith, but three were more constant, and sentenced to death.

The narrative of their defrocking and execution contains elements used in the 1554 and 1555 editions. Crespin took time to outline the hearing that the three men faced, and the ceremonies surrounding their trial. The youngest of the three, presumably Thoren, was separated from the other two; his fate is not entirely clear, but Luther wrote to him the next year, so he was not executed with the others.[93] When describing the fate of the remaining two, Voez and Esch, the account rejoins the version of events seen in the two earlier editions. While some elements are new, for example, the two request to be delivered from the 'false and abominable priesthood', as they believe in the 'holy universal church', rather than the 'son of God', the bulk of their narrative is the same as before.[94] Crespin then added to the main account by adding a short paragraph after the execution described as: 'Another witness to the constancy of the two Augustinians, taken from another letter.'[95] This simply, as promised, attested to the behaviour of the two men, and listed their judges.

A further, and more substantial addition, again after the execution, was the nearly two-page confession of faith, which contained forty-eight

Crespin and Lutheran martyrs 135

separate articles derived from those appearing in the *Historia de duobus Augustinenensibus*. Crespin appears to have had access to this material before, but not included it until the larger editions. These articles were generally simply stated as professions of belief, though a couple of articles reveal the ultimate origin of this list in the interrogation of Henry Voez: the sixteenth article begins: 'Having been often asked what opinion he had of Martin Luther ...'; these were forms taken from the original text.[96] Crespin omitted twelve of the original sixty-two articles due to their being, as Brad Gregory has suggested: 'insufficiently derogatory of Catholic errors for a 1560s Calvinist. Others were too patently Lutheran'.[97] The changes he made were primarily to articles touching on purgatory, the Mass, and the adoration of the saints.[98]

Certainly, Crespin excluded the first article found in the Latin edition, which had argued that no-one could be banned from reading the works of Luther.[99] He also cut a series of three articles pertaining to the Eucharist, numbered from 16 to 18 in the Latin text. These argued that the Mass should not be considered as a sacrifice of Christ, but rather a commemoration; that the mass was entirely symbolic, and done as a memorial; and that he does not know if the bread remains after the consecration, admitting to doubts over the exact mechanism of the sacrament, and nature of the Host.[100] The thirty-ninth article also touched on the sacraments, and was also excluded; this had argued that only the recipients of the mass benefitted from its celebration (as opposed to, for example, the dead).[101] Similarly, the fifty-third and fifty-fourth articles were removed, which each dealt with the requirement for the mass to be served to the people *sub utraque specie*, in both kinds, insisting in fact that to refuse to do so was against divine law and the teachings of Christ.[102] Contrary to the trend established to this point of omitting discussion of the Eucharist, Crespin chose to retain the forty-third article, which denied any sacrificial utility of the Mass, as Christ's sacrifice on the cross had been sufficient.[103]

These critiques of the Eucharist ran contrary to Catholic opinion, but were not entirely in line with Reformed belief, either, especially in their expressed doubts over the exact nature of the sacrament.

Other articles which were removed were the twenty-fourth, which argued that there was an equality before God of laity and clergy, and the thirty-fifth, which denied the supremacy of the papacy by recourse to questioning St Peter's mission from Christ.[104] The twenty-sixth article was another interrogation of the role of the sacraments in the era of a priesthood of all believers, and downplayed the importance of clerical consecration.[105] These points all dealt with the powers and status of the established Church, and some of the areas of concern, if not the exact doctrines suggested, are reminiscent of the trial of Jan Hus at Constance.

Another group of articles which were removed from the *Livre des Martyrs* dealt with other sacraments. The forty-first article was also removed, this expressed doubt as to whether or not there was a purgatory.[106]

136 *Crespin and Lutheran martyrs*

The forty-fourth rejected the idea of ecclesiastical judgement for private sins, arguing instead that the process of confession and absolutism were the only parts of penance, leaving no space for the system of ecclesiastical jurisprudence.[107] Finally, Crespin's version of the articles omitted the fifty-fifth and fifty-sixth ones, which respectively stated that the consecration of the mass must be offered in a high, clear voice; and a refusal to answer any questions about the veneration of the saints.[108] This last, might be considered, given the circumstances, as an indication that Voez did not subscribe to that particular view, or simply as an instance of happenstance, an indication that he had tired of his interrogation. Given his willingness to criticise so many other aspects of the Catholic cult, however, it might also suggest to a reader that Voez was conflicted about the point, or that he lacked the conviction of his beliefs in this one field.

After this extensive exhibition of the faith for which the two men died, the compendium editions of 1564 and 1570 were further expanded by the addition of a six-page (in folio) section entitled: 'Christian complaint made against one, who by the tyranny of infidels & by the fear & horror of death, was finally constrained to deny the truth which he had professed.'[109] This was taken from a later part of the *Historia De Duobus Augustinensibus*, a lengthy passage which concluded that pamphlet. In this, the unidentified author, whom we are presumably meant to identify with either Voez or Esch, lodges complaint against his companions who have abjured. The text is laden with scriptural references, which were cited in the margins, along with small pieces of commentary indicating the direction of the argument. Although the references themselves had been present in the Latin pamphlet, these glosses were inserted by Crespin.

The text is presented in the form of a letter to those who had abjured, hoping to impress upon them the error of their ways, and justifying the decision of the author to defend his faith at the risk of the stake. Drawing upon the ideas of St Augustine, who is cited at length in the first pages, the letter contrasts the worldly benefits of abjuration against the spiritual costs, and ends with a citation from Matthew 16: What shall it profit a man if he gains the world, but at the loss of his soul?[110] Its author is frequently scathing towards his former colleagues, figuring them as the heirs of Judas, and lamenting the opportunity their failure has given to the Antichrist.[111] The letter ends with an enjoinment to turn towards God, and a request that: 'Tell us by letters how your conscience is.'[112] This was the conclusion of their section; there was no afterword or conclusion, their deaths having been described before the insertion of the confession of faith and the correspondence.

Heindrichs van Zutphen

Heindrichs van Zutphen was another martyr who was included from the first, 1554 edition as part of the introduction Crespin presents to the

Reformation era, which follows the sections on Jan Hus and Jerome of Prague, and was thus the first Lutheran martyr to be included in that edition.[113] He did not receive a heading of his own, but was introduced after the paragraph telling of the constancy of martyrs in 'these times', showing that the 'persecutions of the primitive Church had recommenced'.[114] It is depicted as a time of mass conversion, for 'the number of the faithful multiplyed from day to day'.[115] Still in this narrative mode, Crespin tells us that van Zutphen, whom he rendered as 'Henry Supphen', was an excellent martyr, and died at Dietmar, in modern Schleswig-Holstein. Gaspar Tambard and 'another named Jean' are also introduced at this point.

Returning to van Zutphen, we find he originally preached at Autdorff, and had links with Meldorf, which seems to have been the major religious centre for the region, and was an important site for reformers.[116] He had been the head of the Augustinian monastery in Antwerp through its more Lutheran period, when the monks were arrested, and Henry Voez and Jean Esch were burned at the stake.[117] Neither his connection to the Augustinians or, through them, to the two martyrs of Brussels is mentioned in Crespin. Van Zutphen was burned by a mob supposedly stirred up against him in late 1524 by the local ecclesiastical authorities.[118]

Van Zutphen was known personally to Luther, who lamented his death in a pamphlet entitled *The Burning of Brother Henry*, published in early 1525.[119] This text was addressed directly to van Zutphen's congregation in Bremen. Despite strong thematic similarities, and some borrowings, Crespin's introduction does not rely entirely on Luther's. The pamphlet began with an introduction explaining the exceptional nature of the times, stressing that 'in many places both preachers and hearers are daily being added to the number of the saints'.[120] Crespin again introduced the theme of a return to the persecutions of the primitive church, while omitting references to 'the saints'. Like Luther, he uses the introduction to mention in passing a series of other martyrs, several of whom were collected in Crespin: John and Henry at Brussels (this is Voez and Esch), Gaspard Tamber (or, in Luther, Casper Tauber), George ('Buchfuhrer') in Hungary, and an unnamed ex-monk, in Prague.[121] This is followed, in each version, by more praise for the importance of these martyrs, though Crespin follows a different rhetorical line to Luther. Where Luther expresses confidence that: '[t]hese are the ones who, with their own blood, will drown the papacy and its god, the devil', Crespin opts for the less combative: 'It is a very certain thing, that all these and others who suffer such a death, endure a passion which is truly Christian, and not such a death as thieves and brigands endure.'[122]

Similarly, both narratives go on to praise the institution of martyrdom, Luther stressing the legitimacy that martyrs gave to his cause: 'we read of no instance where a Christian died for the doctrine of free will and of works, or for anything but the Word of God', and that 'to die for God's

138 *Crespin and Lutheran martyrs*

Word and faith is a priceless, precious, and noble death'.[123] Crespin stresses the suffering of the martyrs as part of 'the people of God', and the mockery 'for the name of the Lord Jesus' before setting up an awkward comparison with Moses, who was honoured in Egypt.[124] The two accounts then diverge further. Luther addresses the congregation of Bremen, and explains his purpose in publishing the pamphlet, which is to commemorate van Zutphen, and to hope that his death spurs more conversions, as God must have intended 'to use this murder for the benefit of many in that land and by it lead them to eternal life'.[125] He then gives a short, twenty-point exposition on the Ninth Psalm (which in the pamphlet Luther cited as the Tenth).[126]

For the narration of the death of Heindrichs van Zutphen, Crespin follows Luther's pamphlet relatively closely. Both accounts introduce him as arriving (only Luther specifies that it is in Bremen) in 1522, having been expelled from his previous post. In Luther this is given as Antwerp, in Crespin, it is Autdorff.[127] Luther spends much time describing how the Bishop of Bremen attempted to have van Zutphen arrested, but was defeated by Henry's learning and procedural manoeuvring, all of which Crespin omits.[128] In 1524, citizens from Meldorff (near Dithmarschen, in Schleswig-Holstein) approached van Zutphen and asked him to preach there. Both accounts make it clear that he asked the permission of his Bremen parish before leaving; again, Luther's account is longer, and devotes more time to Henry's discussions with his parishioners, presenting genuine cases for and against.[129] Having accepted, and moved to Meldorff, van Zutphen came to the attention of the local Jacopins, who came to agreement with the forty-eight regents or governors of the district to 'put this heretic monk to death' in Luther's words, or as Crespin has it, they: 'secretly took, by night, this good person Henry [van Zutphen], and without any dey burned him, before the men of the country could be alerted',[130] This embellishment by Crespin aside, it is Luther's account, again, which goes into detail about the meeting of the regents, and the specific dates and places of events. The order to have Heindrich arrested took nearly a week to be acted upon, partly because the population of Meldorff rejected it; in the meantime he was able to preach several sermons, whose subjects are related. Van Zutphen apparently preached especially on justification by faith, using text from Matthew 1, and Hebrews 7, which contained themes of rejection of the existing priestly orders.[131] Crespin, again, cut all mention of this delay and of the sermons, let alone their content, and instead follows the initial decision with action: 'Around five hundred peasants, whom they assembled a half-league from Meldorf, apparently initially reluctant, move on the town.'[132] From this point on, when the primary action is the capture and death of Heindrichs, the two accounts are much closer in content.

Both versions are careful to detail that the Jacopins themselves had taken an active role in preparing the mob, 'Furnished with torches & light

Crespin and Lutheran martyrs 139

for their lighting', and giving them 'three casks of beer from Hamelburg'.[133] The mob's pillaging and destruction of the curate's house is also emphasised in each. Henry was soon dragged naked into the street, bound. Crespin omits passages from Luther describing Heindrichs' long night locked in a cellar while the crowd grew drunk and boisterous.[134] In the morning, he was condemned to be burned alive (Luther notes that he had not even had a hearing, while Crespin does not) by a bribed magistrate. Heindrichs van Zutphen was accused of 'Preaching against the Christian faith, and the mother of God.'[135] At the site of the execution, the crowd became uncontrollable, attacking Heindrichs before he could be burned. This torture lasted for two hours (Luther notes that the fire would not light) before he was finally led up a ladder to be thrown into the fire. At this point Luther tells us that Heindrichs began to recite the Creed, while Crespin simply says that he was 'invoking the name of God'.[136] With van Zutphen still alive, one of the mob attempted to strangle him, while another's halberd slipped and pierced his chest before he was finished off by a man with a club. Crespin reproduces all of these painful details from Luther, though the description of this botched killing as a 'glorious end' is his alone. Luther's description in the final lines of Heindrichs as a 'holy martyr' is retained as 'happy martyr' in Crespin's rendering, though it would soon be changed.[137]

The depiction of Heindrichs van Zutphen remained stable throughout its publication in four editions of the *Livre des Martyrs*, although there were alterations to the format in which it was presented. The 1555 edition was divided more clearly into sections, and the early mentions of other martyrs were separated from the story of Heindrichs van Zutphen, with a separate header reading 'Gaspar Tamber and others'. This gap is further expanded by the insertion of the account of the deaths of Henry Voez and Jean Esch.[138] When van Zutphen was mentioned again, he was granted his own title, and header. Numerous minor changes were made to the text in 1555, perhaps the most notable of which was the change of the final line from describing Henry as a martyr, as would be expected from this edition.[139]

In 1564, more substantial changes were made, most of them small cuts with the result that the account is noticeably shorter. Much of van Zutphen's brutal treatment at the hands of the mob was removed from this edition: the specific claim that the people: 'did not cease to hit him with pikes and halbards' becomes 'did not cease to torment him in all ways'.[140] However, the designation of Heindrichs van Zutphen as a martyr was restored. The 1570 edition changed very little from this version, though it emphasised that the mob was initially forced to march on Meldorff, and a line which underlined their later hostility towards van Zutphen was omitted.[141] These changes suggest Crespin was concerned with portraying him as a pure martyr, which would involve the intervention of the authorities and some sort of trial, rather than as the victim of a lynch mob.

140   *Crespin and Lutheran martyrs*

Overall, Crespin drew the major events of van Zutphen's death from Luther, but on almost every subject he seems to have lost specificity. Luther's text named a great number of the actors in it, gave dates, details of Heindrichs' preaching, and much more information about the various discussions which took place (most notably, the mission by the mob to arrest van Zutphen, and the various manoeuvers undertaken by the Dominicans to have him arrested). These changes are perhaps explicable given the different contexts of the two works. Luther's was written in Germany, within a couple of years of the events depicted, and such naming and shaming gave the work more veracity, but would also have increased its impact. Crespin's work, a generation later, and in another country, would have had less interest in naming names. In addition, though not surprisingly, Luther's entire exposition on the Ninth Psalm was removed. This makes the account of Heindrichs van Zutphen's martyrdom a much more narrative-based passage, and one which is very light on any sort of doctrinal content. In addition, some of the omissions and alterations seem to have been made to no clear purpose, such as the alteration of Antwerp to Autdorff. Crespin would have known Antwerp, and may well have already associated van Zutphen with it, so the reasons for the name being changed remain unclear. This and other small errors and omissions may well be the result of an intervening work or translation which transmitted Luther's pamphlet to Geneva, providing Crespin with a rather different text.

Leonard Kaiser

Another well-known Lutheran martyr to be included in Crespin's first edition was Leonard Kaiser, a former student of Luther's who was burned at Passau in 1527. Luther had written both to Kaiser and about him, and this writing was included as a postscript to the German-language pamphlet produced about Kaiser's martyrdom in 1527: *Histori oder das warhaftig geschicht, des leydens vnd sterbens Lienhart Keysers seligen, etweñ Pfarrers zü Waytenkirchen, von des heyligen Euangelij vnd Götlicher warheyt wegen zü Passaw verurteylt, vnd zü Scherding verbrandt, am Freytag nach Laurentij, im jar MDXXVII.*[142] The Lutheran pamphlets of 1527 seem to have been the original source material for the narrative which appeared in the *Livre des Martyrs*. These saw multiple publications in multiple locations, all dated 1527; their content was consistent, even through changes in printing format.[143]

At least one hostile pamphlet was produced as well. Johann Eck, who had been one of Kaiser's interrogators, published in 1527 a pamphlet in quarto entitled: *Warhafftige handlung, wie es mit herr L. Käser zu Schärding verbrent ergangen ist wider ain falsch, erdicht und erlogen büchlin vormals dar von, in namen des dichters aussgangen,* but it would appear that Crespin made no attempt to engage with this work, even to rebut it.

Crespin and Lutheran martyrs 141

Given the nearly thirty-year interval and the linguistic divide between these works and Crespin, it is also quite possible that there was an intermediary work. The pamphlet briefly explains that Kaiser, from Raab, near Passau, became a student at Wittenberg (he apparently held holy orders). On being informed that his father was dying, he returned home, where he was arrested, tried, and executed. The focus, as one would expect, is on the trial of Kaiser, and on his pronouncements at the time of execution, including within it a detailed confession of faith. The final three pages of the pamphlet are given to a document which is titled: *Eyn trostbrieff Doctor Martini Luthers/gemeltem Lienhart Keyser seligen in seynem gefenctnus zugeschickt.*[144] This was the letter of consolation to Kaiser, which Luther wrote to him in prison.

The main narrative makes clear how seriously the authorities took the trial of Kaiser: listed as attending are the Bishop of Passau, the *Weybischoff*s of Passau and Regensberg, two abbots, two provosts, and assorted other ecclesiastical figures.[145] The central section of the pamphlet focuses on Kaiser's confession of faith, presented in eighteen separate articles. Uncontroversially for a Protestant, he argues that man is justified solely by belief in God (article 1), that only the sacraments of baptism and of the Eucharist should be accepted (article 2), that the sacrament in both kinds, the *Sacrament zu Wittenberg* as he termed it, was appointed by Christ (article 5).[146] The third article attacks the Eucharist quite strongly, arguing that the Mass is no sacrifice for the living, and cannot help the dead.[147] The fifteenth article stated that Christ was the sole intermediary between man and God, the eighteenth argued that 'man has no free will in divine matters'. Several argue for clerical marriage. The sixteenth, in phrasing very similar to Jerome of Prague's, rejected holy days, and perhaps even the Sabbath, by declaring that 'all days are the same before God'.[148]

Crespin's account, which remained stable throughout the editions, is significantly shorter than that of the pamphlets. Of the three paragraphs, one is dedicated to the arrest of Kaiser, and one to his execution. This leaves little room for his trial, which made up the bulk of the original source, but which in Crespin only took a single paragraph. Instead of the eighteen articles included in the German pamphlets, Crespin gives four articles of faith confessed by Kaiser. These are first, that faith alone saves, which matches the first article in the German pamphlet. The second is that works are the fruits of faith. The third is that the Eucharist is neither an offering, nor a sacrifice, which may be a truncated reading of the third article. Fourth, that there are three kinds of confession (of faith, of charity, and to solicit council and consolation), a statement which has no obvious counterpart in the original.[149] These represent a series of alterations and redactions from the pamphlet. Not all of the articles which Crespin removed were necessarily ones which might be expected to cause trouble for his project. Many were minor from his point of view, such as the second article, arguing for only two sacraments. Yet he changed Kaiser's

142   Crespin and Lutheran martyrs

confession out of all recognition, in distinct contrast to his handling of the confession of Heinrich Voez, and again we may speculate about intermediate texts.

Crespin made editorial decisions as well. The consolatory letter by Luther, which concluded the pamphlets, was never included in Crespin, despite Luther's commentary on Kaiser being alluded to in the introductory sentence. The scene of Kaiser's burning, too, was altered. In Crespin, Kaiser's execution was depicted as being somewhat botched.

> And because it was not a large fire, the executioner threw his body, half-burned, on the wood again: then he took his pole and again cast it into the fire: & in this way completed the burning. Witness the end of the days of this good Martyr Kaiser, dying for the testimony of the truth of the Son of God.[150]

This is a rather toned-down version of what had appeared in the pamphlet, which described Kaiser's body refusing to burn, necessitating the executioner to cut him to pieces while still alive.[151] This may reflect a move away from the depiction of the miraculous and providential by Crespin, who did occasionally distance himself from tall tales told about the deaths of his martyrs. It is also a decision which finds parallels in the toning down of the depiction of the gory end of Heindrichs van Zutphen in later editions of the martyrology.

The presentation of Kaiser's notice was little changed between the 1554 and 1555 editions of the *Livre des Martyrs*. Alterations were made to the first line of the account, which changed from 'the martyrdom' to 'the constance of M Leonard Kaiser'. Other similarly small changes were made to the language: the early description of Kaiser as 'good and holy' becomes simply 'good', and a second mention of him as a 'martyr' was removed in accordance with the changes ordered by the Council of Geneva.[152] In 1554 Kaiser was introduced, without separation from the account before (of Heindrichs van Zutphen), as 'Leonard Keyser, dict l'Empereur'.[153] The account itself was newly placed in the 1555 edition, appearing after the material on the Peasants' War, as Kaiser's death in 1527 would demand.

In 1564, the account was again altered. The introductory line, in keeping with the increased emphasis given to historical context in the folio editions, read: 'Since Germany has been cultivated by the word of God, she has given great persons, who not only have taught this truth, but also have been cruelly killed by the Princes holding to the party contrary to it.'[154] In 1570, the introductory line was expanded to explain the source of the information about Kaiser: 'Martin Luther and others give witness to the present Martyr.'[155]

George (Winckler), Ministre de Hall

George (Winckler), Ministre de Hall was first included as a sort of footnote to Heindrichs van Zutphen in 1554's edition of the *Livre des Martyrs*. Van Zutphen's notice had concluded with a single paragraph noting that 'In this same time many were secretly drowned for the word of God, in the Rhine as in other rivers, in which the dead bodies of those have since been found.'[156] Among them was a certain M. George, who preached at Hall.[157] All we are told of his preaching in this edition is that he administered communion in both kinds, which enraged the priests enough that they incited 'brigands and murderers' to beset him, giving an example 'of what rage leads those that the Antichrist has in his pay, to band against the Gospel'.[158]

The changes of 1555, which added titles and discrete sections to the accounts, did not touch Winckler, who remained in the final paragraph of Henry's account, just before the title for Jean Castellan.[159] Winckler is deployed to stand in as an example for these supposed masses, a technique of synecdoche which Crespin used elsewhere.

> And among others there was a certain master George, who preached at Halle; who, especially as he gave the Eucharist in the two kinds, was [hunted] by the brigands & murderers appointed by the priests, & villainously killed near to Aschembourg.[160]

This short account remains the same in the compendium editions as well, changing only a final line which refers to the rage of the Antichrist against the Gospel, and, in the final edition, brigands and murderers becomes brigands & thieves.[161]

It would appear that George of Hall was George Winckler, for whose sake Luther had written another tract, *Trost-brief an die Christen zu halle*, which was published in 1527 in at least three locations. It initially ran to fourteen pages, and saw multiple editions printed at Wittenberg and elsewhere.[162] Winckler had been a priest, and when he began serving the mass in both kinds and married, he was brought for a hearing before the Archbishop of Mainz in Aschembourg.[163] Winckler was released, and on his trip back to Halle, murdered. Luther argued in his pamphlet that 'it was the tyrants of the chapter in Mainz who perpetrated Winckler's murder'.[164] Like the account of the death of Heindrichs van Zutphen, Luther's commentary on Winckler only contains minimal mention of the narrative of his killing. Luther gives a lengthy defence of communion in both kinds, which is many times the length of the narrative directly relating to M. George. More minor points of contention argued that 'if he could choose to be restored to life or to have remained alive, he would reject both and rebuke us for such thoughts', for it would be better to die than to risk falling into error, while there is a suggestion that the deaths of martyrs

144 *Crespin and Lutheran martyrs*

means that 'a great catastrophe is at hand'.[165] It is an instructive point to note the emphasis that Luther placed on the comfort his readers could take from the fact George was killed 'while obeying those in authority', even making a virtue of his co-operation with the Catholic bishop during the Peasants' War 'and opposed the rebels with all his might, to the admiration and love of the bishop'.[166]

Crespin does not appear to have used much of this material, if at all; only the location of Winckler's death, and his doctrine of the communion in both kinds, are included in the account. Much of Luther's text would not have been usable for his purposes, being theological argument by the German reformer; there is no confession of faith from George himself. Combined with the paucity of information provided on the martyrdom, as well, it is unsurprising that George's account in Crespin is so short. However, it also has to be considered that Crespin probably drew his information from an intermediary source. It would be difficult to understand why he might omit useful pieces of information such as George's last name, or the fact that he had been called before the Archbishop, if they had not previously been omitted or muddled in some fashion.

In his 1556 edition, Crespin added only two German martyrs. These were included together as the first two accounts in the volume, possibly on the grounds of chronology, or geography. Indeed, there seems to have been little compelling reason to group them together unless the two accounts came to Geneva together. They were also listed alongside each other in the index, which was arranged by country of origin.

George Carpentier

George Carpentier was the first martyr to appear in the 1556 edition, and was given five octavo pages. His account is apparently that of Jorgen Wagner, given here under an altered name.[167] Carpentier/Wagner's story was given shortly after his death, in a 1527 German-language pamphlet entitled *Eyn new warhafftig vnd wunderbarlich geschicht oder hystori von Jörgen wagner zu München in Bayern als eyn Ketzer verbrandt im Jar M.D.xxvij*, printed possibly at Nuremberg. This six-page work focussed primarily on his confession of faith, which consisted of four articles. These were all included, modified to varying degrees, by Crespin; they are a critique of the Catholic sacraments. Carpentier/Wagner denied that priests could absolve as part of confession, and that God had any Real Presence in the bread of the Eucharist. Most strikingly, he questioned whether one could become blessed through baptism.[168]

In Crespin's rendering, a short subtitle immediately makes a claim for Carpentier/Wagner; he was: 'of Emering, who was burned in Münich, a city in Bavaria, for the doctrine of the Gospel'; this was expanded in 1564 to include a description: 'by which he surmounted the wit of some worldly sages, who subtly approached him to bend'.[169] The passage begins with a claim about German Protestantism which places Germany at the centre of the battle for the truth in these years: 'many excellent persons have been found from the country of Germany, through which the Lord has willed, not only to manifest his truth, but also by the effusion of their blood, witness it, & confirm it'.[170] When the reader is first introduced to Carpentier/Wagner in 1527, he has already been imprisoned, and 'could not stray from the true doctrine, such that there was no question of not proceeding to his condemnation'.[171]

Without any description of a hearing, accusation, or trial, we are told that the sentence of death was pronounced against him, and he was taken to be executed. It was at this stage that his articles were read to the crowd.[172] Crespin included these, from 1564 describing them in the margin as 'Summary of the trial of Carpentier [Wagner].'[173] The first held that he did not believe the priest could, through confession, pardon sins.[174] The second, that he did not 'believe that man could make God descend from heaven'.[175] The third argued that he: 'did not believe that God was enclosed in the bread, that the priest kneads, turns, and re-turns, at the altar'.[176] These first three were very similar to their presentation in the German pamphlet. The fourth article, as presented by Crespin, stated that: 'He does not believe that the Baptism of water itself can make a man blessed.'[177] This had, originally, been rendered in German as: 'claims that Baptism of water does not make a man blessed'.[178] Crespin's rendition, as noted by Brad Gregory, is subtly but significantly softened, by claiming that baptism with water in itself does not make a man blessed.[179] Carpentier/Wagner's views on baptism were potentially Anabaptist, and his death was indeed used in Anabaptist songs.[180] His critiques of the Eucharist were also radical by the standards of 1520s Protestantism, verging towards that used by Karldstadt or Zwingli's conception of the Eucharist as a symbolic gesture, but they were acceptable, even useful, to 1550s Reformed thinking.

The second half of his account shows Carpentier/Wagner challenged by a Master Conrad Sceitter, apparently the priest and preacher of the community. Carpentier/Wagner turns down a chance to return to his home and his family, and is enjoined to: 'believe the sacrament of the altar, & not only the sign'.[181] He also offers a line-by-line commentary on the Lord's Prayer and the Nicene Creed as it is read at his execution. Some of these interjections reiterate his Protestant themes, as when he replies to Conrad's invocation of 'give us this day our daily bread', with: 'Jesus Christ the true bread will today be my food'.[182] Other parts of it are less doctrinal in inspiration; the martyr replies to Conrad's 'deliver us from evil' with a plea to God: 'without any doubt you deliver me: for I in you alone fix my hope'.[183] Finally, offered a mass to pray for his soul, Carpentier requests that the onlookers pray for him until his death (that is, during the burning), rather than after, for when: 'the soul wil be separated from the body, I shall have no need', an implicit denial of the power of intervention, as well.[184] This

146   *Crespin and Lutheran martyrs*

line-by-line commentary on the Lord's Prayer and formal process against Carpentier/Wagner, which became part of his running debate with Sceitter, is also present in the original. In this case, however, Crespin seems to have made a number of cuts which reduced this section, noting about the comments on the Creed that the remainder: 'would be too long to describe'.[185]

The case of Carpentier/Wagner shows Crespin acknowledging, and indeed even promoting, the importance of the German contribution to the opening years of the Reformation, while at the same time obscuring some of the exact details of the doctrine being contested. In this instance, only one of Wagner's four articles posed a challenge to Genevan understanding, and therefore had to be changed.

Pierre Flistede and Adolph Clarebach

Flistede and Clarebach (Clarenbach) were executed in Cologne in 1529. They first appeared in Crespin in the third volume, in 1556, immediately behind Carpentier/Wagner. The account was fairly straightforward. The two were arrested because they 'Did not agree with the Papists, concerning the Eucharist of the Lord and other points.'[186] After being imprisoned for a year and a half, they were finally executed with 'Great regret, lamentation, & compassion of many.'[187] Crespin's account suggests that the clergy of the city – the 'theologians' – were recommending this sentence as necessary to appease God in the face of a new sweating sickness currently spreading, 'commonly called the English sickness', as well as the assaults of the Turks.[188] At their death the two men were said to have defended their faith 'By texts and testimonies of the Gospel.'[189] Clarebach, especially, is mentioned for his youth, eloquence, and learning.[190] In 1564, and 1570, the two appear again, the only alteration being the addition of some marginal notes, and a subtitle explaining that 'the common people blamed the plagues, which the country of Germany sustained then, on the change of Religion'.[191]

Clarebach and Flistede had appeared (with the emphasis on Clarebach) in a pamphlet of 1528 entitled *Ernstliche handlung zwische den hochgelerten Doctorn inn der gotheyt, als mann sie zu Cölln nennt, oder ketzermeyster, vnnd eynem gefangnen genant, Adolph Clarenbach, geschehen zu Cöln erstlich vff Franckenthurn*. This work does not seem to have been consulted at all, however. The two also appeared in Book IV of Rabus' martyrology, along with many of the other German martyrs included in Crespin; Book IV was published in 1556, making it possible, though unlikely, that Crespin could have used it.[192]

Crespin's approach to these German martyrs was driven by the established tradition concerning them. These were figures who had already been given attention by major figures of the Reformation, often in widely distributed and reprinted pamphlets, rather than from the work of Rabus and others. As has been seen, he was not averse to making dramatic changes to these accounts, especially what might be regarded as their most important content: the confessions of faith. However, Lutheran doctrines were not the only reason he might alter the account of a German martyr of the 1520s. The German Peasants' War of 1524–25 also revealed a deep unease about insurrection and violence amongst those who attacked the Catholic Church.

Conclusion

The Lutherans as a group were not central to the *Livre des Martyrs*. There were relatively few of them, appearing in shorter accounts, and of course, these accounts depicted events which had happened decades previously. They are, however, revealing of Crespin's attitudes on a range of issues. First, it is clear that he regarded the Lutherans as part of the same Church as himself, and Luther as an instrumental figure in the history of that Church. Luther was depicted as the 'great restorer of the Gospel', a figure who helped to put an end to centuries of abuse and darkness before him, and who was compared to Saint Augustine.[193] This, and the cautious approach taken towards Lutheran doctrine, accords with Bodo Nischan's view that 'Calvinists ... interpreted [Luther's] earlier reforms in historical, evolutionary terms; Luther's own disciples, by contrast, were wont to dogmatize and absolutize the reformer's achievements.'[194] That Luther should be regarded as so important, and yet not appear in any meaningful way before 1564, was a reflection of the change in direction which Crespin took after the *Cinquieme Partie*. This more historically minded approach was borrowed from Foxe and from Rabus, who led Crespin in including not only more pieces of context, but in including amongst the martyrs, major 'confessors', who had advanced the faith in other ways. Crespin added very few historical elements to the *Livre des Martyrs*, but he inserted Luther into a prominent role at his earliest opportunity. Other leading figures, Lutheran or Reformed, such as Zwingli, Melanchthon, or Bucer, were not included in the historical sections, even in the guise of confessors.

In addition to Crespin's inclusion of Luther as a pivotal figure in history, he took care to present Lutheran martyrs as holding entirely acceptable doctrine. Whereas the Vaudois were depicted with caveats about the quality of their beliefs, Lutherans were not identified as such, and their beliefs were transmitted as holding the same value and importance as those of any other martyr in the book. Crespin took this line despite his participation in a major, and long-standing, polemical battle against the Lutherans on a central issue of doctrine. To do so meant that in many cases he omitted parts of their confessions of faith. In the case of Henry Voez, this meant omitting ten of the sixty-two articles of faith. Leonard Kaiser's eighteen articles were reduced to four, one of which does not bear resemblance to anything which appears in the original confession. The primary

148 *Crespin and Lutheran martyrs*

target for these was naturally the areas where the martyrs did not agree with Reformed teaching, chief among them, the Real Presence of Christ in the Eucharist, a subject which Crespin might be expected to understand in some detail, due to his polemical work on the subject. Discussion of other sacraments was also subject to intervention, as the editing of George Carpentier/Wagner's comments on baptism show. Other subjects were edited for reasons which are less clear, such as Crespin's removal of Henry Voez' article stating that no-one should be banned from reading Luther; Crespin, of course, was a publisher of Luther himself, and presumably in agreement with Voez on this point.

This sensitivity to Lutheran doctrine seems to have extended to some of Luther's writings about the martyrs. Crespin certainly used some of Luther's work. As we have seen, he was an influential printer of Luther in other fields, and he relied on Luther's *The Burning of Brother Henry* for his account of van Zutphen's martyrdom, and pamphlets which had included Luther's writing for his accounts of Voez and Esch, and for Leonard Kaiser. However, the martyrology only used parts of those documents; the parts most prominently by Luther – even when not dealing with serious theological topics – were often omitted. Luther's letter to Kaiser, the *Trostbrieff Doctor Martini Lutheri gemeltem Leinhart Keiser*, was excluded from the *Livre des Martyrs*, despite the section advertising Luther's testimony in the passage.[195] Luther's letter of consolation to the people of the Low Countries on the occasion of the deaths of Voez and Esch was never published in Crespin, and his devotional passages which had accompanied *The Burning of Brother Henry* were excluded, and if Crespin had access to any of Luther's writing on the death of George Winckler, he used almost none of it. Most of this Lutheran writing which Crespin excluded was not central to the telling of the martyr's story; instead it consisted of letters to congregations and communities after the martyrdom, or letters of consolation to the martyr himself. Much of it was devotional in content, rather than doctrinal, or narrative. Nonetheless, the *Livre des Martyrs* included several such letters by other reformers in other contexts, most notably those of Calvin.

It seems that Crespin worked in an entirely different way regarding the Lutherans compared to other Protestant groups, such as the Vaudois, to whom he granted a separate identity. His objective seems to have been to create an image of a coherent and united Protestant movement; the changes and omissions he made to the Lutheran martyrs were largely made in order to efface differences between the denominations, which were operating in theological and political debates. The various critiques of the Real Presence made by numerous martyrs were never directly aimed at the Lutherans, but instead at Catholics, though the effect was still to assert and to teach Reformed doctrine over all others. His approach appears to have closely matched that recommended by Calvin himself in his 1544 letter to Bullinger: to avoid conflicts which would give Catholic opponents an opening of the sort Bossuet exploited a century later, while at the same time advancing Reformed teaching.

Crespin had to balance these priorities largely through the editorial process, as his source material consisted primarily of pamphlet literature published by Lutheran authors. While there must have been many decisions which remain opaque to us today, which resulted in his choosing the works that he did, and omitting others of which we are not aware, comparison between the successive editions, and to their original sources where possible, shows a great deal of editorial interference in the text. The alterations, and they almost always involved the removal of text, reflected the Genevan approach to the differences between the major Protestant denominations.

Notes

1 Brad Gregory, *Salvation at Stake* (Cambridge, MA: Harvard University Press, 2001), p. 185.
2 Jean Crespin, *Recueil de plusieurs personnes qui ont constamment enduré la mort pour le nom de nostre Seigneur Jesus Christ* ([Geneva: Jean Crespin], 1554), p. 144.
3 Crespin, *Recueil de plusieurs personnes* (1554), p. 144.
4 Jean Crespin, *Recueil de plusieurs personnes qui ont constamment enduré la mort pour le nom de Nostre Seigneur* ([Geneva]: Jean Crespin, 1555), Vol. I, p. 395.
5 Crespin, *Recueil de plusieurs personnes* (1555), Vol. I, p. CXXXIIII.
6 Crespin, *Recueil de plusieurs personnes* (1555), Vol. I, p. CXXXI.
7 Jean Crespin, *Actes des Martyrs* ([Geneva]: Jean Crespin, 1565), sig. ∂i verso.
8 Compare Crespin, *Recueil de plusieurs personnes* (1555), Vol. 1, p. CXXXI with Crespin, *Actes des Martyrs* (1565), p. 80.
9 John Foxe, *The Unabridged Acts and Monuments Online* (1576 edition). Editorial commentary and additional information, re. 1563 edition, p. 454. (HRI Online Publications, Sheffield, 2011). Available from: hwww.johnfoxe.org [accessed 18 August 2015].
10 John Foxe, *The Unabridged Acts and Monuments Online* (1563 edition), p. 456 (HRI Online Publications, Sheffield, 2011). Available from: www.john foxe.org [Accessed 18 August 2015].
11 Foxe, *The Unabridged Acts and Monuments Online* (1563 edition).
12 Crespin, *Actes des Martyrs* (1565), p. 84.
13 Crespin, *Actes des Martyrs* (1565), p. 84.
14 Crespin, *Actes des Martyrs* (1565), pp. 84–85.
15 Crespin, *Actes des Martyrs* (1565), p. 85.
16 Crespin, *Actes des Martyrs* (1565), p. 85.
17 Crespin, *Actes des Martyrs* (1565), p. 85.
18 Crespin, *Actes des Martyrs* (1565), p. 85.
19 Crespin, *Actes des Martyrs* (1565), p. 85.
20 *TAMO*, 1563, p. 458 [accessed 20 August 2011]. Crespin, *Actes des Martyrs* (1565), p. 85.
21 Jean Crespin, *Histoire des vrays tesmoins de la verité de l'Evangile* ([Geneva]: Jean Crespin, 1570), p. 56 verso.
22 Crespin, *Histoire des vrays tesmoins* (1570), p. 57 recto.
23 Crespin, *Histoire des vrays tesmoins* (1570), p. 57 recto.

150 Crespin and Lutheran martyrs

24 Crespin, *Histoire des vrays tesmoins* (1570), p. 57 recto.
25 Crespin, *Histoire des vrays tesmoins* (1570), p. 57 recto.
26 Crespin, *Histoire des vrays tesmoins* (1570), p. 57 verso.
27 Crespin, *Histoire des vrays tesmoins* (1570), p. 57 recto.
28 Crespin, *Histoire des vrays tesmoins* (1570), p. 57 verso.
29 Crespin, *Histoire des vrays tesmoins* (1570), p. 57 verso.
30 Crespin, *Histoire des vrays tesmoins* (1570), p. 58 recto.
31 Crespin, *Histoire des vrays tesmoins* (1570), p. 58 recto.
32 Crespin, *Histoire des vrays tesmoins* (1570), p. 58 verso.
33 Crespin, *Histoire des vrays tesmoins* (1570), p. 58 verso.
34 Alister McGrath, *Reformation Thought: An Introduction* (Oxford: Blackwell, 2000), p. 189.
35 E.g. Luke 22.69.
36 Mark Edwards, *Luther and the False Brethren* (Stanford, CA: Stanford University Press, 1975), pp. 82–83.
37 Edwards, *Luther and the False Brethren*, pp. 82–83.
38 Lee Palmer Wandel, *The Eucharist in the Reformation: Incarnation and Liturgy* (Cambridge: Cambridge University Press, 2005), pp. 95–96.
39 See Bodo Nischan, 'The "Fractio Panis"', *Church History*, 43:1 (1984), pp. 17–29.
40 Jean Calvin, *Institutes of the Christian Religion*, Book IV, Chap. XVII, 16 (Grand Rapids, MI: Eerdman, 1958), p. 569.
41 Calvin, *Institutes*, Book IV, Chap. XVII, 16.
42 Calvin, *Institutes*, Book IV, Chap. XVII, 31, p. 587.
43 Calvin, *Institutes*, Book IV, Chap. XVII, 30, p. 585.
44 Wandel, p. 162.
45 Calvin, *Institutes*, Book IV, Chap. XVII, 18, pp. 570–71.
46 Calvin, *Institutes*, Book IV, Chap. XVII, 31, p. 587.
47 Crespin, *Histoire des vrays tesmoins* (1570), p. 80 recto.
48 Arthur Cochrane, *Reformed Confessions of the Sixteenth Century* (London: SCM Press, 1966), p. 138.
49 Trans. Cochrane, p. 157.
50 Cochrane, p. 124.
51 Calvin, *Petit Traicte de la Cene*, in Francis Higman (ed.), *Three French Treatises* (London: Athlone, 1970), p. 128.
52 Calvin, *Petit Traicte de la Cene*, in J. Dillenberger, *John Calvin: Selections from his Writings* (Oxford: Oxford University Press, 1975), pp. 538–95.
53 Letter to Melanchthon, 28 June 1545. *Letters of John Calvin, Selected from the Bonnet Edition* (Edinburgh: Banner of Truth Trust, 1855/1980).
54 Calvin to Bullinger, 25 November 1544. Jules Bonnet (ed.), *Letters of John Calvin* (Philadelphia: Presbyterian Board of Publication, [1858]). Vol. I, pp. 433–34.
55 Calvin to Bullinger, pp. 434.
56 Calvin, '3 Forms of Exposition', in Dillenberger, *John Calvin: Selections from his Writings*, p. 539.
57 Calvin, '3 Forms of Exposition', p. 540.
58 Crespin, *Histoire des vrays tesmoins* (1570), p. 87 verso.
59 Crespin, *Recueil de plusieurs personnes* (1554), p. 310.
60 Gilmont, *Jean Crespin: Un éditeur réformé du XVIe siècle* (Geneva: Droz, 1981), p. 146.
61 Gilmont, *Jean Crespin*, p. 147 n.
62 Gilmont, *Jean Crespin*, p. 147. Gilmont, *Bibliographie des éditions de Jean Crespin* (Verviers: Gason, 1981), Vol. I.
63 Gilmont, *Bibliographie*, Vol. I.

Crespin and Lutheran martyrs 151

64 Gilmont, *Jean Crespin*, p. 141.
65 Gilmont, *Jean Crespin*, p. 141.
66 Jean Crespin, *Troisieme Partie du recueil des martyrs* ([Geneva]: Jean Crespin, 1556), p. 199.
67 Gilmont, *Jean Crespin*, p. 141.
68 Gilmont, *Jean Crespin*, p. 125.
69 Gilmont, *Bibliographie*, pp. 82–83.
70 William Moore, *La Reforme Allemande et la Literature Française* (Strasbourg: Faculté des lettres à l'Université, 1930), pp. 333–34.
71 Moore, p. 128.
72 Moore, p. 128.
73 Robert Kolb, *For All the Saints: Changing Perceptions of Martyrdom and Sainthood in the Lutheran Reformation* (Macon, GA: Mercer, 1987), pp. 55–56.
74 William Monter, *Judging the French Reformation: Heresy Trials by Sixteenth-Century Parlements* (London: Harvard University Press, 1999), pp. 55–56.
75 Martin Luther, *Works*, Vol. 53 (Philadelphia: Fortress Press, 1965), p. 211.
76 *Bibliographie des martyrologes protestants neerlandais*, Vol. 1 (Ghent: 1890), p. 473.
77 *Bibliographie des martyrologes protestants neerlandais*, p. 473. See also *TAMO*, 'German Martyrs'.
78 *Bibliographie des martyrologes protestants neerlandais*, p. 473. See also *TAMO*, 'German Martyrs'. Marcus Gielis, 'Leuven Theologians as Opponents of Erasmus and of Humanistic Theology', in Erika Rummel (ed.), *Biblical Humanism and Scholasticism in the Age of Erasmus* (Leiden: Brill, 2008), p. 61.
79 Gielis, p. 62. This was Martin Luther's *Die artikel warumb die zwen Christliche Augustiner munch zu Brussel verprandt sind, sampt eyenem send-brieff an die Christen ym Holland und Braband* (Wittenburg: Nickel Schirlentz, 1523).
80 Luther, *A New Song Here Shall Be Begun*. Luther, *Works*, Vol. 37 (Philadelphia: Fortress Press, 1961), p. 212.
81 Crespin, *Recueil de plusieurs personnes* (1554), p. 152.
82 Crespin, *Recueil de plusieurs personnes* (1554), p. 152.
83 Crespin, *Recueil de plusieurs personnes* (1554), p. 152.
84 Crespin, *Recueil de plusieurs personnes* (1554), p. 154.
85 Crespin, *Recueil de plusieurs personnes* (1554), p. 154.
86 Crespin, *Recueil de plusieurs personnes* (1555), Vol. I, p. 146.
87 Crespin, *Recueil de plusieurs personnes* (1555), pp. 146–47.
88 Crespin, *Recueil de plusieurs personnes* (1555), p. 147.
89 Compare Crespin, *Recueil de plusieurs personnes* (1554), p. 154 with Crespin, *Recueil de plusieurs personnes* (1555), Vol. I, p. 147.
90 Crespin, *Actes des Martyrs* (1565), p. 87.
91 *Bibliographie des Martyrologes*, p. 473.
92 Crespin, *Actes des Martyrs* (1565), p. 87.
93 Kolb, 'God's Gift of Martyrdom: The Early Reformation Understanding of Dying for the Faith', *Church History*, 64:3 (1995), p. 402 records one such letter from 1524, a year after the burning of Voez and Esch.
94 Crespin, *Actes des Martyrs* (1565), p. 88. Compare with Crespin, *Recueil de plusieurs personnes* (1555), Vol. I, p. 147.
95 Crespin, *Actes des Martyrs* (1565), p. 88.
96 Crespin, *Actes des Martyrs* (1565), p. 89.
97 Gregory, p. 185.
98 Gregory, p. 185.

152 Crespin and Lutheran martyrs

99 Compare Crespin, *Actes des Martyrs* (1565), p. 88 to *Historia de Duobus Augustinenensibus, ob evangelii doctrinam exustis Bruxellae, die trigesima Iunii. 1523* (via electronic media, Universitat-Bibliothek Basel), p. 9.
100 *Histoiria de duobus Augustinen*, p. 4.
101 *Histoiria de duobus Augustinen*, p. 12.
102 *Histoiria de duobus Augustinen*, p. 13.
103 *Histoiria de duobus Augustinen*, p. 12.
104 *Histoiria de duobus Augustinen*, p. 12.
105 *Histoiria de duobus Augustinen*, pp. 10–11.
106 *Histoiria de duobus Augustinen*, pp. 10–11.
107 *Histoiria de duobus Augustinen*, pp. 12–13.
108 *Histoiria de duobus Augustinen*, p. 14.
109 Crespin, *Actes des Martyrs* (1565), p. 90.
110 Crespin, *Actes des Martyrs* (1565), p. 90. This phrase from Mark 8 frequently appears uncited in Crespin, being an understandable favourite of his subjects.
111 Crespin, *Actes des Martyrs* (1565), pp. 91–92.
112 Crespin, *Actes des Martyrs* (1565), p. 96.
113 Crespin, *Recueil de plusieurs personnes* (1554), p. 144.
114 Crespin, *Recueil de plusieurs personnes* (1554), p. 144.
115 Crespin, *Recueil de plusieurs personnes* (1554), p. 144.
116 Crespin, *Recueil de plusieurs personnes* (1554), p. 146.
117 Luther, *Works*, Vol. 53, p. 211. Luther, *Works*, Vol. 32 (Philadelphia: Fortress Press, 1958), p. 263.
118 Crespin, *Recueil de plusieurs personnes* (1554), p. 146.
119 Luther, *Works*, Vol. 32, p. 264.
120 Luther, *Burning of Brother Henry*, trans. Steinhauser, revised Forell, in Luther's *Works*, Vol. 32, p. 265.
121 Crespin, *Recueil de plusieurs personnes* (1554), p. 145. Compare to Luther, *Burning*, p. 266.
122 Luther, *Burning*, p. 266. Crespin, *Recueil de plusieurs personnes* (1554), p. 145.
123 Luther, *Burning*, p. 267.
124 Crespin, *Recueil de plusieurs personnes* (1554), pp. 145–46.
125 Luther, *Burning*, pp. 267–68.
126 Luther, *Burning*, p. 265.
127 Luther, *Burning*, p. 265. Crespin, *Recueil de plusieurs personnes* (1554), p. 146.
128 Luther, *Burning*, p. 276.
129 Luther, *Burning*, p. 278.
130 Luther, *Burning*, p. 279. Crespin, *Recueil de plusieurs personnes* (1554), p. 146.
131 Luther, *Burning*, p. 280.
132 Crespin, *Recueil de plusieurs personnes* (1554), pp. 146–47.
133 Crespin, *Recueil de plusieurs personnes* (1554), p. 147.
134 Luther, *Burning*, p. 284.
135 Crespin, *Recueil de plusieurs personnes* (1554), p. 148.
136 Luther, *Burning*, p. 286. Crespin, *Recueil de plusieurs personnes* (1554), p. 149.
137 Luther, *Burning*, p. 286. Crespin, *Recueil de plusieurs personnes* (1554), p. 150.
138 Crespin, *Recueil de plusieurs personnes* (1555), Vol. I, p. 146.
139 Crespin, *Recueil de plusieurs personnes* (1555), Vol. I, p. 152.
140 Compare Crespin, *Recueil de plusieurs personnes* (1555), Vol. 1, p. 151 to Crespin, *Actes des Martyrs* (1565), p. 98.

Crespin and Lutheran martyrs 153

141 Crespin, *Histoire des vrays tesmoins* (1570), p. 91 verso.
142 *Histori, oder das warhaftig geschicht des leydens und sterbens L. Keyser's seligen* (Wittenberg, 1527). Robert Kolb, 'Kaiser, Leonhard', *The Oxford Encyclopedia of the Reformation*, edited by Hans J. Hillebrand (Oxford: Oxford University Press, 1996, 2005).
143 Quarto and octavo editions of the same text were printed in 1527 in Nuremberg and Wittenberg. As many as nine editions in total may have been produced.
144 *Histori ... L. Keyser* (Wittenberg).
145 *Histori ... L. Keyser* (Wittenberg), p. 4.
146 *Histori ... L. Keyser* (Nuremburg), sig. A (iii) recto.
147 *Histori ... L. Keyser* (Nuremburg), sig. A (iii) recto.
148 *Histori ... L. Keyser* (Nuremburg), p. A iii verso.
149 Crespin, *Histoire des vrays tesmoins* (1570), p. 69 verso.
150 Crespin, *Recueil de plusieurs personnes* (1554), p. 152.
151 *Histori ... L. Keyser* (Wittenberg), p. 11. This scene is described in Robert Scribner, 'Incombustible Luther', *Past and Present*, 110 (1986).
152 Compare Crespin, *Recueil de plusieurs personnes* (1554), p. 151 with Crespin, *Recueil de plusieurs personnes* (1555), Vol. I, p. 200.
153 Crespin, *Recueil de plusieurs personnes* (1554), p. 150.
154 Crespin, *Actes des Martyrs* (1565), p. 109.
155 Crespin, *Histoire des vrays tesmoins* (1570), p. 68 verso.
156 Crespin, *Recueil de plusieurs personnes* (1554), p. 150.
157 Crespin, *Recueil de plusieurs personnes* (1554), p. 150.
158 Crespin, *Recueil de plusieurs personnes* (1554), p. 150.
159 Crespin, *Recueil de plusieurs personnes* (1555), Vol. I, p. 152.
160 Crespin, *Recueil de plusieurs personnes* (1554), p. 150.
161 Crespin, *Actes des Martyrs* (1565), p. 98. Crespin, *Histoire des vrays tesmoins* (1570), p. 62.
162 Luther, *Works*, Vol. 43 (Philadelphia: Fortress Press, 1968), p. 144.
163 Luther, *Works*, Vol. 43, p. 141.
164 Luther, *Works*, Vol. 43, p. 147.
165 Luther, *Works*, Vol. 43, pp. 160–62.
166 Luther, *Works*, Vol. 43, p. 149.
167 Thomas Freeman, 'Text, Lies and Microfilm', *Sixteenth Century Journal*, 30:1 (1999), p. 34 n.
168 *Eyn new warhafftig vnd wunderbarlich geschicht oder hystori von Jörgen wagner zu München in Bayern als eyn Ketzer verbrandt im Jar M.D.xxvij* (Nuremburg: Hans Hergot, 1527), p. 2.
169 Crespin, *Troisieme Partie du recueil des martyrs* (1556), p. 5. Crespin, *Actes des Martyrs* (1565), p. 110.
170 Crespin, *Troisieme Partie du recueil des martyrs* (1556), p. 5.
171 Crespin, *Actes des Martyrs* (1565), p. 110.
172 Crespin, *Actes des Martyrs* (1565), p. 110.
173 Crespin, *Actes des Martyrs* (1565), p. 110.
174 Crespin, *Troisieme Partie du recueil des martyrs* (1556), p. 6.
175 Crespin, *Troisieme Partie du recueil des martyrs* (1556), p. 6.
176 Crespin, *Troisieme Partie du recueil des martyrs* (1556), p. 6.
177 Crespin, *Troisieme Partie du recueil des martyrs* (1556), p. 6.
178 *Eyn new warhafftig ...*, p. 2.
179 Gregory, p. 185.
180 Gregory, p. 185.
181 Crespin, *Troisieme Partie du recueil des martyrs* (1556), p. 7.
182 Crespin, *Troisieme Partie du recueil des martyrs* (1556), p. 8.

154 Crespin and Lutheran martyrs

183 Crespin, *Troisieme Partie du recueil des martyrs* (1556), p. 8.
184 Crespin, *Troisieme Partie du recueil des martyrs* (1556), p. 9.
185 Crespin, *Troisieme Partie du recueil des martyrs* (1556), p. 8.
186 Crespin, *Troisieme Partie du recueil des martyrs* (1556), p. 10.
187 Crespin, *Troisieme Partie du recueil des martyrs* (1556), p. 10.
188 Crespin, *Troisieme Partie du recueil des martyrs* (1556), p. 10.
189 Crespin, *Troisieme Partie du recueil des martyrs* (1556), p. 11.
190 Crespin, *Troisieme Partie du recueil des martyrs* (1556), p. 11.
191 Crespin, *Actes des Martyrs* (1565), p. 111.
192 Rabus, IV, p. 488 recto, according to Kolb, *For All the Saints*, p. 164. Kolb, *For All the Saints*, p. 82.
193 Crespin, *Recueil de plusieurs personnes* (1555), p. CXXXIII. Crespin, *Actes des Martyrs* (1565), p. 85.
194 Bodo Nischan, *Lutherans and Calvinists in the Age of Confessionalisation* (Aldershot: Ashgate, 1999), p. xi.
195 Crespin, *Histoire des vrays tesmoins* (1570), p. 68 verso.

5 The German Peasants' War

The German Peasants' War of 1524–26 had been a subject of controversy, particularly amongst Protestants, from its beginning. It was perhaps the greatest upheaval of the century, involving an estimated 300,000 people and 100,000 deaths across the southern areas of the Holy Roman Empire, and briefly appeared to present a serious threat to the existing social and political orders.[1] Peasant grievances included the tithe, and many of the peasant bands attacked monasteries and clerical landlords, giving the uprising an anti-clerical character. The stated aims of the peasant bands helped to give the uprising a Protestant appearance. The Twelve Articles of the peasant bands embraced a principle of appeal to the Bible that suggested an inspiration from the Reformation, and as James Stayer has noted, a great many of the peasants themselves 'thought of the enterprise as their contribution to the Reformation'.[2]

On the Peasants' War, Crespin was joining a controversy that had already been in progress for decades. The question of the role played by the Reformation in sparking the unrest had indeed been immediately raised by Catholic controversialists such as Cochlaeus, and is still a topic of academic debate.[3] Luther's *Admonition to Peace*, a response to the Twelve Articles of the peasantry, was written early in 1525, in part to answer the peasants, who had promised to withdraw any articles found to be against the word of God. Luther felt compelled, as a leader of the Reformation, to give his opinion:

> I do this in a friendly and Christian spirit, as a duty of brotherly love, so that if any misfortune or disaster comes out of this matter, it may not be attributed to me, nor will I be blamed before God and men because of my silence.[4]

Although not unsympathetic to the demands of the peasants (the *Admonition* told the princes and lords that: 'The peasants have just published twelve articles, some of which are so fair and just as to take away your reputation in the eyes of God and the world'), Luther's advice to the rebels was to act temperately, and avoid violence, so as not to threaten their

156 *The German Peasants' War*

standing before God, advice which also had the effect of drawing a clear line between himself and the rebels.[5]

When the uprising continued to grow, and became associated with religious radicalism, as well, Luther took a further step, and sided decisively against the rebels with 1525's *Against the Robbing and Murdering Hordes of Peasants*. As they had broken their vows to their rulers, started a campaign of rebellion and pillage, and falsely called themselves 'Christian brethren', Luther decided that the peasants must be crushed: 'I will not oppose a ruler, who, even though he does not tolerate the gospel, will smite and punish these peasants without first offering to submit the case to judgment.'[6] He even figured the conflict as a holy war: 'anyone who is killed fighting on the side of the rulers may be a true martyr in the eyes of God ... anyone who perishes fighting on the peasants' side is an eternal firebrand of hell, for he bears the sword against God's word.'[7] These strong views were hardly retracted when later in the same year, he attempted to explain them in: *An Open Letter on the Harsh Book Against the Peasants*.[8] Blickle considered this stance vital to the success of Lutheranism within the Holy Roman Empire: 'Ideologically, Luther defeated Bucer and Zwingli.... After this date, Zwinglianism was linked with upheaval and forced to surrender its bastions.'[9] Subsequently, religious policy became entwined with concerns for order and fears of another uprising.[10]

Luther did not escape accusations of responsibility for the rural uprisings, however. As Mark Edwards has noted, Catholic commentators pointed to his history of anti-clerical writings; in 1525, Johannes Cochlaeus included an entire appendix of such statements to one of his pamphlets.[11] Cochlaeus' 1527 *Answer to Luther's Treatise against the Robbing and Murdering Hordes of Peasants*, also blamed Luther's conception of Christian freedom for giving the peasantry ideas that they were beyond the law.[12] Hieronymous Emser, with whom Luther was already engaged in a long polemical rally, offered five proofs that Luther had incited the Peasants' War.[13] These argued that Luther had wrongly juxtaposed the secular and spiritual estates, had attacked human laws and the Catholic hierarchy, committed *lèse majesté* against secular authorities (by criticising interventions in spiritual affairs), and incited rebellion through his incendiary language.[14] The debate continued for years: Cochlaeus' 1529 *Sieben kopffe Martin Luthers, von sieben sachen das Christlichen glaubens*, argued that 'There were many peasants slain in the uprising, many fanatics banished, many false prophets hanged, burned, drowned, or beheaded who perhaps would still all live as good obedient Christians had Luther not written.'[15]

French Protestants had been spared direct involvement in these events, but one legacy of peasant revolt was to increase suspicion of popular involvement in reform movements. It also made the task of the martyrologist difficult. From Crespin's point of view, it was imperative to prove that anyone who was included from that period had been killed for the

The German Peasants' War   157

correct reasons, and if possible, in the correct manner, in order to qualify as a martyr under his criteria. The death of a rebel would obviously be disqualified, but it could also be difficult to prove the motivations behind the killing of a pastor in the heat of combat, or a convert caught up in a wave of reactionary violence, and these motivations were important. Even after the introduction of the *Récits d'histoire* after 1563, which gave him scope to include the victims of massacres like Vassy, Crespin appears to have had some doubts about the suitability of some of the martyrs presented in this section.

As a result, Crespin's engagement with the Peasants' War showed an abundance of caution. The *Livre des Martyrs* engaged with the central issues of the Peasants' War as little as possible: Crespin did not include any figures who had been killed in the uprising itself, and one of the martyrs repeatedly disavowed any knowledge of the contents of the Twelve Articles, even while on the scaffold.[16] It is possible that the question of genre played a part in this: Crespin referred his readers to histories for the narrative of the uprising and, especially, its defeat, while there was little pedagogic or doctrinal value to be had in discussing the religious aspects of the uprising. It would also have been quite difficult, under his criteria, to include the victims of the peasant bands as martyrs, and this may explain why the four accounts that he does include all come from the end of the conflict, when the authorities were reasserting their control. Three of the four figures he discusses were Protestant clergy, and Crespin paints them in the best possible light, as dutiful, honest, and brave men, even as good hosts. Their theology, however, is not a focus of these accounts, aside from some broad Protestant statements, and a narrative of conversion from Catholicism.

Although the Peasant's War did not play a major role in Crespin's history of the period, he included several martyrs who had been connected with it in some capacity, as well as, in his final edition, a short history of the Anabaptists, whom he tied to the uprising, using the figure of Thomas Müntzer as a key link. These accounts show a great deal of alteration from edition to edition, with one of the martyrs being written out of the martyrology after 1564, seemingly very close to publication. This was, notably, the sole farmer amongst them, a man accused of some level of involvement in the uprising. Crespin's own position on the Peasants' War was primarily one of condemnation. He refers to it in several places as 'sedition', 'mutiny', and a 'tumult', and showed a deep concern for the reputational harm it could cause to Protestantism. He describes attacks on Catholic institutions as occurring 'under colour of defending the Gospel', and above all, laments the 'great prejudice to the cause of the Gospel' that followed.[17] Indeed, in the outline of the contents of the 1570 edition of the *Livre des Martyrs*, Crespin explicitly framed the Peasants' War as an obstacle to Protestantism, writing that: 'despite the sedition of the peasants, the Gospel continued its progress, overcoming all obstacles'.[18]

158   *The German Peasants' War*

Crespin only included a handful of figures involved in the Peasants' War, the origins of which he described in the 1564 and 1570 editions in a section titled 'History of some cruelties committed in the sedition of the Rustics' (which also included two of the Peasants' War martyrs):

> at the end of the year 1524, the peasants had begun to quarrel because of charges which they complained were oppressive; a great sedition was launched against the great Ecclesiastical prelates & many gentlemen of Germany, under colour of defending the doctrines of the Gospel & to set them at liberty. In addition to the murder & damage which carried this popular tempest, it caused great prejudice to the cause of the Gospel & to many good Ministers who began to announce it.[19]

This last point became particularly important in the *Livre des Martyrs*, as several of his martyrs were victims of repression in the aftermath of the revolt. Crespin included three martyrs from this period in the 1554 and 1555 editions of the *Livre des Martyrs*, with two of them continuing into the 1564 and 1570 volumes. In 1554 and in 1555, they were introduced with a small header reading: 'This history has been put in writing by [Oecolampadius].'[20] These are fairly vague accounts which do not always name their subjects, and in two cases, do not even specify a location.

In the octavo editions of 1554 and 1555, the accounts were placed together; each had its own title, and was a distinct entity, grouped with the others and preceded by the note about Oecolampadius. In 1564, only two of these accounts were included, as *Récits d'Histoire*, presented separately from each other, and introduced with a claim that they were 'attributed' to Oecolampadius.[21] This changed these accounts from martyrdoms to historical events, and placed less emphasis on the doctrine and behaviour of the subjects. This is a relatively rare example of the *Récit d'Histoire* format being used to 'downgrade' a martyr; in most cases, they were used to add events, particularly from the French Wars of Religion, which would not have otherwise qualified for inclusion in the martyrology.

In 1564's *Récit d'Histoire*, Oecolampadius' credentials are burnished, and he is described as the: 'founder of the true religion in the city of Basel', and Crespin explains why he has included the accounts in this fashion:

> Because the punishment does not make the Martyr, but the cause, which in these narrations is mixed with facts that could render it suspect & impure, we have inserted them here in the form of a narrative of the history, as at the beginning of this edition we have promised to do, when the death is not for the cause of Religion, but is mixed with another accusation.[22]

In 1570, this became:

The punishment does not make the martyr, but the cause, which in these three [accounts] is mixed with some deeds little suitable to the martyrs of the Lord, we have here inserted them in the form of a narrative of the history, as in the beginning of this edition.[23]

Suspicion of the content of these three martyrs' beliefs, and their possible activities during the Peasants' War, was thus the apparent cause of this demotion in status. We cannot know whether some change of opinion occurred between 1555 and 1564 which caused Crespin to re-evaluate his view of these three accounts, or whether it was the development of the *Récit d'Histoire* format which spurred this change.

These martyrdoms appeared in John Foxe's *Actes and Monuments* from 1563 onwards, credited, as in Crespin, to Oecolampadius.[24] There are few major differences between the accounts in the two martyrologies: part of Crespin's version of the second account, describing the ominous approach of troops to arrest the pastor of Bisgoye, does not appear in Foxe. Similarly, two sections describing the depredations of soldiers suppressing the Peasants' War in the third of the Oecolampadius notices were omitted from the English work: Foxe appears to have shied away from representing such military action in these cases. From 1570 onwards, Foxe seems to have gained access to information which Crespin did not have. In that year, he was able to put a name to the second martyr, the 'pastor of Brisgoye', who was apparently a Peter Spengler, of the village of Schlat, in Württemberg.[25] The name was apparently added after consulting Pantaleone's *Martryium Historia*.[26]

Having been given a separate title in the early editions: 'Of the cruel death of a certain minister or pastor, who was cruelly killed for having maintained the truth, 1525', the first of the three subjects is described simply as one who: 'Faithfully performed the office of pastor', who at the time: 'that the peasants having being moved to sedition, did something which was not of great importance, as those who know, have well related', a deeply ambiguous statement about his actions during the uprising.[27] In return, his prince (who is not identified) was 'irritated by that deed, and even so much that he had given him some rude remonstrations. And even though all this deserved no punishment', the prince condemned him to death.[28]

In 1564's version, the prince's reaction is modified, in that in his condemnation of the preacher: 'forgets all friendship and the reverence that he had always borne the said Pastor'.[29] The prince then sends a gentleman and some servants (in early editions the servants appear to be the gentleman's; in 1564 they are the prince's) to the house of the cleric to carry out this sentence, where they are received with great hospitality by the pastor, which increases the servants' 'horror of this deed'.[30] Indeed, they remonstrate with their master to spare him. It is in this passage that we are finally given some idea of the charges against the pastor, for he: 'protests that he

160 The German Peasants' War

had faithfully and purely taught the doctrine of the Gospel'.[31] He had 'rebuked, bitterly and in public, the horrible vices of the Gentlemen' in places where they should 'give example of faith, true religion, and all sobriety: the Gentlemen strongly and firmly resisted'.[32] Indeed, they threatened him, saying that:

> that they were the lords, & they could kill him if they wanted: that all that they did was laudable, and could not be contradicted or resisted: & that he plotted some things in his sermons, that would soon come to a bad end.[33]

His final words are figured in a traditionally martyrological way. He: 'said nothing else except: Jesus Christ, give me mercy, Jesus Christ, save me'.[34] Crespin concluded his account with a brief note comparing the character of the hangmen, who were described as being like 'a Turk against his mortal enemy' in the early editions, and like barbarians in 1564, with those of the martyrs.[35] One has a hanging on their conscience, while the other comes away with an immortal crown.[36] In 1570, Crespin tried to underline the demonstrative value of the account: 'This act, among others, merits reciting here, to show the great cruelty...', before going on to accuse the killers of barbarian behaviour.[37]

It is the cruelty of the execution that Crespin stresses the most in this account. The pastor has shown his killers hospitality and generosity, and this presents the gentleman's servants with real problems. The execution of an evangelist pastor who had criticised the local nobility, in the aftermath of the Peasants' War, also suggests the backlash against the Reformation which Crespin had identified as one of the uprising's worst effects.

The second of the three martyrs attributed to Oecolampadius also had his own heading in 1554 and 1555, which was lost in the 1570 agglomeration: 'Another history of the martyrdom of a minister or pastor, which was drowned in the year 1525. Collected by the said author Jean Ecolampade.'[38] In 1564 this was changed to: 'Account of the history of a pastor of the land of Brisgoye'.[39] In the final edition, in 1570, it was incorporated into a section entitled: 'Gaspar Tambar, and others executed in several places'.[40]

This pastor, who was later named by Foxe as Peter Spengler, tended to a village in the Brisgoye (Breisgau) area near Freiburg-im-Breisgau, and was granted high praise by Crespin for being well-versed in Scripture, and dedicated to his office, as being 'courteous, humane, and kind, excellent in good doctrine'.[41] None of these complimentary adjectives survived in 1564, and indeed, that edition drops any reference to 'the good' pastor and also omits the line describing his manner: 'with authority toward all, and peaceful with all those with whom he had to deal'.[42] Crespin begins by presenting us with a classic conversion narrative. With the coming of reform elsewhere, he was inspired to revisit the Gospels, which he had previously

The German Peasants' War 161

read: 'without any intelligence, without thinking of words and sentences'.[43] When he had 'recovered some judgement, he began to teach by continual preaching'.[44]

He began to regret: 'in what deep darkness, and in what tragic errors the entire order of priests had been plunged for a long time'.[45] The account laments the failures of earlier generations to grasp the truth, and the abuses of the established Church in apocalyptic language:

> now however he saw, that the priests lived in great prosperity: & no-one dared to keep a holy & good cause against them without great danger ... he saw the hour had come, that the Gospel could widely spread its virtue, that the cross was next, that the enemies of the truth frothed their rage.[46]

The persecutions and executions of the modern era are invoked, and compared to those of the ancients, which spurred the pastor into action, when he: 'Saw that so many of the bodies of the saints & faithful were every day being whipped, beaten with rods, banished, torn, beheaded, hung, drowned, & burned.'[47] The good pastor therefore 'saw all things went topsy-turvey (for also by then the peasants had raised a great mutiny)' and took action by taking a wife, to 'avoid the sin of fornication', thus definitively breaking from the Catholic Church.[48]

The 'rage of the peasants continued to grow', however, and 'they went among the monestaries and the houses of the priests, as if they had undertaken some pilgrimage, sparing nothing of what they found'.[49] In time, a group of rebels descended on Breisgau, and took all that he had, as these bands 'had no point of difference between bad priests and the good'.[50] Spengler tried to use his moral authority to shame his assailants, but to no purpose, and he prophetically warned them that 'sedition has never had a good issue, which envelops the good and honest people amongst the wicked'.[51] The peasants are accused of betraying the Gospel for which he stands:

> All these excesses & dissolutions under the shadow of the Gospel ... you pretend the truth of the Gospel ... that it thus overflows in fury and inhumanity? Your Gospel is sooner a Gospel of the Devil, which troubles all to wrong and to disorder, ravaging and pillaging without regard for any justice.[52]

They taunted him, replying that he had taken money for Masses, under fear of Purgatory, and asked when he would repay it.[53]

Having ridden out the local uprisings, which in the Breisgau region mainly took place in the spring of 1525, when: 'the rebellion of the peasants was appeased', and some of the leaders captured, the pastor returned to spreading the Word, and was captured by 'some apostate soldiers', who

162　*The German Peasants' War*

were 'angry that he was freely announcing the word of God' and taken away (Foxe tells us to Freiburg, and then Eguisheim).[54] There he was tortured, and condemned to death, apparently because of his marriage (which would have meant he died for his faith), rather than because of sedition, or robbery, or theft, which are specifically excluded.[55]

He denounced the monks for their 'foolishness' (later changed to 'false doctrines'), but mainly sticks to wider terms of debate, introducing ideas such as 'for my part, I do not want only to glorify the cross of our Lord Jesus Christ', without presenting specifically theological arguments.[56] His sentence was to be executed by drowning in the local river, a fact remarked upon in the introduction to his notice. On being thrown into the water, it became red with his blood.[57] According to the narrator of this account, this was taken as a potentially providential sign: 'Those who were present saw which had been done, were all dumbfounded, were grieved in themselves, wondering what this water signified, tinted with blood. Each one returned thoughtful to his house, considering what had been done.'[58] The account ends with the truth-claim that: 'I have had all of this by one who saw with his own eyes that which has been written above.'[59]

In this account, and especially in 1564's edition, nearly as much space was devoted to documenting the pastor's clashes with the peasants as his persecution by the authorities. Indeed, they are central to this account, although they were ultimately irrelevant to his execution. They may thus serve the purpose of acting as a testament to the pastor's holy life, and good conduct at this difficult time: the Peasants' War would be in this sense a test of Spengler's suitability for the title of martyr.

These themes are stressed by the marginal notes which Crespin added to the 1564 and 1570 editions. Of the ten, only two marginal notes cite biblical passages. The rest provide commentary on the text. The initial praise of the pastor is marked with a note reading: 'Marks of a Good Minister', while the description of the Peasants' War was annotated: 'Overflowing fury of the peasants.'[60] Most interestingly, his torture and spell in prison, after his arrest by soldiers, was marked by marginalia reading: 'Torments which the pastor endured from the Peasants.'[61]

The third and final of the Peasants' War accounts also appeared in the first and second editions with its own heading, which read: 'Another history, of a villager slain wrongly, collected by the same author, Oecolampadius.'[62] Unlike the previous two, who were clergy, this man is described as being a peasant, a: 'Lover of justice, & mortal enemy of the exactions of the gentlemen, which oppress the poor people, & trample on more than reason, [who] saw that the privileges given by Kings and Princes did not allow it.'[63] The last clause was omitted from Foxe's version. Holding these somewhat radical views, he was caught up in the Peasants' War, or its aftermath:

> After the noise & tumult of the peasants was appeased, this man was seized: & the reason was, that he had cried to arms when in all the

The German Peasants' War 163

nearby country & fields there were numbers of horsemen who searched with great diligence those who had been authors of the sedition.[64]

It seems that everyone had believed that they were in danger: a village had already been burned, and many were fleeing their homes for the forests.[65] The knights killed all who they found, so that all in the area were afraid of them (it was this section which was omitted from Foxe).

Meanwhile, the peasant was apparently persuaded to surrender by promises and tricks, in the face of which he consented to their demands, thinking he would avoid the gallows.[66] He was tortured in a variety of ways, and incarcerated, seemingly with the aim of getting him to sign a confession that he steadfastly denied.[67] His captors eventually suborned a witness to testify that: 'he is worthy of death, all that he had cried the alarm after that truce was given, & had wanted to raise a new sedition'.[68] He was indeed sentenced to death, and the reader is given a detailed rendering of the ceremonies around this peasant's final hours.

Crespin depicts the man as having some religious motivation in his actions. He accuses the monk who accompanies him to the scaffold, at some length, of 'having the heart of a fox', and of deceiving simple folk; the peasant decries the wooden crucifix as being 'your doll of wood: my Saviour lives in heaven'.[69] The villager denies the need to confess to the monk, insisting that he has already confessed his sins before God himself.[70] His confession was read aloud, containing nothing other than the statement that: 'This man had been seditious, & then in the time of the truce he had cried the alarm, indeed at night, while the others rested in their beds.'[71] Demanding the right to speak, the villager launched into a monologue defending himself:

> There were horsemen, who seized many men of good life & simplicity, whether they laboured, sowed, cut the vines, slept at night with their women and children, & did not think of such surprises: for my part I gathered all of my parents & friends in my house, to protect them from this violence & oppression, & not to stir up sedition ...[72]

He insists again and again that he is innocent of the charges, that he has been unjustly condemned by the gentry and the judges in collusion, before returning to the question of his role in the uprisings:

> I have been adherent to the noise & tumult of the villagers, as did everyone else who has lived around here. But so what? Have there not been many gentlemen who followed the army of peasants, & many strong towns who have allied with them? I have not been the author of any rebellion, which I always mortally hated.... We had asked advice of our genteman as to what we should do, when the bands of peasants

164   *The German Peasants' War*

gathered on the fields, but he did not give us council or consolation ... I never knew what was in the articles that were published, and neither has any man told me why one has published such articles. I also do not know why this band of villagers was raised, and why each one incited his neighbour to take up arms.... Why have I been held like a brigand? Why have I endured such tortures? The main reason is because I have adhered to the peasants ... I have not pillaged or ravaged any goods, I have not done wrong, I have not burned the house of another. Of what crime, therefore, am I accused of more than the other, who also have been seditious?[73]

He insisted, however, that having grabbed arms and raised the alarm, he had not known he was acting against knights. This, he says, is not sedition.[74] As he argued, however, the judge ordered the executioner to behead the condemned man, in order to curtail his harangue: 'his tongue moved in his head for a long time, from the vehemence of the words which he had given'.[75] This case stands apart from the other two, as an example of a layman executed for a seemingly seditious act. His defence was not to deny the charge, but to try to justify it, and to mitigate his actions. At no point was there an indication that his religious views were relevant to the trial, or to his actions, and indeed, we are given hardly any insight into what they might be. As such, this peasant can be said to fail to fulfil most of the criteria for martyrdom suggested by David El Kenz; certainly it would appear that Crespin, and Foxe after him, had second thoughts on the topic.

After 1564 this account was removed from the martyrology, despite the introductory note before the first Oecolampadius notice, which promised: 'The history of three who were cruelly oppressed during the times of the sedition of the Peasants of the country of Germany.'[76] In the *Actes and Monuments*, this 'certaine man of the Countrey' was retained only with strategic cuts to his confession. In Foxe's version, the executioner cuts the man off before he can confess his links with the peasants, or to taking up arms.

This was the most significant of the changes which Crespin made in 1564 to his depiction of the Peasants' War, but it was part of a pattern of downplaying the importance of the Peasants' War. In 1564 and 1570, the Oecolampadius accounts, in addition to being reduced from three to two, were changed from full martyrdoms to *Récits d'Histoire*. The first notice, the minister attacked in his home, was prefaced with a short note alluding to this change. As described above, Crespin explained that these three accounts had been changed because one could not be certain that their deaths had been purely for religious reasons, and not 'mixed with other accusations'.[77] Indeed, the ability to include the victims of massacres and battles was one of the attractions of the new format. That Crespin felt compelled to make this lukewarm defence of these accounts even after

The *Récit* introducing the Peasants' War, however, only includes the first of Oecolampadius' martyrs before ending; the 1564 edition then moves on to the separate (but contemporary) account of Wolfgang Schuch, who is described below.[78] It is only after the lengthy section on Schuch, and a very brief one on Gaspar Tambar, that the second of the three, the pastor of Brisgoye, is included.[79]

Crespin did not often remove entire items from the *Livre des Martyrs*, and neither did he often cut the length of items too much from edition to edition. This makes the cuts to Oecolampadius' account of deaths in the Peasants' War particularly interesting. These interventions show a clear desire to avoid identification of his martyrs with the Peasants' War. His inclusion of two of the Oecolampadius martyrs as *Récits d'Histoire* is coupled with an acknowledgement that their deaths might have been for reasons other than simply their beliefs; his exclusion of the third is a de facto admission that the man was executed for his deeds, not his doctrine. The pastor of Brisgoye, however, was portrayed as being in conflict with the rebels, who robbed, mocked, and abused him. His case seems to present an excellent example of a virtuous Protestant beset by both Catholic authorities and rebellious peasants, and yet Crespin continued to treat it with great caution.

Wolfgang Schuch

The Peasants' War was similarly unaddressed in the account of Wolfgang Schuch, a minister executed in early 1525, in an area of Alsace which was affected by the Peasants' War that same year. This account first appeared towards the end of the 1554 edition, away from the other victims of the 1520s, on page 627 of 687. This suggests that he was a late addition, as does the short length of the passage itself, which is only thirty-three words long. It sits as the first entry in the final section of the *Livre des Martyrs*, which was a collection of various pieces which had not found a place elsewhere:

> Being a declaration of some other Martyrs, who have also endured constantly for the confession of one same doctrine of Jesus Christ & this in diverse places & times, & by many sorts of torments: of some faithful men & worthy of faith have rendered certain witness, & true authentication.[80]

The entry reads: 'Wolfgang Schuch, pastor of the town of St. Hippolite in Lorraine, had faithfully announced, & constantly sustained the word of the Son of God, was burned at Nancy, in the month of June, 1525.'[81] This

166   *The German Peasants' War*

brevity is worth noting, because Crespin may well have had access to much more information. A French-language pamphlet about Schuch's death was issued at Strasbourg in 1526; an example tentatively dated 1527 exists at the British Library.[82] This was introduced by a Theodulus Philadelphus (apparently an alias for the reformer François Lambert), in a sixteen-page passage preceding the seventeen-page letter, and followed by an untitled three-page afterword.[83] There is also a contemporary, hostile, French-language work by the historian to the Duke of Lorraine, Nicolas Volcyr.[84]

If he had not already had it, Crespin must have received this information within months, it would seem, for in the 1555 edition we find a much longer account – more than fourteen octavo pages (the 1555 sextodecimo edition incorporated the information less fully – the letter was included, but only at the end of the book). While most new additions in 1555 were added to the *Deuxieme Partie*, for reasons of chronology, Schuch's account was moved forward to sit just after those of Oecolampadius. This placed it with other accounts from 1524 and 1525, and shortly after Jan Hus and the earliest Lutheran martyrs. Indeed, the introduction to Schuch's account is smaller and less bold than most others of its sort, reducing the sense of separation from the previous section. He does, however, have his own running headers to set him apart.[85]

In its 1555 incarnation, Schuch's account consists entirely of a letter of January 1525 written by him to Antoine, the imperial Duke of Lorraine (and thus a cousin of the Guise clan), and a short afterword informing the reader of Schuch's fate.[86] The letter itself, which would remain the central part of the account in all later versions, is a defence by Schuch of his actions as the pastor of St Hippolyte (St Pilt in German), a village between Strasbourg and Mulhouse, and dominated by the castle of Haut-Konigsbourg. The text is very similar in content to that of the letter printed in the 1526 pamphlet, but different in almost every particular of language. For example, where in the Philadelphus version Schuch arrives to minister to 'people like lost sheep', Crespin has it as 'a wandering and errant peple'; where in the earlier version, 'the Kingdom of God is near', in Crespin it is 'the Kingdom of Heaven' that is nearby.[87] It is possible that the two accounts represent parallel French translations of an original document, perhaps in Latin or German (Crespin claims in a later version that Schuch did not speak any Latin).[88] Kolb regards it as 'remotely possible' that Rabus drew his account of Schuch not from Crespin but from a common source; the differences between Crespin and the 1526 document suggest that such a source at least existed.[89]

As the address of the letter to the Duke had been set as a sort of title, Schuch's letter begins *in media res*, explaining that when he arrived in St Hippolyte, he found: 'A people wandering and lost like sheep without a shepherd, and being miserably lost by many abominable errors & superstitions.'[90] In passages full of Biblical imagery (glossed by Crespin), Schuch described his actions:

The German Peasants' War 167

I began ... impatient like the good worker to uproot all the thorns and errors which little by little increased against the Lord and his word: to demolish, dissipate, and destroy all highness and weapons laid against the doctrine of God: to plant trees giving fruit in our time: to build a hoouse neither transitory nor terrestrial.[91]

He went out to preach the Gospel. That these changes were essentially Protestant in nature is indicated by his stinging condemnation of works, and of traditional religion: 'God condemns and judges the damned who have believed according to commandments and doctrines of men', which evolves into a wholesale attack on the theology and the practice of the Catholic Mass, which degrades the proper Eucharist by being 'sold for a daily sacrifice, counter to the most salutary institution of Christ'.[92]

All of this defence of his reforming project, however, is preparation for a plea for mercy. Schuch is accused of being a 'seducer, misleading, seditious, heretic', by those who cannot refute his criticisms, and so resort to the 'aid of the secular arm'.[93] He begs the prince not to listen to his accusers, who 'cannot pretend falsely that the people are moved by the preaching of the Gospel to sedition and disobedience, to disdain the Princes and Magistrates. One cannot give this dishonour to the word of God.'[94] Keen to prove his own loyalty to the 'Most Merciful Prince' Schuch reiterates the importance of rendering what is Caesar's unto Caesar and deploys a number of scriptural references to stress that 'for where the will of God ... is most purely understood, there one understands the command of Princes most sincerely' so long as it is 'not against God, against whom one must not have any obedience'.[95] Indeed, 'nothing renders a kingdom more tranquil and peaceable, than the word of Christ'.[96]

In the 1555 martyrology, the only information given outside of the letter was a short afterword, stating that Schuch was taken by a 'A gentleman of Lorraine, named Gaspard d'Hassonville, governor of Blamont' to Nancy, where he was burned in August 1525, showing no fear, and invoking God's name to the end.[97]

The later editions of the martyrology, although still centred on this letter of Schuch, provide more context on his execution. In the 1564 *Livre des Martyrs*, Schuch retained his place amongst the Peasants' War martyrs, this time placed after the first of Oecolampadius' martyrs (the pastor hanged at his house). It was prefaced with a single paragraph introducing Schuch and his situation. This appears to be distinct from the introduction supplied in Philadelphus's tract. Philadelphus' introduction had contained a long meditation on martyrdom from the time of St Stephen before setting the stage for Schuch's letter.[98] It shows Schuch publically joining the cause of reform by marrying, as had the pastor of Brisgoye and other former priests.[99] This earlier tract had also denounced the Catholic Mass in the strongest possible terms, as 'infected and Pharisitical, placing the doctrines of men over those of Christ'.[100]

168   *The German Peasants' War*

Crespin's 1564 introduction, by contrast, first places Schuch within the martyrology, praising him for being amongst the first in Germany to come to knowledge of the Gospel, and to drive out the idolatries and superstitions of his parishioners.[101] He acted in a practical fashion, abolishing 'Lent, images, and finally the abomination of the Mass', an approach which was eased by his education of the people in the Gospel.[102] None of these fundamental changes to his church were mentioned in Philadelphus, meaning that Crespin either elaborated on the pamphlet, or that he had another source for the actions of Schuch.

Schuch's local reforms led, in turn, to his position in early 1525, when the letter to the Duke of Lorraine was written: 'The news of this revolt of the Papal doctrine, gave occasion to the enemies of truth to slander and accuse them before the Prince ...'.[103] As a result, Antoine of Lorraine reacted violently, seeing this as a challenge to his authority 'such that the town was menaced by the Prince with being put to fire and blood', and Schuch responded with his plea for mercy, in order to 'assure the Prince of the good will & obedience of the people towards him'.[104] This respect for authority was an attitude approved by Luther in his account of George Winckler, but it also may be seen as a placatory move in the context of the Peasants' War, which reached its peak in Alsace a few months later in the spring of 1525, before being crushed by Duke Antoine.[105] Crespin's introduction differs from the more contemporary Philadelphus' on the matter of the reforms which Schuch had introduced to St Hippolyte – it describes attacks on a much wider range of Catholic practices, such as Lent and the veneration of images.

The compendium edition of 1564 added to the conclusion to the section, as well. This was expanded from a few dozen words to almost a full page in folio.[106] It describes how, his letter having had no effect on the Duke, Schuch: 'seeing that Duke Antoine persisted in this willingness to sack the town of St. Hippolyte, went to Nancy'.[107] There is no longer any mention of his arrest by the nobleman d'Hanssonville, as in the earlier version, and Schuch is now portrayed as acting in a spirit of heroic self-sacrifice. Schuch's interrogation is described, being undertaken by the Duke's grand confessor. The Duke, so respectfully addressed by Schuch in his letter, is now attacked by Crespin as 'ignorant', one who would: 'exterminate all the wise men of the court & of his country', and who remarks 'that it suffices to know the Paternoster and Ave Maria: and that the greatest doctors were the cause of the greatest errors and trouble'.[108] The Duke personally attended some of the questioning of Schuch, and himself: 'said that it was not necessary to argue more, but he needed to proceed to execute him, as he denied the sacrament of the Mass'.[109] It is worth noting that the Philadelphus tract did not end with such emphasis on the Mass. Instead, the three concluding pages in that work discussed the meaning of martyrdom, and the importance of spreading the faith by words, not conquest. Again it becomes clear that for the passages on the life and death of Schuch, outside of the letter to the Duke, Crespin must have been drawing on another source.

The account concludes by describing Schuch's execution, which followed the traditional pattern. His books were burned, and he declared his faith that God would see him through the ordeal.[110] He clashed with the monks over what he perceived as their idolatry, and sang psalms at the stake. A sort of divine stamp was placed on things with the final sentences of the notice, which explain that the judge in Schuch's trial, and an abbot, the suffragant of Metz, both died suddenly, soon after the execution. The marginal note suggests that this was an: 'example of the judgement of God upon his enemies'.[111] Schuch's was a much more official, and more orthodox, execution than the lynchings and drowning which had characterised the deaths of the Oecolampadius martyrs. This official condemnation of Schuch, combined with this conclusion's strong emphasis on his sacrifice, his doctrinal stubbornness, and the doctrines for which he was condemned, helped paint Schuch as a strongly conventional martyr, in word and in deed. In both the introduction and conclusion added in 1564, Schuch's opposition to idols and to the Mass are stressed, in a way in which Philadelphus, for example, does not. Indeed, it was his answers on the Mass which eventually led the Duke to condemn him to death. Where the 1564 edition had played down central aspects of the Oecolampadius accounts, it played up several of Schuch's attributes.

Anabaptists

In the final edition of the *Livre des Martyrs*, Crespin also included a five-page discussion of the Anabaptists, associating them directly with the Peasants' War. He professed to have drawn much of it from a book titled *Une belle & profitable admonition & correction au magistrat & à tous estats*, a work also cited by Guy de Brès in his own writing against Anabaptism.[112] He also cites Bullinger, who had written a history of the Anabaptists in 1561, and who insisted on the essential connection between Müntzer and Münster, a decade later.[113]

Crespin's discussion of the 'discord of the Anabaptists' made reference to them as 'weeds amongst the wheat of the Gospel'.[114] Like the Peasants' War, to which Crespin closely links them, the Anabaptists are dangerous because of the damage that they do to the Reformed Church, both in substance and in reputation:

> The pernicious sect of the Anabaptists strongly troubled the Churches where the Gospel had been newly announced ... it rendered the simple doubtful and uncertain, and on the other side the preaching of the truth suspect and odious to the ignorant.[115]

Crespin repeatedly emphasises the division in the Anabaptist movement, 'divided not only into sects and assemblies, but also one finds amongst them as many opinions as they have heads'.[116]

170   *The German Peasants' War*

Crespin placed the beginning of Anabaptism in Saxony, in 1522, where a group of 'mutinous and seditious men' was led by Nicholas Storch.[117] Crespin is thus tracing the birth of the Anabaptist movement back to the Zwickau Prophets, a group with links to both Martin Luther and Thomas Müntzer, who was to play a notorious role in the Peasants' War. Indeed, Müntzer is mentioned in Crespin's brief narrative, as one of several radicals, who also included the Anabaptist leaders Jan Hut, Balthazar Hubmaier, Hans Denck, and Melchior Rink.[118] These men believed in the coming of a new world, and 'for that cause they must exterminate from the earth all the wicked, with their infidel Princes and Magistrates'.[119]

Crespin draws a direct line between early leaders like Storch and Müntzer, and the apocalyptic thinkers of the late 1520s and 1530s, whose teachers are shown to lead to the siege of Münster in 1535.

Crespin writes that:

> Müntzer with his enraged [comrade] Pfeiffer put in train ... the year 1525, the peasants and labourers were in arms in Swabia and Franconia, up to the number of a quarter million. Now, of the miserable end of the said Müntzer and Pfeiffer, and of the sedition of the Peasants, there is no need to write more here, but to have recourse to the histories of our times which speak of them more fully.[120]

In the margins, he suggests the work of Johannes Sleidan, which he himself had published, and which likely provided Crespin with his sources for this section. Instead, this work is intended only to show the trouble that the Anabaptists had caused the Reformation, with Müntzer's followers continuing to spread 'their dreams and their books', on visions and revelations, on the Community of Goods, and on adult baptism.[121] With this, and with his references to Denck, Hut, and Hubmaier, Crespin captures something of the Anabaptist movement in Germany in the years between the Peasants' War and the siege of Münster.

The narrative soon leaves Germany, however, to focus on Zürich, whose reformation was 'afflicted in its beginning by the Anabaptists'.[122] Crespin describes how the Anabaptists were driven by a desire to form a 'pure church of those who had the spirit of God'.[123] Zwingli's view was that this was schismatic, and the debates in the streets in Zürich became ever more disruptive. This agitation forced Zwingli and the magistrate (the two are depicted as working closely together) to hold a disputation on 6 November 1525.[124] Although known to scholars as the Third Baptismal Disputation, Crespin's narrative does not place baptism as a major issue leading up to the debate.[125] Instead it is the disorder, and the challenges to authority represented by the Anabaptists, which pose the major problem for Zwingli. The debate is brought to an end with the publication of letters and ordinances against the 'damned and miserable sect'.[126] That the city of Zürich soon imposed the death penalty on several of the Anabaptist leaders

The German Peasants' War 171

is not mentioned; although Crespin clearly felt the Anabaptists to be a dangerous group, the *Livre des Martyrs* was not concerned with occasions where the Reformed Church participated in the execution of others.

The final, and longest topic of this section on Anabaptism is on the spread of Anabaptism like 'a plague' across Switzerland, Germany, and the Netherlands, which allowed Crespin to engage with the most disruptive of the Anabaptist uprisings, 1534–35's siege of Münster. The narrative starts with Balthazar Hubmaier, described as a minster seduced by 'that sect'.[127] Anabaptists also trouble Oecolampadius in Basle, publish material in Worms, and debate the authorities in Basle and Berne.[128] They even make it to Geneva and Neuchatel. A short passage is given over to a spectacular murder of one Anabaptist by his brother, in St Gall, and Joachim Vadian's intervention in the case.[129] The narrative is drawn to the spectacular and the strange: a woman in 'Appasel', Switzerland, 'taught and persuaded many of that sect that she was Christ, & Messiah of women, and elected twelve Apostles'.[130]

The next passage deals with the Netherlands, where Satan had turned his attentions, being 'too well known in these areas of Switzerland'.[131] This allows Crespin to discuss the Anabaptist seizure of Münster, in Westphalia, from 1534 to 1535. He notes, as he has at several other places in this section on Anabaptism, that he will leave the actual narration of events in the city to the historians. Instead, he focusses on the disorder and social chaos within the city, and the pretensions of the 'tailor-king', Jan van Leiden.[132] As one might expect, the introduction of polygamy plays a major role in Crespin's description of the Anabaptist regime, as do the commonplace divorces.[133] Crespin does not, however, dwell on the violence within the city, or the siege and eventual taking of the town.

Instead, he writes so that 'all faithful hear that this damned sect is not only out of control one time or two, or in the city of Münster only'; he moves on to yet more vignettes of Anabaptist subversion and disorder.[134] Nudist preaching in Amsterdam, and the separate sect of the Adamites, lead up to a final denunciation of the dangers of Anabaptism, particularly their schismatic qualities.[135] The Anabaptists, he says: 'build a tower of Babel and God has confounded their tongues', causing them to 'excommunicate and condemn each other'.[136] Despite an ostensible fear of boring his readers, Crespin claims that he can name at least fifteen separate sects, and proceeds to do so, moving from the band of 'Thomas Müntzer, their first father', to the 'spiritual Anabaptists, separate from the world', the 'glorious and triumphant Anabaptists of Münster', the Huttites, Melchoirites, and even the Mennonites.[137] He closes this account by addressing himself directly to the Anabaptists, and (seeming to anticipate much later historiographical debates) insisting that they cannot distance themselves from the actions of their more violent co-religionists.[138] Even Menno Simons, he says, does not deny the link to Münster and Amsterdam.[139]

172   *The German Peasants' War*

As with the wider question of the Peasants' War, Crespin stressed the disorder and danger of the Anabaptists. He placed the Reformed Church on the side of order, and made the case for obedience to the magistrates, while stressing the division, and lack of serious theological credentials, of the other groups. Indeed, the beliefs of the Anabaptists are of more interest to him than their history. Crespin insists on a direct link from the first Anabaptists, particularly Müntzer, through a series of disputes and disorders to the present enthusiasts, spiritualists, and Mennonites. This takes precedent over giving a detailed account of the events themselves. As with the Peasants' War, Crespin does not depict the end of the siege of Münster, referring the reader instead to works of history (sometimes with a recommendation), a decision into which may have been driven by the demands of genre. Even in this late edition, historical sections were carefully defined, and kept separate; the focus of the *Livre des Martyrs* remained on religious matters.

Conclusion

The four martyrdoms associated with the Peasants' War presented in Crespin all took place after the end of the hostilities themselves. As the genre demanded, the focus was on the martyrs themselves. All three of the martyrs who were included in the 1570 edition were clergy, and were given some chance to express their doctrinal views, which were duly critical of the Catholic Church. All three were, in some fashion, killed by the authorities. By these standards they fulfilled most of the criteria to be included as martyrs.

The revolt of the peasantry is hardly discussed at all; nor is the suppression of the peasants (Crespin refers to them at least twice as 'being appeased'), or the end of the siege of Münster. All of these accounts instead take place in the chaotic aftermath of the Peasants' War, each of the martyrs being caught up in the restoration of order. Indeed, in some of the cases, the Peasants' War seems like a pretext to strike at Protestant clergy, who represent the bulk (and later the entirety) of Crespin's martyrs from this period.

The martyrology reveals fears that the war, as well as the actions of the Anabaptists, will affect the perception of the Reformation as a whole, both in their doctrines, and in their rejection of hierarchy (a tendency Crespin particularly identifies with the Anabaptists). Obedience to authority, on the other hand, had already been praised in the case of George Winckler, whom Luther made a point of commending. Even the third Oecolampadius martyr, accused of fomenting revolt, and a man who was described as: 'a mortal enemy of the exactions of the gentlemen, which oppress the poor people' protested: 'I have not been the author of any rebellion, which I always mortally hated ... I never knew what was in the articles which were published.'[140] This is the only mention in Crespin of the Twelve

The German Peasants' War   173

Articles of the peasants. There is little attempt to engage with the uprisings, and why they happened; they were a piece of history outside of the lives of the martyrs, and thus a subject more suited for pure histories, rather than the martyrology.

Notes

1 James Stayer, *The German Peasants' War and Anabaptist Community of Goods* (Montreal: McGill-Queen's University Press, 1991), p. 20.
2 Stayer, p. 35.
3 Cochlaeus, *Historia Martini Lutheri* (Ingolstadt, 1582). Heiko Oberman, 'The Gospel of Social Unrest', in Robert W. Scribner and Gerhard Benecke (eds), *The German Peasant War of 1525: New Viewpoints* (London: Allen and Unwin, 1979) argues that Lutheran ideas of godly law were essential to the beginning of the revolt. Peter Blickle, in *From the Communal Reformation to the Reformation of the Common Man*, trans. Kumin (Leiden: Brill, 1998) argues that 'The divine law of the peasants derived from the Reformation ... not in Luther's Wittenberg, but among the Christian humanists around Zwingli, who trusted the gospel's capability to improve the ways of the world', p. 160. Hans Hillerbrand, 'The German Reformation and the Peasants' War', in L.P. Buck and J.W. Zophy (eds), *The Social History of the Reformation* (Columbus: Ohio State University Press, 1972).
4 Luther, *Admonition to Peace: A reply to the twelve articles of the peasants in Swabia*, in Luther, *Works*, Vol. 46 (Philadelphia: Fortress Press, 1967), p. 17.
5 Luther, *Admonition to Peace*, p. 22.
6 Luther, *Against the Robbing and Murdering Hordes*, in *Works*, Vol. 46, p. 53.
7 Luther: *Against the Robbing and Murdering Hordes*, p. 53.
8 Luther, *Works*, Vol. 46, pp. 63–85.
9 Blickle, p. 200.
10 Blickle cites Wohlfeil's studies of the Imperial Diets to 1530.
11 Henry J. Cohn, 'Anticlericalism in the German Peasants' War 1525', *Past & Present*, 83 (1979), pp. 4–5.
12 Mark Edwards, *Printing, Propaganda, and Martin Luther* (Minneapolis: Fortress Press, 2005), p. 155. Cohn, p. 4.
13 Edwards, p. 150. The Emser tract is 1525's *Answer to Luther's 'Abomination' Against the Holy secret prayer of the Mass, also how, where and with which words Luther urged, wrote, and Promoted rebellion in his books* (Dresden, 1525).
14 Edwards, pp. 151–53.
15 Edwards, p. 149. Cochlaeus' tract was published at Dresden, 1529.
16 Jean Crespin, *Recueil de plusieurs personnes qui ont constamment endure la mort pour la nome de N. S. Jesus Christ* ([Geneva], 1554), pp. 174–75.
17 Jean Crespin, *Histoire des vrays tesmoins de la verité de l'Evangile*, ([Geneva]: Jean Crespin, 1570), p. 63 verso. Crespin, *Actes des Martyrs* ([Geneva]: Jean Crespin, 1565), p. 102.
18 Crespin, *Histoire des vrays tesmoins* (1570), f. a [vii] verso.
19 Crespin, *Histoire des vrays tesmoins* (1570), p. 63 verso.
20 Crespin, *Histoire des vrays tesmoins* (1554), p. 158. Jean Crespin, *Recueil de plusieurs personnes qui ont constamment enduré la mort pour le nom de Nostre Seigneur* ([Geneva]: Jean Crespin, 1555), Vol. I, p. 164.
21 Crespin, *Actes des Martyrs* (1565), p. 100.
22 Crespin, *Actes des Martyrs* (1565), p. 100.

174   *The German Peasants' War*

23 Crespin, *Histoire des vrays tesmoins* (1570), p. 63 verso.
24 John Foxe, *The Unabridged Acts and Monuments Online* (1576 edition). Editorial commentary and additional information, re. 1563 edition, pp. 483–87. (HRI Online Publications, Sheffield, 2011). Available from: www.johnfoxe.org.
25 TAMO, 1570, p. 1052.
26 TAMO, Apparatus, German Martyrs.
27 Crespin, *Recueil de plusieurs personnes* (1554), pp. 154–55. Crespin, *Recueil de plusieurs personnes* (1555), Vol. I, pp. 164–65.
28 Crespin, *Recueil de plusieurs personnes* (1554), p. 155.
29 Crespin, *Actes des Martyrs* (1565), p. 101.
30 Crespin, *Recueil de plusieurs personnes* (1554), p. 156.
31 Crespin, *Recueil de plusieurs personnes* (1554), pp. 156–57.
32 Crespin, *Recueil de plusieurs personnes* (1554), p. 157.
33 Crespin, *Recueil de plusieurs personnes* (1554), p. 157.
34 Crespin, *Recueil de plusieurs personnes* (1554), p. 158.
35 Crespin, *Recueil de plusieurs personnes* (1554), p. 158. Crespin, *Actes des Martyrs* (1565), p. 101.
36 Crespin, *Recueil de plusieurs personnes* (1554), p. 158.
37 Crespin, *Histoire des vrays tesmoins* (1570), p. 64.
38 Crespin, *Recueil de plusieurs personnes* (1554), p. 158.
39 Crespin, *Actes des Martyrs* (1565), p. 107.
40 Crespin, *Histoire des vrays tesmoins* (1570), p. 64.
41 Crespin, *Recueil de plusieurs personnes* (1554), p. 158.
42 Compare Crespin, *Recueil de plusieurs personnes* (1554), p. 158 with Crespin, *Actes des Martyrs* (1565), p. 107.
43 Crespin, *Recueil de plusieurs personnes* (1554), p. 159. Crespin, *Recueil de plusieurs personnes* (1555), Vol. I, p. 168.
44 Crespin, *Recueil de plusieurs personnes* (1554), p. 159.
45 Crespin, *Recueil de plusieurs personnes* (1554), p. 159.
46 Crespin, *Recueil de plusieurs personnes* (1555), Vol. I, p. 169.
47 Crespin, *Actes des Martyrs* (1565), p. 107.
48 Crespin, *Recueil de plusieurs personnes* (1554), p. 160. Crespin, *Recueil de plusieurs personnes* (1555), Vol. I, pp. 169–70.
49 Crespin, *Recueil de plusieurs personnes* (1555), Vol. I, p. 170.
50 Crespin, *Recueil de plusieurs personnes* (1555), Vol. I, p. 170.
51 Crespin, *Recueil de plusieurs personnes* (1555), Vol. I, p. 170.
52 Crespin, *Recueil de plusieurs personnes* (1554), p. 161.
53 Crespin, *Actes des Martyrs* (1565), p. 108.
54 Crespin, *Recueil de plusieurs personnes* (1555), Vol. I, p. 171. Tom Scott and Bob Scribner, *The German Peasants' War: A History in Documents* (Atlantic Highlands, NJ: Humanities Press, 1991), p. vi. TAMO, 1570, p. 1052.
55 Crespin, *Recueil de plusieurs personnes* (1555), Vol. I, p. 172.
56 Crespin, *Recueil de plusieurs personnes* (1555), Vol. I, p. 174. Crespin *Recueil de plusieurs personnes* (1554), p. 164 changed to 1565, p. 108.
57 Crespin, *Recueil de plusieurs personnes* (1555), Vol. I, p. 174.
58 Crespin, *Recueil de plusieurs personnes* (1555), Vol. I, p. 174.
59 Crespin, *Recueil de plusieurs personnes* (1554), p. 165.
60 Crespin, *Actes des Martyrs* (1565), p. 107.
61 Crespin, *Actes des Martyrs* (1565), p. 108.
62 Crespin, *Actes des Martyrs* (1565), p. 166. Crespin, *Recueil de plusieurs personnes* (1555), Vol. I, p. 175.
63 Crespin, *Recueil de plusieurs personnes* (1555), Vol. I, p. 175.
64 Crespin, *Recueil de plusieurs personnes* (1555), Vol. I, p. 175.

The German Peasants' War 175

65 Crespin, *Recueil de plusieurs personnes* (1555), Vol. I, p. 175.
66 Crespin, *Recueil de plusieurs personnes* (1555), Vol. I, p. 175.
67 Crespin, *Recueil de plusieurs personnes* (1554), p. 168.
68 Crespin, *Recueil de plusieurs personnes* (1555), Vol. I, p. 177.
69 Crespin, *Recueil de plusieurs personnes* (1554), pp. 170–71.
70 Crespin, *Recueil de plusieurs personnes* (1555), Vol. I, p. 179.
71 Crespin, *Recueil de plusieurs personnes* (1555), Vol. I, pp. 179–80.
72 Crespin, *Recueil de plusieurs personnes* (1555), p. 180.
73 Crespin, *Recueil de plusieurs personnes* (1554), pp. 173–74.
74 Crespin, *Recueil de plusieurs personnes* (1554), p. 174.
75 Crespin, *Recueil de plusieurs personnes* (1554), p. 175.
76 Crespin, *Actes des Martyrs* (1565), p. 100.
77 Crespin, *Actes des Martyrs* (1565), p. 100.
78 Crespin, *Actes des Martyrs* (1565), p. 101.
79 Crespin, *Actes des Martyrs* (1565), p. 107.
80 Crespin, *Actes des Martyrs* (1565), p. 627.
81 Crespin, *Actes des Martyrs* (1565), p. 627.
82 Wolfgang Schuch, *Epistre Chrestiene envoyée a trèsnoble Prince monseigneur le duc de Lorayne*, Theodulus Philadelphus (ed.), ([Strasbourg?, 1527]).
83 Schuch, *Epistre Chrestiene*. Gregory, p. 411.
84 Athenase Coquerel, 'Vie et mort du martyr Wolfgang Schuch', *BHSPF*, 2 (1852), p. 634. Volcyr's work is the *L'histoire et recueil de la triumphante et glorieuse victoire obtenue contra les seduyclz et abusez Lutheriens mescreans du pays d'Aulsays et autres* (Paris, 1526).
85 Crespin, *Recueil de plusieurs personnes* (1555), Vol. I, p. 184.
86 Crespin, *Recueil de plusieurs personnes* (1555), pp. 198–99.
87 Schuch (1527), p. B[1] recto. Crespin, *Histoire des vrays tesmoins* (1570), p. 102 *recto*.
88 Crespin, *Actes des Martyrs* (1565), p. 106.
89 Robert Kolb, *For All the Saints: Changing Perceptions of Martyrdom and Sainthood in the Lutheran Reformation* (Macon, GA: Mercer, 1987), p. 65. Kolb regards it as more likely that Rabus' fourth volume, published in 1556, simply drew upon Crespin's 1555 edition.
90 Crespin, *Recueil de plusieurs personnes* (1555), Vol. I, pp. 184–85.
91 *Recueil de plusieurs personnes* (1555), Vol. I, p. 185.
92 *Recueil de plusieurs personnes* (1555), Vol. I, pp. 189, 192.
93 *Recueil de plusieurs personnes* (1555), Vol. I, p. 194.
94 *Recueil de plusieurs personnes* (1555), Vol. I, p. 194.
95 Crespin, *Recueil de plusieurs personnes* (1555), Vol. I, p. 195.
96 Crespin, *Recueil de plusieurs personnes* (1555), Vol. I, p. 195.
97 Crespin, *Recueil de plusieurs personnes* (1555), Vol. I, p. 199.
98 Schuch (1527), pp. A–[Aiii verso].
99 Schuch (1527), pp. Aiiii–[Aiiii verso].
100 Schuch (1527), p. [Aiiii verso].
101 Crespin, *Actes des Martyrs* (1565), p. 101.
102 Crespin, *Actes des Martyrs* (1565), p. 102.
103 Crespin, *Actes des Martyrs* (1565), p. 102.
104 Crespin, *Actes des Martyrs* (1565), p. 102.
105 Scott and Scribner, pp. 44, 48.
106 Crespin, *Actes des Martyrs* (1565), p. 106.
107 Crespin, *Actes des Martyrs* (1565), p. 106.
108 Crespin, *Actes des Martyrs* (1565), p. 106.
109 Crespin, *Actes des Martyrs* (1565), p. 106.
110 Crespin, *Actes des Martyrs* (1565), p. 106.

176　*The German Peasants' War*

111 Crespin, *Actes des Martyrs* (1565), p. 107.
112 Guy de Brès, *La racine, source, et fondement des anabaptistes* (Strasbourg, 1589), pp. 24–25.
113 Sigrun Haude, *In the Shadow of 'Savage Wolves': Anabaptist Münster and the German Reformation During the 1530s* (Leiden: Brill, 2000), p. 25.
114 Crespin, *Histoire des vrays tesmoins* (1570), p. 83 recto.
115 Crespin, *Histoire des vrays tesmoins* (1570), p. 83 recto.
116 Crespin, *Histoire des vrays tesmoins* (1570), p. 83 recto.
117 Crespin, *Histoire des vrays tesmoins,* (1570), p. 83 recto.
118 Crespin, *Histoire des vrays tesmoins* (1570), p. 83 recto.
119 Crespin, *Histoire des vrays tesmoins,* (1570), p. 83 recto.
120 Crespin, *Histoire des vrays tesmoins* (1570), p. 83 verso.
121 Crespin, *Histoire des vrays tesmoins* (1570), p. 83 verso.
122 Crespin, *Histoire des vrays tesmoins* (1570), p. 83 verso.
123 Crespin, *Histoire des vrays tesmoins* (1570), p. 83 verso.
124 Crespin, *Histoire des vrays tesmoins* (1570), p. 83 verso.
125 G.H. Williams, *The Radical Reformation* (Kirksville, MO: Truman State University Press, 1995), pp. 233–34.
126 Crespin, *Histoire des vrays tesmoins* (1570), p. 83 verso.
127 Crespin, *Histoire des vrays tesmoins* (1570), pp. 83 verso–84 recto.
128 Crespin, *Histoire des vrays tesmoins* (1570), p. 84 recto.
129 Crespin, *Histoire des vrays tesmoins* (1570), p. 84 recto.
130 Crespin, *Histoire des vrays tesmoins* (1570), p. 84 recto.
131 Crespin, *Histoire des vrays tesmoins* (1570), p. 84 recto.
132 Crespin, *Histoire des vrays tesmoins* (1570), p. 84 recto.
133 Crespin, *Histoire des vrays tesmoins* (1570), p. 84 recto.
134 Crespin, *Histoire des vrays tesmoins* (1570), p. 84 recto.
135 Crespin, *Histoire des vrays tesmoins* (1570), p. 84 recto.
136 Crespin, *Histoire des vrays tesmoins* (1570), p. 85 recto.
137 Crespin, *Histoire des vrays tesmoins* (1570), p. 85 recto.
138 Haude, p. 2.
139 Crespin, *Histoire des vrays tesmoins* (1570), p. 85 recto.
140 Crespin, *Recueil de plusieurs personnes* (1554), pp. 175, 173–74.

Conclusion

Crespin's *Livre des Martyrs* served several purposes. It acted as a history of the Reformed Church, describing a continuous line of martyrs and ideas back to the fourteenth century. Its principal focus, however, was on contemporary Protestant martyrs, whom it compared explicitly to the martyrs of the Apostolic Church.[1] This was the rationale for recording their words and deeds, which were deserving of memorialisation, but also of study.

Through its description of these martyrs and their persecution, often in great detail, the *Livre des Martyrs* also acted as a guide to both theology and behaviour, as Andrew Pettegree has suggested in reference to other martyrologies.[2] It helped to define a Reformed identity by describing the ways in which Protestants acted differently, the ways in which Catholic beliefs were flawed, and by building up a family history of Protestantism. Readers were presented with exemplars of brave behaviour, which was framed as being specifically Protestant. In the form of the trials and interrogations of the martyrs, readers were given examples of how Protestant theology could be used to counter Catholic claims; these were effectively catechisms in action.

The geographical and temporal range of these accounts helped to underline the idea that the beliefs and behaviours they described were somehow essential to being a member of the Reformed Church. Martyrs from Jan Hus to Anne Askew, and from John Wyclif to de Bourg, were largely depicted as holding a single, coherent, set of beliefs, and as being consistently persecuted for these by the Catholic hierarchy. As we have seen, Crespin sometimes altered his source documents (most usually through a process of elimination, rather than fabrication), in order to maintain this sense of doctrinal purity, and therefore the utility of the collection. By their nature, foreign or stranger groups were essential to building this image of a long-standing and wide-spread Protestant movement. The study of the Vaudois, active since the twelfth century, or the Hussites, prominent in the fifteenth, was also a study of the Protestant past. These outside elements were therefore subservient to the practical needs of the martyrology. As we have seen, this often meant that their distinctive elements were worn away, as they were presented as relatively conventional members of the Reformed

178   *Conclusion*

Church. All of this can allow us some insight into the way in which Genevan books and messages were helping to shape Reformed identity during its period of greatest growth in France.

The means by which Crespin worked to create this identity can be difficult to unpick at times. The *Livre des Martyrs* was certainly not a homogenous text. Crespin compiled the book from a variety of other sources, from printed histories to personal letters, and does not appear to have composed much of the text himself. Indeed, it does not appear that he claimed to, instead placing himself more as the book's editor and publisher.[3] Indeed, in the passages borrowed from Rabus, or martyrology's *Quatrieme Partie*, which was largely adapted directly from Foxe, it is difficult even to place the editorial decisions in a single pair of hands.

During Crespin's lifetime, the martyrology also appeared in seven different French editions over a period of sixteen years, evolving in its content and focus throughout this period. Through this process, new information replaced older or less-detailed accounts, and new techniques changed the composition of the text itself, influenced by the work of Foxe, Rabus, and van Haemstede. It is this instability, however, which has allowed us to observe the changes Crespin made and the emphases that he placed on his material. Most of the significant changes that were made to the text were on topics that either affected the right of the account to be included in the martyrology, or were on topics that affected the doctrinal content being conveyed to the readers.

For Crespin, doctrine was 'a certain mark, amongst many others' in defining one's status as a martyr and it was, in turn, a mark of pure doctrine that it was always persecuted.[4] Knowing this doctrine, and remembering these martyrs, was important for the faithful, and the *Livre des Martyrs* was deliberately created to aid in this task. Key catechismical elements were repeated in the confessions and disputations of the martyrs, making it a useful tool for defining the details of its faith. As Crespin stated in the introduction to his 1561 edition:

> One can see by the preceding books and parts of the Collection of Martyrs, the profit brought by the instruction of the examples that God daily gives us in the form of those who die firm and constant for the Gospel;

in 1563, he wrote that these testimonies would 'console, fortify, and defend us against the hard assaults of the most wicked enemies of the truth of the gospel'.[5] This was not simply a memorialisation of a person, but a collection of their words and deeds for the good of others.

Because of these aims, the content of the *Livre des Martyrs* had a particular focus on those doctrines that most clearly separated the Reformed and Catholic Churches. One key reason for this was the source material, which was largely based on trials, interrogations, and other documents

Conclusion   179

that recorded confrontation. The effect was not only to educate the reader, but to frame those tenets in terms of difference from Catholic norms. This was a key strength of the *Livre des Martyrs* in building a sense of a distinct Reformed community, but as we have seen, it was also the key challenge in presenting outside groups.

The example of the Eucharist gives perhaps the clearest example of this. The *Livre des Martyrs* displays a particular interest in the subject of the Real Presence of Christ in the bread and the wine of the Eucharist. It was central to Reformed understanding that there was no such presence, and throughout the martyrology, defendants single this topic out as a central one, arguing again and again that as Christ is, in the biblical phrasing: 'at the right hand of God', he cannot also be descending constantly to earth to participate in Mass. This emphasis on the Real Presence was a difficult topic to apply to the histories of Hussite or Lutheran martyrs, however; both groups held views at odds with Reformed thinking, as Crespin (who had published Calvin's pamphlets against the Lutherans on the topic) would have known well.[6] As we have seen, however, Crespin worked to make sure that, at the minimum, the confessions that he reproduced did not contradict conventional Reformed teaching on the subject. Other issues that were important to Crespin were less difficult to state clearly. Lutheran attacks on clerical celibacy, or on a priest's powers of absolution, were easy to place alongside the Reformed criticisms of Catholic doctrine on saints, justification, or Papal authority, which appear again and again in the martyrology.

In rare circumstances Crespin illustrated and explained a conflict of opinion, usually by reference to incomplete or corrupted knowledge on the part of the outside group. Most notably, he repeatedly made reference to the relative ignorance of the Vaudois (though they were still 'more clear and pure than the common'), who needed guidance from their Reformed partners.[7] In part, this schema reflects the situation in the Alps and Provence, where missionaries from Geneva were dealing with exactly these sorts of issues, as reflected particularly in the books written by men like Lentolo.

This idea of imperfect knowledge on the part of the Vaudois also reflected the martyrology's sense of time, and ecclesiastical history. Like Bale and Foxe, Crespin's history of the Reformation itself suggests a long decline from the ancient church of the apostles, with only a few small groups (such as the Vaudois) keeping alive a continuous chain of true belief. As Agrippa d'Aubigné later put it in his *Histoire Universelle*, continuity with the Apostolic Church came through doctrine, not personal succession.[8] Wyclif and Hus represented a renaissance for this true church, and Crespin suggested (drawing on his Lutheran sources), that Luther and 95 Theses represented the beginning of its fully realised return. These groups, then, had an important role to play in the history of the church, and were worth the conceptual challenges they could pose to Crespin.

180   *Conclusion*

They represented several hundred years of its history, and the crucial link between the first Christians and readers of the martyrology.

Perhaps the key function of these groups in the martyrology was their testimony to the continuous history of the Church. Crespin insisted that this Church had been consistent from the time of the Apostles through to the present day, though suffering from some impurities and deviations during the medieval period, at the height of the Papacy's power. This viewpoint could be found in a number of other Protestant histories of the Church, although Crespin's discussion of this scheme was far less detailed than that in the work of Foxe, Bale, or James Ussher.[9] It was, however, the central organising principle of his discussion of groups who emerged before Luther.

While, unlike some of his contemporaries, Crespin did not illustrate the medieval period in any detail at all, choosing to begin his narrative with Hus, and later with Wyclif, he was always careful to remind his readers that this was effectively a choice made for practical reasons, and that he could have extended the martyrology farther into the past if he had wanted to.[10] Crespin's use of the Lollards and, especially, the Hussites had an important genealogical element to it. As Krumenacker and others have pointed out, it was important to be able to show that the Reformed Church had a long history.[11] For Crespin, it was important that these predecessors were more than simply opposition to the Catholic Church; it was necessary to demonstrate some conformity of doctrine as well. As we have seen, it was not essential for this conformity of belief to be perfect, or for Hus and Wyclif to be fully fledged Protestants *avant-la-lettre*, but it is also clear from the changes made to Hus' statements of faith during his trial that Crespin wanted him to be understood as a straightforward critic of the Catholic Church. As a result, as we have seen, many of Hus' statements before the Council of Constance were altered to make them more radical in their theology, or appear to accept the criticisms of him being made at the Council. This brought Hus into the Reformed fold not only in terms of his doctrine, but also his behaviour. Reformed martyrs were usually portrayed as openly debating theological points with their prosecutors, rather than claiming innocence of the charges against them. Crespin's alteration of Hus' defence placed him more clearly as a forerunner of the Reformation in both the style and the substance of his trial.

The same motives appear to have worked in a different way with regard to Crespin's treatment of the Vaudois. The *Livre des Martyrs* gave them an important place in the history of the Church, suggesting that they had helped to keep alive the true faith through the medieval period. This element of their history was not, however, emphasised. Instead, Crespin's discussion of the Vaudois was largely restricted to contemporary events, between 1530 and 1565. The Vaudois were placed in the martyrology according to these dates, and the history of their movement in earlier times was presented simply as background, or context. For all that the Vaudois

Conclusion 181

occupied an important place in Reformed history, especially within France, this appears to have been somewhat secondary for Crespin. His focus on contemporary events also meant that the primary doctrinal focus in the *Livre des Martyrs* was on the Vaudois as full members of the Reformed Church. Reference was made in several places to the deficiencies in Vaudois teaching and practice, but the central understanding was that this had been resolved, with advice from senior reformers, in the 1530s. Increasingly the doctrines presented in reference to the martyrdoms of the 1540s and 1550s were orthodox Genevan ones, and for the accounts from the 1550s and 1560s in Piedmont, it was primarily Genevan ministers presenting religious ideas to the reader. At least in the pages of the martyrology, the independent voice of the Vaudois was subsumed into the church they had joined.

Even the Lutherans, a more distinct group with their own publishing history and their own political leaders, lost some of their identity to Crespin's conception of a unified Protestantism. Although the coming of Luther, and his break with Rome, clearly marked a watershed in the return of 'the light' for Crespin, the Lutherans themselves were not treated as a separate confession: for example, key elements of Lutheran teaching were omitted from the confessions of Lutheran martyrs. This was not so much a continuation of the polemical battles between Calvinists and Lutherans as it was an attempt to rise above them. Crespin's handling of Luther's doctrine and his legacy appear to reflect the approach taken by Calvin himself, which was predicated on the idea that the divisions between the groups were temporary, and capable of resolution, while the shared history and ties between the denominations were more important and long-lasting. This sense of unity with the Lutherans was strengthened by the martyrology's reliance on accounts of Lutheran martyrs in its coverage of the 1520s and 1530s, a period in which there were few French, or Reformed, figures on which to focus.

All of these factors were important in what histories were presented in the *Livre des Martyrs*. It is clear that there was more to being included than simply being persecuted by the Catholic Church, as the question of relationships with secular authority helps to illustrate.[12] Clearly, some, but not all, episodes of violence were capable of disqualifying an individual martyr from the collection; the rejection of violence and open resistance had been an important feature of Calvin's contact with the communities in France. The treatment of the martyrs of the Peasants' War, and the later removal of one of these accounts from the *Livre des Martyrs* suggests his concern about those who were 'mixed with deeds which could render them suspect and impure'.[13] The inclusion in later editions of massacre victims, whom Crespin did not consider to be full martyrs, demonstrates some of the difficulties that a straightforward application of these principles created for the project.

Crespin's view of Reformed history, and the means by which he communicated Reformed teaching, proved to be influential and durable, lasting

182   Conclusion

well into the seventeenth century. We have seen some indications that the *Livre des Martyrs* was a widely read and prestigious book for French Protestants, as the Foxe's *Actes and Monuments* was in England, and for similar reasons. Later examples of Protestant history, such as the Genevan *Histoire Ecclesiastique*, and Agrippa d'Aubigné's *Histoire Universelle*, or foreign-language martyrologies like those from Foxe and Rabus, directly drew on Crespin's sources and his interpretations. His shift in later editions, to include narratives of the French Wars of Religion alongside martyrdoms, also paralleled a wider movement in French Protestant history writing, which saw greater interest in narrative histories of the kingdom of France.

The most obvious way that Crespin's influence continued was through the later editions of the *Livre des Martyrs*, which was printed until 1619 by Crespin's son-in-law Eustache Vignon and, later by Simon Goulart, Calvin and Beza's successor as the moderator of Geneva's Company of Pastors. The connection of Goulart in particular, a major religious figure and an accomplished historian in his own right, suggests the importance that the *Livre des Martyrs* held for the Reformed Church in the early seventeenth century. The later editions of the martyrology, which were published in 1582, 1597, 1608, and 1619, continued the move Crespin had already begun towards including more narrative history (indeed, all of these editions were titled *Histoire des Martyrs*), particularly in the wake of 1572's St Bartholomew's Day massacres.

Under Goulart's direction, the first book of the 1597 martyrology attempted to fill the gap Crespin had left between the biblical martyrs and Wyclif. Persecutions under Nero, Trajan, and a host of other Roman Emperors were followed by those by Vandals, Muslims, and eventually the Papacy.[14] Amongst the victims of the Papacy, Goulart included the Albigensians, or Cathars, who had previously been omitted by Crespin. They were included alongside the Vaudois, and indeed conflated with them, as a group 'villainously calumnised by the histories', and this edition of the *Livre des Martyrs* gives a brief account of their history.[15] Goulart included a short history of the Vaudois and Albigensians in the martyrology's Book VIII, outlining their medieval history, including Vualdo's establishment in Lyon, and the crusade against the Cathars in Languedoc after 1200.[16] This development was part of a wider integration of the Albigensians into Protestant history that was taking place in the early seventeenth century.[17] Outsider groups, then, continued to be central to the *Livre des Martyrs*, and to Reformed histories of the Church, well into the seventeenth century. The framework in which they were presented, although continuing to evolve, was one that Crespin's martyrologies had done a great deal to create.

From the first editions of the *Livre des Martyrs* onwards, outsider groups were an integral part of the way the martyrology was conceived and presented. Crespin's insistence that there was only one true church

Conclusion   183

meant that there was an important basis to include them. They testified to the fact that there was no place, and no time, where the Gospel was not persecuted.[18] They gave the Church a history, and a geographical spread, that a more narrow focus on the French Reformed Church, or the Reformed community, would not have done. In addition to this historical context, the martyrologies did important work in defining the attributes and boundaries of Reformed belief and behaviour. They provided role models, and templates for argument that could be used in the village square or around the table.

These arguments would not have been as effective, however, and the book's educational ends would not have been met, if Crespin had not carefully edited and presented the theological contents of the accounts he had collected. By design, the *Livre des Martyrs* provided a series of examples of good behaviour, and of proper doctrine, in the face of Catholic tricks and errors. It demonstrated to its generations of readers a community of Protestants that was much larger, and more ancient, than simply the French Reformed Church, giving that community a history, a mission, examples of expected behaviour, and the details of the faith that defined it. The outsider groups helped to define this community's limits in time, space, conduct, and doctrine, demonstrating what it meant to be a member of the True Church.

Notes

1 Jean Crespin, *Histoire des vrays tesmoins de la verité de l'Evangile* ([Geneva]: Jean Crespin, 1570), sig. *a* iiii recto.

2 Andrew Pettegree, 'Adriaan van Haemstede: The Heretic as Historian', in Bruce Gordon (ed.), *Protestant History and Identity in Sixteenth Century Europe* (Aldershot: Scolar Press, 1996), p. 69.

3 Jean-François Gilmont, *Jean Crespin: Un éditeur réformé du XVIe siècle* (Geneva: Droz, 1981), pp. 179–87.

4 Jean Crespin, *Recueil de plusieurs personnes qui ont constamment enduré la mort pour le nom de Nostre Seigneur* ([Geneva]: Jean Crespin, 1555), Vol. I, sig. ii recto, p. I.

5 Jean Crespin, *Quatrieme partie des actes des martyrs* (Geneva, 1561), sig. *ii recto. Jean Crespin, *Cinquieme partie du recueil des martyrs* ([Geneva: Jean Crespin], 1564 [1563]), sig. *ii verso.

6 Gilmont, *Jean Crespin*, p. 125.

7 Jean Crespin, *Actes des Martyrs* ([Geneva]: Jean Crespin, 1565), p. 189.

8 Agrippa d'Aubigné, *Histoire Universelle … Tome Premier* (Amsterdam: Commelin, 1626), col. 75.

9 Luc Racaut, *Hatred in Print, Catholic Propaganda and Protestant Identity During the French Wars of Religion* (Aldershot: Ashgate, 2002), p. 124.

10 Crespin, *Recueil de plusieurs personnes* (1555), Vol. I, p. II.

11 Yves Krumenacker, 'Les genealogie imaginaire de la Reforme Protestante', *Revue Historique*, 638 (2006), p. 262.

12 David El Kenz, *Les bûchers du roi: la culture protestante des martyrs (1523–1572)* (Paris: Seyssel, 1997), pp. 110, 128.

13 Jean Crespin, *Actes des Martyrs* (1565), p. 100.

184 *Conclusion*

14 Jean Crespin and Simon Goulart, *Histoire des Martyrs persécutez* (Geneva, 1597), p. 20 verso.
15 Crespin and Goulart, *Histoire des Martyrs persécutez* (1597), p. 25 verso.
16 Jean Crespin and Simon Goulart, *Histoire des Martyrs persécutez et mis a mort pour la vérité de l'Évangile, depuis le temps des apostres jusques à présént* (1619), pp. 600 recto–602 recto.
17 Racaut, p. 126.
18 Crespin, *Recueil de plusieurs personnes* (1555), sig. iii recto.

Bibliography

Printed sources before 1700

d'Aubigné, Agrippa, *Histoire Universelle ... Tome Premier* (Amsterdam: Commelin, 1626).

Bossuet, Jacques-Bénigne, *Histoire des Variations des Eglises Protestantes* (Paris: Veuve Mabre Cramoisy, 1688).

Bracciolini, Poggio, *Epistula de morte Hieronymi Pragensis ad Leonardum Brunum* ([Leipzig]: Conrad Kachelofen, 1490]).

Bracciolini, Poggio, *Historia Johannis Hussi et Hieronymi Pragensis* ([Nuremberg], [1528]).

Bracciolini, Poggio, *Pogii Florentini De Hieronymi Pragensis obitu & supplicio descriptio* [1535].

de Brès, Guy, *La racine, source, et fondement des anabaptistes* (Strasbourg, 1589).

Cochlaeus, Johannes, *Historiae Hussituram libri duidecim* (Mainz, 1529).

Cochlaeus, Johannes, *Historia Martini Lutheri* (Ingolstadt, 1582).

Crespin, Jean, *Actes des Martyrs* ([Geneva]: Jean Crespin, 1565).

Crespin, Jean, *Cinquieme partie du recueil des martyrs* ([Geneva: Jean Crespin], 1564 [1563]).

Crespin, Jean, *Histoire des vrays tesmoins de la verité de l'Evangile* ([Geneva], Jean Crespin, 1570).

Crespin, Jean, *Histoire memorable de la persecution de Merindol et Cabrieres* ([Geneva: Jean Crespin], 1555).

Crespin, Jean, *Histoire memorable de la persecution de Merindol et Cabrieres* ([Geneva: Jean Crespin], 1556).

Crespin, Jean, *Recueil de plusieurs personnes qui ont constamment enduré la mort pour le nom de Nostre Seigneur* ([Geneva]: Jean Crespin, 1555).

Crespin, Jean, *Recueil de plusieurs personnes qui ont constamment enduré la mort pour le nom de nostre Seigneur Jesus Christ* ([Geneva: Jean Crespin], 1554).

Crespin, Jean, *Recueil de plusieurs personnes qui ont constamment enduré la mort pour le nom du Seigneur* ([Geneva]: Jean Crespin, 1556).

Crespin, Jean, *Troisieme partie du recueil des martyrs* ([Geneva]: Jean Crespin, 1556).

Crespin, Jean, *Quatrieme partie des actes des martyrs* ([Geneva]: Jean Crespin, 1561).

Crespin, Jean and Simon Goulart, *Histoire des Martyrs persécutez et mis a mort pour la verite de l'Evangile* (Geneva, 1597).

186 Bibliography

Crespin, Jean and Simon Goulart, *Histoire des Martyrs persécutez et mis a mort pour la verite de l'Evangile* (Geneva, 1619).

Crespin, Jean and Eustache Vignon, *Histoire des Martyrs persécutez et mis a mort pour la verite de l'Evangile* (Geneva, 1582).

Ernstliche handlung zwische den hochgelerten Doctorn inn der gotheyt, als mann sie zu Cölln nennt, oder ketzermeyster, vnnd eynem gefangnen genant, Adolph Clarenbach, geschehen zu Cöln erstlich vff Franckenthurn. Item wie nachuolgends die Doctores inn der gotheyt vnd ketzermeyster den selbigen gefangnen im glaube examinirt oder ersucht zu Cölln vff der Erenporten. ([Worms?, *c.*1528]).

Eyn new warhafftig vnd wunderbarlich geschicht oder hystori von Jörgen wagner zu München in Bayern als eyn Ketzer verbrandt im Jar M.D.xxvij (Nuremburg: Hans Hergot, 1527).

Foxe, John, *Commentarii rerum in ecclesia gestarum ... Autore Ioanne Foxo Anglo. Hiis incalce access erunt Aphorismi Joannis Vuilevi, com collectaneis quibusdam, Reginaldi Pecki Episcopi Cicestrensus* (Strasbourg: Rihel, 1554).

Foxe, John, *Rerum in ecclesia gestarum ...* (Basel: Brylinger & Oporinus, [1559]).

de Hainault, Jean, *L'Estat de l'Eglise Avec le Discours des Temps, depuis les Apostres sous Neron, jusques à Present, sous Charles V* ([Geneva: Jean Crespin], 1556).

Histoire des Persecutions et guerres faites depuis l'an 1555, jusques en l'an 1561, contre le peuple apellé Vaudois qui est auc valées d'Angrongne, Luserne, sainct Martin, la Perouse et autres ... ([Geneva]: Éstienne, 1562) (via Bibliothèque électronique suisse, accessed 20 July 2011).

Historia de Duobus Augustinenensibus, ob evangelii doctrinam exustis Bruxellae, die trigesima Iunii (1523) (via electronic media, Universitat-Bibliothek Basel).

Luther, Martin, *Die artikel warumb die zwen Christliche Augustiner munch zu Brussel verprandt sind, sampt eynem sendbrieff an die Christen ym Holland und Braband* (Wittenburg: Nickel Schirlentz, 1523).

Noel, Etienne, *Histoire des persecutions et guerres faites depuis l'an 1555 jusques en l'an 1561, contre le peuple appele Vaudois ...* ([Geneva], 1562).

Pantaleone, Heinrich, *Martyrum Historia ...* (Basel: Brylinger, 1563).

Perrin, Jean-Paul, *Luther's Fore-runners: Or, a cloud of witnesses, Deposing for the Protestant Faith* (London: Nathanial Newbery, 1624).

Piccolomini, Aeneas Sylvius (Pius II), *Commentariorum Aeneae Sylvii Piccolominei Senesis, de Concilio Basileae celebrato libri duo, olim quidem scripti, nuncuero primum impressi* ([Basel: Andreas Cratander], [1523?]).

Piccolomini, Aeneas Sylvius (Pius II), *De vocatione Bohemorum ad sacrum Basiliense Concilium* [1525].

Piccolomini, Aeneas Sylvius (Pius II), *Historia Bohemica* (Rome: Oppenhym and Shurener de Bopardia, 1475).

Rabus, Ludovicus, *Der Heiligen ausserwöhlten Gottes Zeugen, Bekennern und Martyrern, so inn angender Ersten Kirchen, Alts uñ Newes Testaments, zu yeder zeit gewesen seindt, warhaffte Historien ... Erstmals durch M. L. Rabum ... im Latein ... zusammen getragen, und yetzund durch ihn selbers ... inn Teutsche sprach verdolmetscht* (Strasbourg: Becken, 1552).

Rabus, Ludovicus, *Historien der Martyrer* (Strasbourg: Rihel, 1571).

Schuch, Wolfgang, *Epistre Chrestiene envoyee a tresnoble Prince monseigneur le duc de Lorayne*, Theodulus Philadelphus (ed.). ([Strasbourg?, 1527]).

Scipione Lentolo, *Histoire des Persecution et Guerres faites depuis l'an 1561. Contre le peuple appelé Vaudois, qui est aux valees d'Angrongne, Luserne, sainct*

Bibliography 187

Martin, la Perouse & autres du pais de Piemont (Geneva: Artus Chauvin [1562]).

Severt, Jacques, *L'anti-martyrologe ou Verité manifestée contre les histories des supposés martyrs de la Religion pretendue reformee, imprimees a Geneve onze fois. Divise en douze livres. Monstrant la difference des vrais Martyrs d'avec les faux, corporellement executez en divers lieux* (Lyon: Rigaud, 1622).

Sleidan, Johann, *A briefe Chronicle of the foure principall empires* (London: Roland Hall, 1563).

Sleidan, Johann, *Des Quatres Empires Souverains* ([Geneva]: Jean Crespin, 1558).

Sleidan, Johann, *Histoire entiere d l'estat de la religion et republique sous Charles V.* ([Geneva], 1558).

Van Haemstede, Adriaen, *De Geschiedenisse ende den doodt der vromer Martelaren, die om het ghetuyghenisse des Evangeliums haer bloedt gestort hebben, van den tijden Christi af, totten Jar* ([Emden],1559).

Secondary sources

Aubery, J., *Histoire de l'execution de Cabrieres et de Merindol et d'autres lieux de Provence*, ed. G. Audisio (Mérindol: Association d'études Vaudoises et historiques de Lubéron, 1982).

Audisio, Gabriel, 'How to Detect a Clandestine Minority: The Example of the Waldensians', *Sixteenth Century Journal*, 21:2 (1990), 205–16.

Audisio, Gabriel (ed.), *Les Vaudois des origins à leur fin* (Turin: A. Meynier, 1990).

Audisio, Gabriel, *Les Vaudois: Histoire d'une dissidence XIIe–XVIe siècle* (Paris: Fayard, 1998).

Audisio, Gabriel, *Preachers by Night: The Waldensian Barbes (15th–16th centuries)*, (Leiden: Brill, 2007).

Audisio, Gabriel, *The Waldensian Dissent: Persecution and Survival c.1170–c.1570* (Cambridge: Cambridge University Press, 1999).

Backus, Irena, *Historical Method and Confessional Identity in the Era of Confessionalisation* (Leiden: Brill, 2003).

Barker, Sara, *Protestantism, Poetry, and Protest* (Aldershot: Ashgate, 2009).

Barnett, S.J., 'Where Was Your Church Before Luther? Claims for the Antiquity of Protestantism Examined', *Church History*, 68:1 (1999), 14–41.

Baumgartner, Fredric, *France in the Sixteenth Century* (London: Palgrave Macmillan, 1995).

Benedict, Philip, 'Bibliothèques protestantes et catholiques à Metz au XVIIe siècle', *Annales Économies, Sociétés, Civilisations*, 40:2 (1985).

Benedict, Philip, and Fornerod, Nicholas, 'Les 2, 150 "Eglises" reformées de France de 1561–1562', *Revue Historique*, 651 (2009), 529–60.

Benzing, Josef, *Bibliographie Strasbourgeoise: Bibliographie des ouvrages imprimés à Strasbourg (Bas-Rhin) au XVIe siècle* (Baden-Baden: V. Koerner, 1981).

Betts, R.R., *Essays in Czech History* (London: Athlone Press, 1969).

Biller, Peter, *The Waldenses, 1170–1530: Between a Religious Order and a Church* (Aldershot: Ashgate, 2001).

Blickle, Peter, *From the Communal Reformation to the Reformation of the Common Man* (Leiden: Brill, 1998).

Blum, Claude, *La Representation de la mort dans la littérature Française de la Renaissance Vol. II* (Paris: Librarie Honoré Champion, 1989).

188 Bibliography

Boccassini, Daniela, 'Le massacre des Vaudois des Provence: échos et controversies', *Archiv für Reformationsgeschichte*, 82 (1991), 257–86.

Bonnaire, Pierre, 'Des images à relire et à réhabiliter: l'œuvre gravé de Tortorel et Perrissin', *Bulletin de la Société de l'Histoire de Protestantisme Français*, 138 (1992), 475–514.

Bonnet, Jules (ed.), *Letters of John Calvin* (Philadelphia: Presbyterian Board of Publication, [1858]).

Bowden, John (ed.), *Encyclopedia of Christianity* (Oxford: Oxford University Press, 2005).

Bray, John, *Theodore Beza's Doctrine of Predestination* (Niewkoop: De Graaf, 1975).

Broomhall, Susan, 'Disturbing Memories: Narrating Experiences and Emotions of Distressing Events in the French Wars of Religion', in Erika Kuipers, Judith Pollmann, Johannes Mueller, and Jasper van der Steen (eds), *Memory Before Modernity: Practices of Memory in Early Modern Europe* (Leiden: Brill, 2013).

Calvin, Jean, *Institutes of the Christian Religion*, trans. Beveridge (London: James Clarke & Co, 1953).

Calvin, Jean, *Letters of John Calvin*, ed. Jules Bonnet (Philadelphia: Presbyterian Board of Publication, [1858]).

Calvin, Jean, *Letters of John Calvin, Selected from the Bonnet Edition* (Edinburgh: Banner of Truth Trust, 1855, reprinted 1980).

Calvin, Jean, *Three French Treatises*, ed. Francis Higman (London: Athlone, 1970).

Cameron, Euan, 'Medieval Heretics as Protestant Martyrs', in Diana Wood (ed.), *Martyrs and Martyrologies: Papers Read at the 1992 Summer Meeting and the 1993 Winter Meeting of the Ecclesiastical History Society*, Studies in Church History, 30 (Oxford: Blackwell, 1993), pp. 185–207.

Cameron, Euan, *The Reformation of the Heretics: The Waldenses of the Alps, 1480–1580* (Oxford: Clarendon Press, 1984).

Cameron, Euan, *Waldenses: Rejections of Holy Church in Medieval Europe* (Oxford: Blackwell, 2000).

Cameron, Pierre, *Le martyrologe de Jean Crespin, etude de ses editions au XVIe siecle* (PhD Thesis, Université de Montreal, 1996).

Carroll, Stuart, *Blood and Violence in Early Modern France* (Oxford: Oxford University Press, 2006).

Chaix, Paul, Dufour, Alain, and Moeckli, Gustave (eds), *Les livres imprimés à Genéve de 1550 à 1600* (Geneva: Droz, 1966).

Chartier, Roger (ed.), *Les usages de l'imprimé (XVe–XIXe siécle)* (Paris: Fayard, 1987).

Chartier, Roger, *The Cultural Uses of Print in Early Modern France* (Princeton, NJ: Princeton University Press. 1987).

Chaunu, Pierre, *Le Temps des Réformes* (Paris: Fayard, 1974).

Cochrane, Arthur (ed.), *Reformed Confessions of the Sixteenth Century* (London: SCM Press, 1966).

Cohn, Henry, 'Anticlericalism in the German Peasants' War 1525', *Past & Present*, 83 (1979).

Coquerel, Athenase, 'Vie et mort du martyr Wolfgang Schuch', *Bulletin de la Société de l'Histoire de Protestantisme Français*, 2 (1852), 632–48.

Crouzet, Denis, 'À propos de la plasticité de la violence réformée au temps des premières guerres de Religion', *Bulletin de la Société de l'Histoire de Protestantisme Français*, 148:4 (2002), 907–51.

Crouzet, Denis, *La Genèse de la Réforme Française 1520–1562* (Paris: Sedes Press, 1996).

Cullière, Alain, 'L'Heresie' de Nicolas Volcyr (1534)', *Bibliotheque d'Humanisme et Renaissance*, 71:3 (2009), 433–55.

Davis, Thomas, ' "The Truth of the Divine Words": Luther's Sermons on the Eucharist, 1521–28, and the Structure of Eucharistic Meaning', *The Sixteenth Century Journal*, 30:2 (1999), 323–42.

De Bèze, Théodore, *Histoire Ecclésiastique des Églises Réformées au Royaume de France, Vol. 1*, ed. G. Baum and E. Cunitz (Nieuwkoop: De Graaf, 1974).

Debard, Jean-Marc, 'La Reforme Luthérienne et la langue Française: le cas de la Principauté de Montbéliard du XVIe au XVIIe siècle', *Bulletin de la Société de l'Histoire de Protestantisme Français*, 129:1 (1983), 1–22.

Dillenberger, John (ed.), *John Calvin: Selections from his Writings* (Oxford: Oxford University Press, 1975).

Doucet, Roger, 'Pierre du Chastel, Grand Aumônier de France', *Revue Historique*, 134 (1920), 1–58.

Dubois, Claude-Gilbert, *Le Conception de l'Histoire en France au XVIe siécle (1560–1610)* (Paris: AG Nezet, 1977).

Edwards, Mark, *Luther and the False Brethren* (Stanford, CT: Stanford University Press, 1975).

Edwards, Mark, *Printing, Propaganda, and Martin Luther* (Minneapolis: Fortress Press, 2005).

El Kenz, David, 'Le Roi de Justice et la martyr reformeé', *Bulletin de la Société de l'Histoire de Protestantisme Français*, 141 (1995), 27–69.

El Kenz, David, *Les bûchers du roi: la culture protestante des martyrs (1523–1572)* (Paris: Seyssel, 1997).

El Kenz, David, 'Les usages subversives du martyre dans la France des troubles de religion de la parole ou geste', *Revue des Sciences Humaines*, 269:1 (2003), 33–51.

Evenden, Elizabeth, *Patents, Pictures and Patronage: John Day and the Tudor Book Trade* (Aldershot: Ashgate, 2008).

Evenden, Elizabeth and Freeman, Thomas, *Religion and the Book in Early Modern England: The Making of John Foxe's 'Book of Martyrs'* (Cambridge: Cambridge University Press, 2014).

Faulkner, John, 'Luther and the Real Presence', *The American Journal of Theology*, 21:2 (1917), 225–39.

Febvre, Lucien, *Au cœur religieux du XVIe Siècle* (Paris: Sevpen, 1968).

Fischer, Daniella, 'L'histoire de l'Eglise dans la penseé de Calvin', *Archiv für Reformationsgeschichte*, 77 (1986), 79–125.

Freeman, Thomas, 'Fate, Faction, and Fiction in Foxe's Book of Martyrs', *The Historical Journal*, 43:3 (2000), 601–23.

Freeman, Thomas, 'Text, Lies, and Microfilm: Reading and Misreading Foxe's "Book of Martyrs" ', *Sixteenth Century Journal*, 30:1 (1999), 23–43.

Fudge, Thomas, 'Seduced by the Theologians: Aeneas Sylvius and the Hussite Heretics', in Ian Hunter, John Christian Laursen, and Cary J. Nederman (eds),

190 Bibliography

Heresy in Transition: Transforming Ideas of Heresy in Medieval and Early Modern Europe (Aldershot: Ashgate, 2005), pp. 89–102.

Fudge, Thomas, *The Crusade against Heretics in Bohemia, 1418–1437* (Aldershot: Ashgate, 2002).

Fudge, Thomas, *The Magnificent Ride: First Reformation in Hussite Bohemia* (Aldershot: Ashgate, 1998).

Gaskell, Philip, *A New Introduction to Bibliography* (Winchester: St Paul Bibliographies, 1995).

George, Timothy (ed.), *John Calvin and the Church: A Prism of Reform* (Louisville, KY: Westminster/John Knox Press, 1990).

Gielis, Marcel, 'Leuven Theologians as Opponents of Erasmus and of Humanistic Theology', in Erika Rummel (ed.), *Biblical Humanism and Scholasticism in the Age of Erasmus* (Leiden: Brill), pp. 197–214.

Gilmont, Jean-François, 'Aux origines de l'historiographie vaudoise du XVIe siècle: Jean Crespin, Étienne Noël et Scipione Lentolo', in *Collana della Societa di Studi Valdesi, 9: I Valdesi e l'Europa* (Torre Pellice: Claudiana, 1982).

Gilmont, Jean-François, *Bibliographie des éditions de Jean Crespin, 1550–1572), 2 vols* (Verviers: Gason, 1981).

Gilmont, Jean-François, *Jean Crespin: Un éditeur réformé du XVIe siècle* (Geneva: Droz, 1981).

Gilmont, Jean-François, 'La Correspondence de Jean Crespin (vers 1520–1572)', *Lias*, VI (1979), 3–37.

Gilmont, Jean-François. 'La naissance de l'historiographie protestante', in Andrew Pettegree, Paul Nelles, and Philip Connor (eds), *The Sixteenth-Century French Religious Book* (Aldershot: Ashgate, 2001), pp. 110–26.

Gilmont, Jean-François, 'Les Vaudois des Alpes: mythes et réalités', *Revue d'histoire ecclésiastique*, 83 (1988), 69–89.

Gilmont, Jean-François and Kemp, William (eds), *Le livre évangélique en français avant Calvin: Études originales, publications d'inédits, catalogues d'éditions anciennes/The French Evangelical Book before Calvin: Original Analyses, Newly Edited Texts, Bibliographic Catalogues* (Turnhout, Belgium: Brepols Publishers, 2004).

Gonnet, Giovanni, 'Remarques sur l'historiographie Vaudoise des XVI et XVII siècles', *Bulletin de la Société de l'Histoire de Protestantisme Français*, 120 (1974), 323–65.

Gordon, Bruce, *Protestant History and Identity in Sixteenth-Century Europe, Vol. II* (Aldershot: Scolar Press, 1996).

Gordon, Bruce and Marshall, Peter (eds), *The Place of the Dead: Death and Remembrance in Late Medieval and Early Modern Europe* (Cambridge: Cambridge University Press, 2000).

Greenberg, Devorah, ' "Foxe" as a Methodological Response to Epistemic Challenges: The Book of Martyrs Transported', in David Loades (ed.), *John Foxe at Home and Abroad* (Aldershot: Ashgate, 2004), pp. 237–53.

Greengrass, Mark, 'Scribal Communication and Scribal Publication in Early Calvinism: The Evidence of the "Letters of the Martyrs" ', in Irene Dingel and Herman Selderhuis (eds), *Calvin und Calvinismus: Europäische Perspektiven* (Goettingen: Vandenhoeck & Ruprecht, 2011).

Gregory, Brad, *Salvation at Stake: Christian Martyrdom in Early Modern Europe* (Cambridge, MA: Harvard University Press, 1999).

Bibliography 191

Gribben, Crawford, 'John Knox, Reformation History, and National Self-fashioning', *Reformation and Renaissance*, 8:1 (2006), 48–66.

Haberkern, Philip, *Patron Saint and Prophet: Jan Hus in the Bohemian and German Reformations* (Oxford: Oxford University Press, 2016).

Haude, Sigrun, *In the Shadow of 'Savage Wolves': Anabaptist Münster and the German Reformation During the 1530s* (Leiden: Brill, 2000).

Heal, Felicity, 'The Holinshead Editors: Religious Attitudes and their Consequences', Holinshead Chronicles online (www.cems.ox.ac.uk/holinshed/papers.shtml).

Heller, Henry, 'Nicholas of Cusa and Early French Evangelicalism', *Archiv für Reformationsgeschichte*, 63 (1972), 6–21.

Hempsell, David, 'Languedoc 1520–1540: A Study of Pre-Calvinist Heresy in France', *Archiv für Reformationsgeschichte*, 62 (1971), 235–43.

Heppe, Heinrich, *Reformed Dogmatics: Set Out and Illustrated from the Sources*, ed. Ernst Bizer (Grand Rapids, MI: Baker Book House, 1978).

Herminjard, A.-L., *Correspondance des Réformateurs dans les pays de Langue française* (Nieuwkoop: De Graaf, 1965).

Heymann, Frederick, *John Zizka and the Hussite Revolution* (Princeton, NJ: Princeton University Press, 1955).

Higman, Francis, 'Calvin, le polar, et la propogande: *L'histoire d'un meurtre execrable*', *Bibliothèque d'Humanisme et Renaissance*, 54:1 (1992), 111–23.

Higman, Francis, 'Histoire du Livre et histoire de la Réforme', *Bulletin de la Société de l'Histoire de Protestantisme Français*, 148 (2002), 837–50.

Higman, Francis, *Lire et Decouvrir: La circulaiton des idées au temps de la Réforme* (Geneva: Droz, 1998).

Hillerbrand, Hans, 'The German Reformation and the Peasants' War', in L.P. Buck and J.W. Zophy (eds), *The Social History of the Reformation* (Columbus: Ohio State University Press, 1972).

Hillerbrand, Hans (ed.), *The Oxford Encyclopedia of the Reformation*, ed. Hans J. Hillebrand (Oxford: Oxford University Press, 1996, 2005).

Hotson, Howard, 'The Historiographical Origins of Calvinist Millennnarianism', in Bruce Gordon (ed.), *Protestant History and Identity in Sixteenth-Century Europe* (Aldershot: Scholar Press, 1996).

Hudson, Anne, 'Notes of an Early Fifteenth-Century Research Assistant, and the Emergence of the 267 Articles against Wyclif', *The English Historical Review*, 118 (2003), 685–97.

Hunter, Ian, Laursen, John Christian, and Nederman, Carey J. (eds), *Heresy in Transition: Transforming Ideas of Heresy in Medieval and Early Modern Europe* (Aldershot: Ashgate, 2005).

Jostock, Ingeborg, 'La censure au quotidian: le controle de l'imprimerie a Geneve, 1560–1600', in Andrew Pettegree, Paul Nelles, and Philip Connor (eds), *The Sixteenth-Century French Religious Book* (Aldershot: Ashgate, 2001), pp. 210–38.

Kaminsky, Howard, *A History of the Hussite Revolution* (Berkeley: University of California Press, 1967).

Kaminsky, Howard, 'Pius Aeneas Among the Taborites', *American Society of Church History*, 28:3 (1959), 281–309.

Kavka, Frantisek, 'The Hussite Movement in the Czech Republic', in Mikulas Teich (ed.), *Bohemia in History* (Cambridge: Cambridge University Press, 1998).

192 Bibliography

Kelley, Donald, *The Beginning of Ideology: Consciousness and Society in the French Reformation* (Cambridge: Cambridge University Press, 1983).

Kess, Alexandra, *Johann Sleidan and the Protestant Vision of History* (Aldershot: Ashgate, 2008).

King, J. ' "The Light of Printing": William Tyndale, John Foxe, John Day, and Early Modern Print Culture', *Renaissance Quarterly*, 54:1 (2001), 52–85.

Kingdon, Robert, *Geneva and the Coming of the Wars of Religion in France, 1555–1563* (Geneva: Droz, 1956).

Kingdon, Robert, Bergier, Jean-François, and Dufour, Alain, *Registres de la Compagnie des Pasteurs de Genève au temps de Calvin* (Geneva: Droz, 1962).

Klassen, John, *The Nobility and the Making of the Hussite Revolution* (New York: Columbia University Press, 1978).

Kolb, Robert, *Confessing the Faith: Reformers Define the Church, 1530–1580* (St Louis, MO: Concordia Pub. House, 1991).

Kolb, Robert, *For All the Saints: Changing Perceptions of Martyrdom and Sainthood in the Lutheran Reformation* (Macon, GA: Mercer, 1987).

Kolb, Robert, 'God's Gift of Martyrdom: The Early Reformation Understanding of Dying for the Faith', *Church History*, 64:3 (1995), 399–411.

Kolb, Robert, 'Kaiser, Leonhard', *The Oxford Encyclopedia of the Reformation*, ed. Hans J. Hillebrand (Oxford: Oxford University Press, 1996, 2005).

Krumenacker, Yves, 'La geneologie imaginaire de la Reforme protestante', *Revue Historique*, 638 (2006), 259–89.

Lambert, Malcolm, *Medieval Heresy: Popular Movements from the Gregorian Reform to the Reformation* (Oxford: Blackwell, 1992).

Lambert, Malcolm, *The Cathars* (Oxford: Blackwell, 1998).

Lestringant, Frank, 'Calvinistes et Cannibales: Les écrits protestantes sur la Brésil Français (1555–1580)', *Bulletin de la Société de l'Histoire de Protestantisme Français*, 126 (1980), 167–92.

Lestringant, Frank, *L'experience Huguenot au Nouveau Monde: XVI siècle* (Geneva: Droz, 1996).

Lestringant, Frank, *Lumieré des martyrs: Essai sur le martyre au siècle des Réformes* (Paris: Honore Champion, 2004).

Levene, Mark and Roberts, Penny (eds), *The Massacre in History* (Oxford: Berghahn, 1999).

Loades, David (ed.), *John Foxe at Home and Abroad* (Aldershot: Ashgate, 2004).

Lokkos, Antal (ed.), *Le Livre a Geneve 1478–1978 Catalogue de l'exposition organise par la Bibliothéque publique et universitaire a l'occasion du 500e anniversaire de l'imprimerie a Genéve* (Geneva: Bibliothéque Publique, 1978).

Luther, Martin, *Luther's Works Vol. 24 – Sermons on the Gospel of St. John, Chapters 14–16*, ed. Jaroslav Pelikan (St Louis: Concordia, 1961).

Luther, Martin, *Luther's Works Vol. 37 – Word and Sacrament, 3*, ed. Helmut T. Lehmann (Philadelphia: Fortress Press, 1961).

Luther, Martin, *Luther's Works Vol. 39 – Church and Ministry, 1*, ed. Eric Gritsch (Philadelphia: Fortress Press, 1970).

Luther, Martin, *Luther's Works Vol. 43 – Devotional Writings, 2*, ed. Gustav K. Weincke (Philadelphia: Fortress Press, 1968).

Luther, Martin, *Luther's Works Vol. 44 – The Christian in Society, 1*, ed. James Atkinson (Philadelphia: Fortress Press, 1966).

Bibliography 193

Luther, Martin, *Luther's Works Vol. 46 – The Christian in Society, 3*, ed. Robert C. Schultz (Philadelphia: Fortress Press, 1967).

Luther, Martin, *Luther's Works Vol. 47 – The Christian in Society, 4*, ed. Franklin Sherman (Philadelphia: Fortress Press, 1971).

Luther, Martin, *Luther's Works Vol. 53 – Liturgy and Hymns*, ed. Ulrich S. Leupold (Philadelphia: Fortress Press, 1965).

Lutzow, Francis, *The Life and Times of Master John Hus* (London: J.M. Dent, 1921).

Macek, Joseph, *The Hussite Movement in Bohemia* (New York: AMS, 1958).

Makens, Judith, 'Hugh Latimer and John Forest: Rituals of Martyrdom', *Reformation*, 6 (2002), 29–48.

Matheson, Peter, 'Martyrdom or Mission? A Protestant Debate', *Archiv für Reformationsgeschichte*, 80 (1989), 154–72.

Maynard, Katherine, 'Writing Martyrdom: Agrippa d'Aubigne's Reconstruction of Sixteenth-Century Martyrology', *Renaissance and Reformation*, 30:3 (2007), 29–50.

McGrath, Alister, *Reformation Thought: An Introduction* (Oxford: Blackwell, 2000).

Moore, William, *La Réforme Allemande et la Littérature Française: Recherches sur la Notériéte de Luther en France* (Strasbourg: Faculté des lettres à l'Université, 1930).

Monter, William, *Judging the French Reformation: Heresy Trial by Sixteenth-Century Parlements* (London: Harvard University Press, 1999).

Monter, William, 'Les exécutés pour hérésie par arrêt du Parlement de Paris (1523–1560)', *Bulletin de la Société de l'Histoire de Protestantisme Français*, 142 (1995), 27–69.

Moreau, Georges, 'Contribution à l'histoire de Livre des Martyrs', *Bulletin de la Société de l'Histoire de Protestantisme Français*, 103 (1957), 173–99.

Muller, L., 'Revolutionary Moment: Interpreting the Peasants' War in the Third Reich and in the German Democratic Republic', *Central European History*, 40 (2007), 193–218.

Myers, R., Harris, M., and Mandelbrote, G. (eds), *Books on the Move: Tracking Copies through Collections and the Book Trade* (London: British Library, 2007).

Myers, R., Harris, M., and Mandelbrote, G. (eds), *Fairs, Markets, and the Itinerant Book Trade* (London: British Library, 2007).

Nelles, Paul. 'Three Audiences for Religious Books in Sixteenth-century France', in Andrew Pettegree, Paul Nelles, and Philip Connor (eds), *The Sixteenth-Century French Religious Book* (Aldershot: Ashgate, 2001), pp. 256–85.

Nicholls, David, 'Sectarianism and the French Reformation', *Bulletin of the John Rylands University Library of Manchester*, 70 (1988), 35–44.

Nicholls, David, 'The Theatre of Martyrdom in the French Reformation', *Past and Present*, 121 (1988), 49–73.

Nischan, Bodo (ed.), *Lutherans and Calvinists in the Age of Confessionalisation* (Aldershot: Ashgate, 1999).

Nischan, Bodo, 'The "Fractio Panis": A Reformed Communion Practice in Late Reformation Germany', *Church History*, 43:1 (1984), 17–29.

Novotny, Vaclav, *Fontes rerum Bohemicarum, Vol. VIII* (Prague, 1932).

194 Bibliography

Oberman, Heiko, *Luther Between God and the Devil* (New Haven, CT: Yale University Press, 2006).

Oberman, Heiko, 'The Gospel of Social Unrest', in Robert W. Scribner and Gerhard Benecke (eds), *The German Peasant War of 1525: New Viewpoints* (London: Allen and Unwin, 1979).

Palacký, František (ed.), *Documenta mag. Joannis Hus vitam, doctrinam, causam in Constantiensi concilio actam et controversias de religione in Bohemia annis 1403–1418* (Prague: Tempsky, 1869).

Parker, Charles, 'French Calvinists as the Children of Israel: An Old Testament Self-Conciousness in Jean Crespin's *Histoire des Martyrs* before the Wars of Religion', *Sixteenth Century Journal*, 24:2 (1993), 227–48.

Pettegree, Andrew, 'Adriaan van Haemstede: The Heretic as Historian', in Bruce Gordon (ed.), *Protestant History and Identity in Sixteenth-Century Europe* (Aldershot: Scholar Press, 1996).

Pettegree, Andrew, *The Book in the Renaissance* (New Haven, CT: Yale University Press, 2010).

Pettegree, Andrew, Walsby, Malcolm, and Wilkinson, Alexander (eds), *French Vernacular Books: Books Published in the French Language before 1601*, 2 vols (Leiden: Brill, 2007).

Piaget, Arthur and Berthoud, Gabrielle, *Notes sur le Livre des Martyrs de Jean Crespin* (Neuchatel: Attinger, 1930).

Racaut, Luc, *Hatred in Print: Catholic Propaganda and Protestant Identity during the French Wars of Religion* (Aldershot: Ashgate, 2002).

Racaut, Luc, 'The Polemical Use of the Albigensian Crusade During the French Wars of Religion', *French History*, 13:3 (1999), 261–79.

Randall Coats, Catharine, *(Em)bodying the Word: Textual Resurrections in the Martyrological Narratives of Foxe, Crespin, de Bèze and d'Aubigné* (New York: Peter Lang, 1992).

Roberts, Penny, *A City in Conflict: Troyes during the French Wars of Religion* (Manchester: Manchester University Press, 1996).

Romier, Lucien, 'Les Vaudois et le Parlement français de Turin', *Mélanges d'archéologie et d'histoire*, 30:1 (1930), 193–207.

Rummel, Erika (ed.), *Biblical Humanism and Scholasticism in the Age of Erasmus* (Leiden: Brill, 2008).

Saunders, Alison, 'The Sixteenth-century French Emblem Book as a Form of Religious Literature', in Andrew Pettegree, Paul Nelles, and Philip Connor (eds), *The Sixteenth-Century French Religious Book* (Aldershot: Ashgate, 2001), pp. 38–67.

Schmidt, Charles, 'Actenstucke besonders zur geschichte der Waldenser', *Zeitschrift fur die historische theologian*, 22 (1852), 238–62.

Scott, Tom and Scribner, Bob (eds), *The German Peasants' War: A History in Documents* (Atlantic Highlands, NJ: Humanities Press, 1991).

Scribner, Robert, 'Incombustible Luther', *Past and Present*, 110 (1986), 63–64.

Scribner, Robert (ed.), *Religion and Culture in Germany (1400–1800)* (Leiden: Brill, 2001).

Shepardson, Nikki, *Burning Zeal: The Rhetoric of Martyrdom and the Protestant Community in Refomation France, 1520–1570* (Cranbury, NJ: Associated University Presses, 2007).

Shepardson, Nikki, 'Gender and the Rhetoric of Martyrdom in Jean Crespin's *Histoire des vrays tesmoins'*, *Sixteenth Century Journal*, 5:1 (2004), 155–74.

Smahel, Frantisek, *La Revolution Hussite, une anomalie historique* (Paris: College de France, 1985).

Spinka, Matthew, *Hus at the Council of Constance* (London: Columbia University Press, 1965).

Spinka, Matthew, *John Hus: A Biography* (Princeton, NJ: Princton University Press, 1968).

Spinka, Matthew, *John Hus' Conception of the Church* (Princeton, NJ: Princeton University Press, 1966).

Spinka, Matthew, *Letters of John Hus* (Manchester: Manchester University Press, 1972).

Stayer, James, *The German Peasants' War and Anabaptist Community of Goods* (Montreal: McGill-Queen's University Press, 1991).

Tilley, Maureen, *Donatist Martyr Stories: The Church in Conflict in Roman North Africa* (Liverpool: Liverpool University Press, 1996).

Tinsley, Barbara, 'Pope Joan Polemic in Early Modern France: The Use and Disabuse of Myth', *The Sixteenth Century Journal*, 18:3 (1987), 381–39.

Tingle, Elizabeth, and Jonathan Willis (eds), *Dying, Death, Burial and Commemoration in Reformation Europe* (Aldershot: Ashgate, 2015).

The Unabridged Acts and Monuments Online or TAMO (HRI Online Publications, Sheffield, 2011). Available from: www.johnfoxe.org.

Tucker, Jameson, 'Fire and Iron', in Elizabeth Tingle and Jonathan Willis (eds), *Dying, Death, Burial and Commemoration in Reformation Europe* (Aldershot: Ashgate, 2015).

Van der Linden, David, *Experiencing Exile: Huguenot Refugees in the Dutch Republic, 1680–1700* (Aldershot: Ashgate, 2015).

Van Dussen, Michael, *From England to Bohemia: Heresy and Communication in the Later Middle Ages* (Cambridge: Cambridge University Press, 2012).

Vanderhaegen, Ferdinand, *Bibliographie des martyrologes protestants néerlandais* (Ghent: University of Ghent, 1890).

Venard, Marc, *Réforme protestante, Réforme catholique dans la provence d'Avignon au XVIe siècle* (Paris: Cerf, 1993).

Verveliet, Hendrick, *The Paleotypography of the French Renaissance* (Leiden: Brill, 2008).

Wandel, Lee Palmer, *The Eucharist in the Reformation: Incarnation and Liturgy* (Cambridge: Cambridge University Press, 2005).

Wanegffelen, Thierry, *Ni Rome, Ni Genève: des fideles entre deux chaires en France au XVIe siècle* (Paris, Honoré Champion, 1997).

Watkins, Renee Neu, 'The Death of Jerome of Prague: Divergent Views', *Speculum*, 42:1 (1967), 104–29.

Watson, David, 'Jean Crespin and the Writing of History in the French Reformation', in Bruce Gordon (ed.), *Protestant History and Identity in Sixteenth-Century Europe* (Aldershot: Scolar Press, 1996).

Watson, David, *The Martyrology of Jean Crespin and the Early French Evangelical Movement, 1523–1555* (PhD Thesis, University of St Andrews, 1997).

Watson, Timothy, 'When is a Huguenot Not a Huguenot?' in Keith Cameron, Mark Greengrass, and Penny Roberts (eds), *The Adventure of Religious Pluralism in Early Modern France* (Bern: Peter Lang, 2000).

196 Bibliography

Wiley, David, 'The Church as the Elect in the Theology of John Calvin', in Timothy George (ed.), *John Calvin and the Church: A Prism of Reform* (Louisville, KY: Westminster/John Knox Press, 1990), pp. 96–119.

Williams, G.H., *The Radical Reformation* (Kirksville, MO: Truman State University Press, 1995).

Zdenek, David, 'Utraquism's Curious Welcome to Luther and the Candlemas Day Articles of 1524', *The Slavonic and East European Review*, 79:1 (2001), 51–89.

Index

Actes and Monuments (Foxe) 1, 3, 122, 159, 164, 182
Agricola, Johannes 27, 28, 31, 32
Albigensians *see* Cathars
Amboise, Conspiracy of 111
Anabaptists 145, 157, 167–72
Angrogna Valley, Piedmont 100–1, 103–12
Antichrist 40, 42, 45, 103, 129, 136, 143
Antoine, Duke of Lorraine 166–8
Antwerp 132, 134, 137–8, 140
Apostles' Creed 84–6, 88, 90, 100, 139
Aquinas, Thomas 123
Askew, Anne 177
Aubigné, Theodore Agrippa d' 177, 182
Augustine, St 12, 40–1, 48, 110, 123–5, 147
Audisio, Gabriel 68, 69, 71, 76, 85
Avignon 78, 83, 87, 115

Bale, John 17, 18, 32, 48, 179
baptism 14, 88–90, 109, 141, 144–5, 148, 170–1
Barbes 75, 76, 78, 86, 101, 104, 105
Barnett, S.J. 18
Bataille, Bertrand 103
Baudius, Claude 131
Bellay, Guillaume du 82
Benedict, Philip 16
Bethlehem Chapel, Prague 33, 46
Betts, Reginald 46, 64n172
Beza, Theodore 3, 9, 17, 128, 130, 182
Blanc, Maurizi 80
Blickle, Peter 173n3
Bohemia 35–8, 43, 45–6, 52, 53–9
book burning 45, 51, 169

Bossuet, Jacques-Bénigne, Bishop of Meaux 17, 19, 149
Bourg, Anne de 177
Bracciolini, Poggio 27, 32, 47, 48, 49–51
Broomhall, Susan 17
Brully, Pierre 14–16
Brun, Estienne 99, 102
Brussels 31, 132–4, 137
Bucer, Martin 6, 14, 16, 69, 75, 116, 147, 156
Bullinger, Heinrich 69, 89, 129–30, 148, 169

Cabrières 66, 67, 72, 73, 75, 77–82, 85, 90–2, 95–6, 101, 106–8, 110, 115, 185, 187
Calabria 70–1, 100, 106–7, 115–16
Calvin, Jean 2, 3, 6, 9–18, 22, 24–6, 32, 38, 40, 62, 67, 69, 70, 81, 85, 87, 89, 94, 96–7, 99, 103–5, 108, 114, 117–18, 120–1, 125–31, 135, 147–8, 150, 154, 179, 181–2
Cameron, Euan 66, 68, 70–1, 84–6, 93–7, 99, 115–19
Cameron, Pierre 19
Carpentier, George 144–6
Cathars 3, 11, 18, 38, 68, 70, 182
Catholic Church 16–18, 22, 30, 35, 37–40, 42–3, 52, 57–60, 67, 70–1, 74, 84–5, 88–9, 91, 100, 113–16, 124, 126, 146, 161, 172, 177–81
Chambéry Five 102–4
Chandieu, Antoine de la Roche 5, 128
Chanforan, Synod of 68, 72, 75, 79
Charles University, Prague 46
Chassane, President 82
Chastel, Pierre du 87
Clarebach, Adolph 146

198   *Index*

Coats, Catherine Randall 4, 17, 20
Cochlaeus, Johannes 27, 155–6
Comtat Venaissin 73, 82
Confession (sacrament) 14, 36, 43, 49, 136, 141, 145
Confession of Faith, French 128
Confession of Faith, Genevan 128
Confession of Faith, Vaudois 72, 77, 81, 83–93
Council of Constance 31–44, 46–50, 52, 54, 56, 122, 124, 135, 180
Crespin, Jean: early life 2–3; as publisher 3–9, 16–17, 19, 21–2, 58–9, 66–7, 72, 77, 89, 130–2, 147–9, 156–8, 177–83

Dauphiné 71, 74, 102
defrocking 35, 43, 133–4
Denck, Hans 170
Diaz, Juan 17, 132
Donation of Constantine 39, 70
Donatism 37–40, 43

Edwards, Mark 156
Egypt 125, 138
El Kenz, David 12, 164
Emmanuel-Philibert, Duke of Savoy 108, 111–15
Erasmus 125
Esch, Jean 1, 4, 31, 132–40, 148, 151n93
Eucharist 10, 13–15, 35–8, 43, 48, 50, 53, 58–9, 85, 89, 100, 107, 125–30, 132, 135, 141, 143–8, 167, 179

Farel, Guillaume 69, 74, 81, 99–100
Flistede, Pierre 146–7
Foxe, John 3, 6–7, 11, 13, 15–18, 20, 23, 28–31, 33, 48–9, 51, 57, 59, 67, 88, 104, 122–3, 125, 147, 159–60, 162–4, 178–80, 182
François I, King of France 77–8, 82, 87, 90, 92

Gemets, Odoul 111–13
Geneva 2–4, 6–12, 13, 17, 19, 21–2, 32, 52, 66, 69–70, 73, 79, 84, 93, 98–108, 111, 114, 115–16, 140, 144, 171, 178–9, 181–3; Council of 7, 32, 130–1, 142
Gerson, Jean 51
Gilmont, Jean-François 2–3, 5, 7–8, 20, 28, 68, 76, 84, 98, 104, 108
Girard, Jean 100

Gonin, Martin 78, 99–102, 115–16, 130
good works 41–2, 46, 69, 88, 122, 137, 141, 167
Goulart, Simon 9, 17–18, 182
Graves-Monroe, Amy 20
Gregory, Brad 13, 20, 120, 135, 145
Guardia Piemontese 71, 106–7
Guerin, Jacques 91

Hainault, Jean de 6, 8, 11
Hector, Barthelemy 104–5, 109, 114
Henri II, King of France 9, 19, 87, 90–1
Holofernes 91
Holy Roman Empire 2, 155–6
Hubmaier, Balthazar 170–1
Hus, Jan 11, 30–46, 48–52, 58–60, 121, 135, 137, 166, 177, 179–80; doctrine 35–43, 56; reputation 21, 27–8, 53–5, 121–4; trial 34–5, 37–44, 57
Hussites 2–3, 11, 13, 17, 21, 23, 28, 30–2, 36–7, 44, 53–4, 56, 59–60, 74, 94n52, 114, 120, 121, 126, 131, 177, 180
Hut, Jan 170–1

iconoclasm 54, 58
Illyricus, Matthias Flacius 11, 18, 27, 31–2, 51
images 14, 55, 83, 86, 89, 105, 168
invisible church 17, 40, 49, 85
Israel 20, 45, 91, 125–6

Jerome of Prague 21, 27, 30, 32, 45–55, 57–9, 137, 141
Jews 48, 86–7
justification 14, 86, 123, 179
Judith 91

Kaiser, Leonard 140–2, 147–8
Karlstadt, Andreas 122, 126–7
Kas, Alexandra 6
Kelley, Donald 20
Krumenacker, Yves 18, 180

Laborie, Antoine 103
Lentolo, Scipione 98, 101, 108, 179
Lestringant, Frank 1, 20
Lollards 2–3, 7, 21, 28–31, 33, 48, 59, 74–5, 77–8, 114, 120–1, 126, 132, 180
Lord's Prayer 145–6, 168

Index 199

Lucerne 100, 109–12
Luther, Martin 18–19, 27–30, 54, 60, 99, 120–7, 129–35, 137–44, 147–9, 155–6, 168, 170, 172, 179–81
Lutherans 2, 4, 10–11, 13, 17, 21–3, 27–8, 31, 58, 60, 74, 85, 99, 120–1, 123, 126–7, 130–5, 137–49, 166, 179–81; as synonym for Protestant 74, 78, 81–2, 99, 106, 116
Lyon 67, 70, 76, 182

marks of a martyr 12–13
Marlorat, Augustine 110
Mass 15, 35, 71, 100, 103, 107, 110, 113, 126–8, 135–6, 141, 145, 161, 167–9, 179
Masson, Pierre 69, 75
Melanchthon, Philip 125, 129, 131, 147
Mennonites 171–2
Mérindol 66–7, 69, 72–83, 87, 90–2, 101, 106–8, 110, 114–16; Meynier, Jean *see* Oppède, Jean de Meynier d'
Monter, William 19
Montréal, Aimery de 30
Moravia 53, 57, 70
Morel, Georges 69, 75
Moses 125, 131, 138
Münster 22, 169–72
Müntzer, Thomas 127, 157, 169–72

Nicene Creed 84, 133, 145
Nicodemism 8, 69, 76, 85, 103, 111, 113, 115–16, 130
Noël, Étienne 108
Novotny, Vaclav 31, 42

oaths 14, 86
Ochino, Bernardino 105
Oecolampadius 69, 75, 78, 85, 116, 126, 129–31, 158–67, 169, 171–2
Olivétan, Pierre Robert 66, 79
Oppède, Jean de Meynier d' 80, 82, 90–1
Original Sin 88

Palecs, Stephen 34–5, 37, 39, 41, 44
Pantaleone 159
Papal authority 21, 30, 40–2, 49, 124, 179
Parker, Charles 20
Parlement of Aix (Provence) 73, 78–80, 82–3, 87, 90–2, 116
Parlement of Chambéry 103

Parlement of Turin 104–5, 108–10
Pascal, Jean-Louis 106–7, 109, 111, 114–16
Peasants' War 131, 142, 144, 147, 155–73, 181
Pellenc, Colin 81
Peter of Mladonovice 27–8, 31–44, 58–9
Pettegree, Andrew 9, 16, 20, 177
Piccolomini, Aeneas Sylvius 27, 32–3, 53, 55–6, 58–9
Piedmont 67, 69–70, 74–5, 92–3, 98–116, 181
Poor of Lyon *see* Vaudois
Pope 27, 29–30, 41–2, 45, 44–9, 55–7, 100, 103, 106, 110, 112, 121, 124–6, 131
Pope Pius II *see* Piccolomini, Aeneas Sylvius
Prague 21, 30, 34–5, 37, 39, 44, 46, 54, 56, 58, 137
preaching 15, 29, 33, 41, 43, 53–4, 69–70, 74, 100, 103, 105–7, 109–11, 113, 116, 122, 124, 132, 137–40, 143, 161, 167, 171
primitive Church 1, 2, 39, 45, 75–6, 120, 132, 137
Providence 29, 78–9, 91, 110, 169
purgatory 13–15, 49, 71, 105, 107, 135, 161

Rabus, Ludwig 6, 7, 12, 20, 132, 146–7, 166, 175n89, 178, 182
Racaut, Luc 18
Real Presence 126–7, 144, 148, 179
Reformed Church 1, 3, 6, 10–11, 17, 19, 21–3, 29–30, 37–8, 66–70, 75, 79, 85, 91–2, 98–9, 101, 109, 113, 115–16, 120, 130–2, 169, 171–2, 177–83
relics 4, 17, 35, 44, 51–2; veneration of 40, 83
resistance to authority 22, 52–3, 57, 67, 81, 108, 110–15, 181
Rink, Melchior 170
Roma, Jean de 78, 85, 87, 91–2

Sadoleto, Cardinal Jacopo 84, 87
saints 4, 10, 14, 18, 53, 83, 85, 89, 100, 107, 135–7
San Sisto dei Valdese 71, 106–7
Satan 16, 29, 103, 107, 111, 115–16, 171
Savonarola, Girolama 31, 121–4, 126

200 *Index*

Savoy 19, 22, 66–7, 93, 101, 103, 108, 111–15
Sceitter, Conrad 145
Schuch, Wolfgang 165–9
sedition 12, 53, 81, 87, 91, 115, 157–67, 170
Seisel, Claude de, Archbishop of Turin 76
Seré, Nadia 12
Severt, Jacques 17
Shepardson, Nikki 20
Sigismund, King of Bohemia 34–5, 41, 55–6
Sleidan, Johannes 6, 8, 72, 170
Spengler, Peter 159–62
Spinka, Matthew 31, 33, 37, 42, 46
Stayer, James 163
Storch, Nicholas 170

Tabor 53–4, 56, 58, 59
Taborites 32, 55–6, 71
Tambard, Gaspar 137, 160, 165
Taschart, Martin 105
Tauran, Guyraud 103
Ten Commandments 84–8
torture 30, 78, 112, 139, 162–4
Transubstantiation 18, 34, 38, 43, 48, 58, 105, 126–8, 135, 145; *see also* Real Presence
Treaty of Cavour 108, 111, 113
Trigalet, Jean 103
Truchet, Captain 113
True Church 2, 12, 17–19, 21, 29, 60, 85, 88, 121, 123, 125–6, 132, 179, 180, 182–3
Turks 1, 18, 21, 56, 82, 86, 87, 123, 146

Ussher, James, Archbishop of Armagh 18, 180

Utenhove, Jan 130
Utraquism 32, 35, 37–9, 53, 56, 58–9, 143

van der Linden, David 16–17
van Haemstede, Adriaan 20, 49, 178
van Zutphen, Heindrichs 112, 120, 132–3, 136–40, 142–3, 148
Varagle, Geoffrey 101, 105, 109, 114
Vassy, massacre of 157
Vaudois 2–3, 8–9, 11, 17–19, 21–3, 39, 66–73, 120–1, 126, 131–2, 147–8, 177, 179–82; in Provence 73–93; in the Alps 98–116
Vernou, Jean 98, 102–5, 107, 131
Vignon, Eustache 9, 182
Viret, Pierre 69, 74, 99, 128
Voez, Henry 1, 4, 31, 132–7, 139, 142, 147–8
Vualdo, Peter 29, 70, 75–7, 123

Wagner, Jorgen *see* Carpentier, George
Wandel, Lee Palmer 127
Watson, David 8, 10, 19, 64n159
Wenceslas IV, King of Bohemia 53–4
Westphal, Johannes 130
Winckler, George 143–4, 148, 168, 172
Wyclif, John 7, 18, 28–31, 33–4, 38–41, 44, 46–8, 51, 59, 177, 179–80, 182

Zizka, Jan 32, 55–8, 64–5
Zwickau Prophets 127, 170
Zwingli, Huldrych 126–7, 129–31, 145, 147, 156, 170
Zwinglians 126, 156